by Jennifer Reuting

***Limited Liability Companies* For Dummies®, 3rd Edition**

Published by: **John Wiley & Sons, Inc.,** 111 River Street, Hoboken, NJ 07030-5774, www.wiley.com

Published simultaneously in Canada

Library of Congress Control Number: 2013956850

ISBN 978-1-118-85298-9 (pbk); ISBN 978-1-118-85653-6 (ebk); ISBN 978-1-118-85659-8 (ebk)

Manufactured in the United States of America

10 9 8 7 6 5 4 3 2 1

Contents at a Glance

Table of Contents

Introduction

Individuals are now, more than ever, realizing the power of the limited liability company (LLC). If you're like many people, you probably understand that an LLC can benefit you in one way or another; you just don't know the next steps to take. Maybe you've just purchased a piece of real estate and know that it should be protected in some way; you just don't know how to form the LLC and do the transfer. Or, on a whim, you created an LLC for your current business and can't get any answers on what to do now. How do you transfer assets? What do you do at tax time? How can you take on a partner?

You now hold in your hands the key to some of the most powerful strategies of the rich and successful. This book was written to make your life easier and eliminate the guesswork on forming and owning an LLC. After all, your LLC should work for *you,* not the other way around.

After I get into the basics on LLCs in this book, I go into some more-complex strategies. This info sets this book apart from all the others. The rich have used a lot of these strategies for decades to operate their businesses, protect their assets, and pass on their estates. Now, I'm putting the power in your hands. When you find a strategy that may work for you, I encourage you to sit down with your team (your attorney, accountant, and/or corporate consultant) and figure out how to build on it and how to customize it to your specific situation. Use this book as your starting point. Your possibilities are endless, and your asset protection and tax strategies should grow along with you.

Now get going on your journey to success and don't look back!

About This Book

Although this book was written in an easy-to-understand, concise manner, I didn't limit this book to the basics. You'll find that a lot of other books on LLCs just skim over things, filling their pages with forms and legal statutes. They often just cover the basics of filing your articles and creating your operating agreement without delving into the more powerful uses of LLCs or the strategies that LLCs can be integrated with. Instead, I crammed these pages with valuable information that you'd be hard-pressed to find in other books.

Even though this is a *For Dummies* book, you're no idiot. You don't want to be put to sleep while reading a jargon-laden book on complex strategies that even most attorneys can't understand. You want something that dives deep but keeps it simple, and that's what I strive to give you — well-organized, easy-to-read, and fluff-free information.

I know, I know — you're busy! You operate on a need-to-know basis and the rest is just gibberish. Therefore, to speed things up a little, feel free to ignore anything with a Technical Stuff icon next to it. The information in those paragraphs isn't really necessary to understand the topic. Also, the sidebars are fun, but they're sort of a bonus for those who aren't time-impaired. Feel free to skip those too.

I use a few conventions in this book. They're pretty intuitive and easy to understand, but here's a rundown anyway.

- Any industry terminology that may be new to you will appear in *italics*.
- I **boldface** the action parts of numbered steps and keywords or the main points in bulleted items.
- Sidebars, which are the gray boxes of text, contain fun stories, examples, or other pieces of information that are great to know but not necessary to read if you're in a time crunch.
- Nine times out of ten I won't spell out "limited liability company" but will instead use the abbreviation "LLC." I can't help it — it's just too easy!
- When this book was printed, some web addresses may have needed to break across two lines of text. If that happened, rest assured that I haven't put in any extra characters (such as hyphens) to indicate the break. So, when using one of these web addresses, just type in exactly what you see in this book, pretending as though the line break doesn't exist.

Foolish Assumptions

In order for this book to cater to a broad audience, I needed to make some foolish assumptions about you, the reader, and your skill level. After all, it's not *Limited Liability Companies For Attorneys* or *Limited Liability Companies For Real Estate Investors.* It's *Limited Liability Companies For Dummies* — in other words, "everyone". Let's see if any of these shoes fit:

- You're a budding (or experienced) entrepreneur, looking for the next leg up.
- You have a business, and you want to finally get legit and form an entity to protect yourself.

- You're a real estate investor looking to save some dough and keep your butt out of the courtroom.
- You're an inventor who wants to protect his patents from a random lawsuit that may be just around the corner.
- You have intellectual property, and you want to keep it right where it is — in your name.
- You're old, or young, and are planning your estate.
- You want to raise money for a project and want a vehicle that can keep things in order and sweeten the pot for your investors.
- You were born on a day that ends in the letter *y*.

If any of the above assumptions fits your profile, then this book was written especially for you!

Icons Used in This Book

In this book, I use little pictures, called *icons,* to highlight important information. When you see these, make sure to pay close attention — otherwise, you may miss some really good info!

This icon flags helpful tips, tidbits, and secrets that may give you an upper hand on your road to success.

If I mention a topic more than once and/or use this icon, then you should make an effort to remember the information. These concepts are often the most important.

Whenever I use this icon, you should watch out! Obtain advice that is specific to your situation from a professional. Otherwise, legal or financial snares can ensue.

I use this icon to flag some technical stuff that may be a little advanced and difficult to understand for the LLC novices out there. When you encounter one of these icons, don't worry — just ignore the information or ask a competent professional for advice.

This icon directs you to the *Limited Liability Companies For Dummies* page at `www.dummies.com/extras/limitedliabilitycompanies`. This page on Dummies.com has extra articles and goodies to explore.

When you see this icon, know that I've got you covered. This icon flags the extra information and helpful, time-saving tips that you can find at the online resource center made especially for For Dummies readers at www.docrun.com/dummies. Just enter the password **onesmartdummy** and you're in! See the next section for more info on online content for this book.

Beyond the Book

One of the great things about LLCs is how much you can do with them! Unfortunately, if I were to write everything one could possibly know, this book would rival the length of *War and Peace*. So, in an effort to save some trees, this book you're reading right now comes with digital perks!

First, I have created a password-protected online resource center made specifically for *For Dummies* readers. Every place where I mention state laws throughout the book, I will refer you to this online resource center for more information specific to your state. You can access this information anywhere and you can also be sure that it's up-to-date. The online resource center can be found at www.docrun.com/dummies and the password is **onesmartdummy**.

Want more information on things like estate planning with LLCs and LLC tax distributions? Well, look no further than the *Limited Liability Companies For Dummies* page at www.dummies.com/extras/limitedliabilitycompanies. Here, you can find extra articles and information on topics covered in this book.

And last but not least, make sure to check out the free eCheat Sheet at www.dummies.com/cheatsheet/limitedliabilitycompanies. This will tell you all you need to know about naming your LLC, help you understand the different tax types, and get clear on more of the benefits of LLCs.

Where to Go from Here

One of the many great things about a *For Dummies* book is that you don't have to read it from cover to cover to get to what you need to know. This book was designed to be jumped into, with each chapter standing on its own. Find a topic that interests you and start there! After all, why waste time reading mundane topics that you already know when you can immediately get to the good stuff?

If you're a complete novice and are just dipping your toes into the whole LLC concept, you may want to read Chapters 2 and 3, and then skip to whatever topic interests you most. If you have already formed your LLC and are looking for the next step, you may want to skip to Chapters 9, 10, and 11 to find out how to create or revise your operating agreement. Only interested in the use of LLCs for real estate? Skip to Chapter 18. Ready to dissolve your LLC? Feel free to flip to Chapter 16.

Or, you can read the book cover to cover if you want. You get a lot of juicy info out of every chapter!

Part I

The ABCs of LLCs

getting started
with
LLCs

Visit www.dummies.com for great Dummies content online.

In this part . . .

- Understand what LLCs are and what they're used for.
- Discover the many types of LLCs and the pros and cons of choosing each one.
- Compare LLCs to other types of business structures so you can determine if an LLC is right for you and your business.

Chapter 1

What Is an LLC, Really?

In This Chapter

- Understanding LLC basics
- Creating your plan of attack
- Knowing the essentials for operating an LLC

The Limited Liability Company (more commonly known by its acronym, LLC) is by far the most popular business structure. Only a decade ago, the LLC was the new kid on the block — untrusted and unverified. Luckily, that changed pretty rapidly — LLCs gained popularity and, within a short time, became firmly established in the business world. Since then, LLC has become a household term, and for good reason.

The LLC is a complete divergence from its predecessor, the corporation. While corporations have a fixed management structure, LLCs offer *flexibility.* While corporations have strict rules regarding owners and profit distributions, LLCs are adjustable. While corporations are stuck with corporate taxation (or its limited variant, S corporation taxation), with an LLC you can select whichever form of taxation you prefer. The added flexibility of the LLC enables you to build a solid foundation for your business that works for your *exact* circumstances.

Great, right? Well . . . yes and no. With all the hoopla and the incessant commercials from filing companies, we all know how easy it is to file an LLC. However, very few folks can really explain how an LLC works, or why an LLC is right for your situation, or, even worse, how to actually *structure* it after receiving that one-page filing back from the state. Aside from hiring a pricey attorney (not an option for most people), the majority of your peers don't know how to do simple things like issue the ownership properly or formally agree on what happens if one of the partners wants to leave.

The LLC is a powerful tool, but if you don't know how to use it — how to build that crucial foundation that will support your greatest potential — then it really amounts to nothing more than the piece of paper on which your formation document is printed . . . and possibly a few lawsuits along the way.

I go into detail on setting up an LLC for your specific circumstances later in the book, but first I want to give you an overview — or a refresher, if you're a seasoned pro — on the meat and bones of this awesome business structure.

Understanding How LLCs Work

Think of an LLC as a partnership on steroids. If you and a buddy were to get together and start a business without registering it as any particular business structure with the state, your business would automatically be considered a general partnership. All business income and losses would be reflected on your personal tax returns. No rigid formalities would be required — you could literally draft your agreements on a napkin.

The problem is, what happens if you want to raise capital? The business is comprised of only you and your partner, and possibly some assets that you've acquired along the way. You can't exactly sell pieces of yourself. Or what if your partner ends up being, well, a jerk? Or even worse, a jerk who runs up a lot of debts that you could be personally responsible for? Eek! As unfair as it sounds, that's the reality for partnerships. Until the LLC came along, that is.

The LLC takes all the best features of a partnership (pass-through taxation — defined at the end of this chapter — and no hefty burdens of corporate formalities) and the best features of a corporation (personal liability protection and ownership shares) and then adds a few extra perks for good measure, like the capability to choose your own form of taxation and a formal yet flexible management structure. In addition, the LLC can offer a second layer of liability protection that shields the business from any personal lawsuits that may befall you (referred to as *charging order protection,* which I elaborate on in Chapter 17).

If all this sounds like Martian to you, don't worry. In this chapter, I dive into some of those benefits and other LLC fundamentals a bit more, all while steering you toward other chapters in the book where you can read about specific topics in more detail.

Owners: You gotta have 'em

Although LLCs are separate from their owners in a lot of ways, they still need to have them. An LLC without an owner is like a child without parents: It simply doesn't exist. So, even though you may have called up a filing company and filed your LLC with the state, until you go through the process of doling out ownership in your LLC, it doesn't become its own legitimate entity.

The owners in an LLC are called *members*. They have units of ownership called *membership interests* that show what percentage of the company they own and how much influence they have when voting on important company matters. Membership interests in an LLC are comparable to stock in a corporation. However, unlike the S corporation, which is often compared to the LLC, an LLC can have unlimited members of any type. Members can be citizens of other countries or even entities, such as corporations, partnerships, or trusts.

Unlike corporations, LLCs offer a lot of flexibility in how you issue membership. For instance, your LLC can have many different forms of membership, called *classes*. You can set whatever rules you like for each class. If you structure them properly, classes are a great way to entice investors or partners to join your business — some folks may want a bigger piece of the profits up front, while others may want more control. For example, one class can have priority on the profit distributions, while another class is second in line. Or one class can have a say in managing the company, while another class must remain silent. With an LLC, you can structure the membership in a way that makes everyone happy. And happy partners make for a happier you. Trust me on this.

The owners of an LLC not only own the entire business and all its assets, but also generally have the final say. Although they may not all manage the day-to-day operations of the business, they do elect the managers. They vote on important issues and ultimately control the company's fate. In Chapter 10, I go into more detail on membership, including how to issue it and structure it in a way that works for your business.

The actual term for the members of an LLC and their membership interests varies from one state to another. For example, in some states, the membership interest is called *ownership interest* or *limited liability company interest*. Just keep in mind that no matter what they're called, the concepts are the same.

If your LLC has only one member, it's called a *single-member LLC*. Unless the single member LLC elects corporate taxation (which I'll show you how to do in Chapter 8), the IRS treats it as a sole proprietorship — or *disregarded entity* — for tax purposes.

All states now allow single-member LLCs. (It took a while for a few states to jump on the bandwagon.) However, in some states, because of certain court rulings, single-member LLCs are often disadvantageous — they aren't afforded the benefit of partnership taxation and aren't guaranteed *charging order protection,* which protects the LLC from lawsuits that may be filed against you personally. I discuss this concept in depth in Chapter 17.

Contributions: Where the money comes from

When you buy a share of stock on the stock market, the money you pay is what you are contributing (or *investing*) in return for a percentage (or *share*) of the company's ownership. Well, purchasing ownership in an LLC is very similar: In exchange for a membership interest in the company, a person or company must contribute something of value. This contribution can be in the form of cash, services, hard assets such as equipment, real estate, or even promissory notes (which are allowed in some states).

When a new business is formed, all the initial owners, or *founding members,* come together and pool the value of their contributions. Say Jane contributes $100,000 in cash, Chris contributes $5,000 in cash and $25,000 in services, and Joe contributes an office building worth $150,000. The combined total of their contributions is $280,000. To determine each person's percentage of ownership in the LLC, they simply divide their contributions by the total. The result: Jane gets 35.7 percent, Chris gets 10.7 percent, and Joe gets 53.6 percent.

After you figure out each owner's percentage of ownership, determining her *membership interest* in the company is easy. Given the previous example, if the LLC has a total of 1,000 membership shares, then Jane's 35.7 percent ownership in the company translates to 357 membership shares, Chris's 10.7 percent results in 107 membership shares, and Joe's 53.6 percent results in 536 membership shares. I dive into more details on issuing membership in Chapter 10.

The contributions made by the founding members (the ones who were on board when the company was formed) and their corresponding membership interests are listed in the LLC's operating agreement. That way, it's documented that all the owners know what everyone else is contributing to the business and agrees on the value of those contributions.

Things get a bit more complicated when a new member joins an existing company. Newly formed companies have no value — assets are added as contributions. However, when a business has been in operation for a while and elects to bring on additional contributions (and often new members), things can get weird. I mean, is Apple still worth the $10,000 it took to get things going in Steve Jobs's garage? Ha! Not even close. As businesses evolve, they increase in value. In Chapter 11, I go over the intricacies of taking on new capital and issuing membership in existing businesses.

Some LLCs issue membership certificates that, like stock certificates in a corporation, are paper evidence of the amount of ownership a member has in the company. The membership certificate displays the member's name and the number of membership shares the person owns. However, membership certificates are no longer a legal requirement in most states, and this practice is fading from popularity as our lives go digital. Which is a bit sad, really — there's nothing like the feel and smell of a newly printed stock certificate representing your stake in an exciting new endeavor.

Whether or not your LLC issues membership certificates, your membership interest should be listed in the operating agreement next to your contribution amount. (In Chapter 10, I show you how to properly list your members, their contributions, and their membership interests in your operating agreement.)

Allocations and distributions: Getting what you're due

After an LLC starts turning a profit, the members will no doubt want to benefit. After all, they didn't invest their hard-earned money in the company for nothing — they want to see a return! At certain times — usually at the end of the year, but sometimes at the end of each quarter — company profits can be calculated and doled out to each member, usually in proportion to her percentage of ownership. These payments are called *distributions* and are generally in the form of cash (see Chapters 10 and 14 for more on distributions).

Now, as many of you savvy entrepreneurs know, growing a business is hard enough without draining it of its much-needed cash in the first few years. You'll hold off on sending checks to the investors and instead use that revenue to grow the business. But what happens when your business is still showing a profit at the end of the tax year? Maybe you're saving up to purchase property or other assets pertinent to the business. Well, unfortunately, Uncle Sam still wants his share. And with the partnership form of taxation (how most LLCs elect to be taxed), the owners of the LLC are still *allocated* this revenue and must pay tax on it . . . even though they never saw the cash.

I dive into this topic in more detail in Chapter 8, where I discuss the different forms of taxation that an LLC can elect. Until then, just know that if you elect the most common form of LLC taxation — partnership taxation — then you need to understand the differences between *allocations* and *distributions.* Allocations are the profits on which you and your partners have to pay taxes. Distributions are the money you actually *get,* in your pocket, ready to be spent on that new backcountry snowboard you've been craving.

Unlike corporations, LLCs don't necessarily have to distribute profits in proportion to the members' percentage of ownership. The members can decide to vary the distributions however they want. The IRS generally allows this practice as long as you pass their tests (mainly to prove that you aren't varying the distributions simply to avoid taxes). This strategy gets complex, and I dive into it a bit more in Chapters 10 and 14; however, if used correctly, it can result in some huge incentives for powerful partners and investors to join your team.

Distributions also occur if your LLC goes out of business, but in this case they're handled differently. The LLC's assets are liquidated, the creditors are paid back (including any members to whom the business owes money), and then the remaining amount is distributed to the members according to their membership interests or, more specifically, their *capital accounts.* Capital accounts can be, well . . . complex. But an easy way to think of them is how your percentage interest evolves over time, as more contributions to the company are made. They also tend to keep accountants in business.

The key takeaway here is this: When the final distributions are made, you can't choose how the money is distributed — it must be doled out according to the balance of each member's capital account.

Management: Some folks are just better at it

Just because you own it doesn't mean that you need to know what to do with it. LLCs have a *manager* role — a person who handles the day-to-day operations of the company. All LLCs are required to have at least one manager. They can be the owners themselves or other outside persons or businesses.

Two types of LLCs exist:

- A *member-managed* LLC is managed jointly by all of its members.
- A *manager-managed* LLC is managed by one or more — but not all — of the members or by separate (non-owner) managers altogether.

The birth of the LLC

The LLC didn't come out of nowhere. Business entities with the same characteristics as LLCs have been around for many years. The origin of LLCs can be traced back to 1892, when German law enacted what was called the *Gesellschaft mit beschränkter Haftung* (GmbH) — a modern-day variation of the English private limited company.

Germany's GmbH format was copied throughout Europe and Central and South America. This concept remains popular in many parts of the world.

In the United States, limited partnership associations actually predated the German concept. These entities were formed in several Midwestern states starting as early as 1874. However, this entity structure soon fell out of favor. In 1977, the LLC was born in Wyoming and modeled after the German GmbH and the successful Panama variation. LLCs didn't become popular nationally until 1988, when the IRS ruled that LLCs could be taxed as partnerships. And the rest, as they say, is history!

If you are forming an LLC with only a few owners (members), and each owner is going to have a say in managing the company, then you may want to choose member-management. However, if you decide to take on a silent partner and that person is *not* managing the business day-to-day, then your LLC needs to be manager-managed. All members, except for the silent partner, are listed as manager.

Unless *all* the members are managing the company's day-to-day business, your LLC is considered manager-managed.

Creating Your Own LLC: Your First Step Toward Success

You need to go through a few processes to get your LLC filed, structured, and up and running. You don't have to be a lawyer or an über-savvy entrepreneur to get it right.

If you've listened to the radio or watched TV in the past few years, you're probably well aware that filing an LLC is as simple as "one low fee." However, the important stuff is what comes before and after you call up a formation company or fill out a quick form and send it to the state. That's where the big decisions come into play and the real structuring of your company takes place. So let's get started.

As you flip through this book, the concepts may seem overwhelming at first, but after you get familiar with a little bit of industry terminology, you'll have a basic understanding of LLCs to get started on your own. See the glossary in the back of the book for all the need-to-know terms.

Educating yourself

The first thing to do is gain a little bit of an education about LLCs. I know you're busy, so this doesn't have to be too extensive. You just need to know the basics, and the best way to start is by reading this book. Needless to say, you're on the right track!

You can always use professionals to do the work for you. And that's okay. Hey, I'm all for delegation! Just make sure that you have a basic understanding so that you can have productive and educated conversations with the people you hire. Not to mention that you want to have an idea of whether they really know their stuff. (You'd be surprised how many don't.)

Only after you understand the basics should you call your attorney or accountant and ask about details that pertain to your situation. You may also want to do some research online and set up some free consultations with corporate consulting companies. If you have specific questions, you can ask me directly at `www.myllc.com`, and I'll get back to you as soon as I can.

LLCs, like most entities, are subject to state oversight. The problem is that not all states are on the same page. As much as I wish that I could include information about every state's laws, doing so would result in a page count rivaling *War and Peace.* (My wise editors at Wiley quashed that idea pretty quickly.) So, in an effort to make it easier for you to ensure that you're complying with the laws of the state(s) in which you transact business, I provide state-specific information about LLCs, as well as all state LLC laws on a login-only website especially for Dummies readers. You can access it by going to `www.docrun.com/dummies` and entering the password **onesmartdummy**. This book, in conjunction with these additional resources, should give you everything you need to get started down the right path.

Divvying up the ownership

When you're first starting your business, usually it's pretty clear who the owners are going to be. The real question becomes, how much ownership does an owner actually get? Sometimes, the answer is clear-cut, such as when all the owners are contributing cash and nothing else (see the "Contributions: Where the money comes from" section earlier in this chapter). However, I find that with most businesses, the decision over who gets what isn't so easy.

Often, businesses are started based on just an idea and possibly some savings pooled together. Say three people are in a room and think up an idea, and all three people get excited and decide to pursue it. The first thing that often comes to mind is that all three will be equal partners. After all, it's only fair, right? Each person is valuable and smart and equally excited as the others, so why not share the ownership equally? Right? *Wrong.* In my experience, misjudgments in structuring partnerships are the number-one reason a new business venture fails.

Ideas don't really have much value — at least as far as the law is concerned. It's the *execution* of those ideas that's valuable. So, yes, your crazy cousin Joe might have been in the room when the idea was brought up and thrown in a few asides that got you thinking, but that doesn't mean you need to bring him on as a full partner. In fact, there's a good chance you'll be hating life if you do. You need to choose your business partners as carefully as you choose your spouse. Not only is there a very good chance that you'll see this person as much as — if not more than — your spouse, but the success of your business rides on you and your partners being able to make crucial decisions in a synergistic way.

We entrepreneurs are natural risk-takers. You may encounter a situation where you have a good feeling about a partner and want to take a chance on that person. Luckily, LLC membership enables you to do so by using *membership vesting.* A potential partner can earn (or *vest*) his ownership upon the completion of certain milestones or a fixed amount of time spent with the company. Don't be afraid to have these crucial conversations, and then go to Chapter 10 to find out how to structure the membership in your LLC in a way that promotes accountability.

Deciding who manages

If your LLC is a small business without investors, then chances are it is a *member-managed* LLC, with all members of the company managing the day-to-day business equally. If you have silent partners or want to involve other non-owner managers, then your LLC is likely *manager-managed.* This means one of two things:

- Some, but not all, of the owners are also managers of the company
- An outside party (a person or company that is not an owner) is a manager of the company

All is not always fair and equal in the world of managers. All forms of LLCs allow for *management groups.* When you are structuring your LLC, you can create groups of managers, with each group having a different, clear-cut scope of responsibility and/or powers to make certain decisions or take certain actions pertaining to the day-to-day business of the LLC. These powers include the ability to take out leases in the company's name, the ability to authorize the company to take on debt, and the ability to hire and fire employees.

Now, hearing the word *manager* probably brings you back to your first job slinging pizzas after school . . . and that pock-faced 18-year-old "manager" looking over your shoulder the entire time. But when it comes to LLCs, these low-level employees are not technically managers in the sense that we're talking about here. Managers are the ones *fully* running the company, making the make-or-break decisions. They're the ones who cosign the business loans and leases, for example.

Regardless of how your LLC is structured, when there are multiple managers, I always recommend that a business have a clear leader. If not all the managers are willing to get on board with one leader, then at least make sure that their duties are clearly delineated. Isolating each manager's realm of authority early on saves you a lot of future headaches over disagreements. You draft this delineation of duties in the LLC's operating agreement, and it becomes a set part of the LLC's structure that can be changed only by written agreement of the company's members. I show you how to do so in Chapter 10.

Although not super common, an LLC can also adopt the fixed management structure of a corporation — with a president, secretary, treasurer, and board of directors. This structure can be useful if you are in an industry or have an investor that is more comfortable with those common titles. You elect a corporate management structure in your LLC's operating agreement.

Choosing your registered agent

Before you can file any formation paperwork for your LLC, you need to choose a *registered agent* (sometimes known as a *resident agent* or *statutory agent* or by its acronym RA). A registered agent is a person or company that's *always* available during business hours, every single day, to accept formal legal documents for your company in the unfortunate instance that you are sued. Your LLC needs a registered agent in its home state (its *domicile*) and every other state in which it transacts business.

Most registered agents allow you to use their office address for all your mail and other correspondence. A good registered agent should also stay on top of your state filings for you and make sure that you remain in good standing in each state in which you are registered. If you are registered in many states, this task can be onerous, so you're better off leaving it to a professional service company or an attorney (a more expensive option). See Chapter 5 for more on using a registered agent.

Even if your state allows you to serve as your own registered agent, I don't recommend it. Unless you plan on being at your office during business hours every single day, without exceptions, and you have a good grasp of all the state filings that need to be done, I suggest that you leave it to the pros. If you are not available when a lawsuit is served, you could lose the case by default — without knowing about it until it's too late! Another consideration is that if you were sued, would you really want a process server or sheriff serving you a lawsuit in front of your customers? I wouldn't!

Bringing your LLC into existence

After you decide on a management structure for your LLC (member-managed or manager-managed) and on a registered agent, you are ready to file your LLC. Your LLC needs to be registered and receive approval in any state in which it is transacting business. Your LLC doesn't need to reside in the same state as you — it should reside wherever its headquarters is going to be. In the case of a company that doesn't have a headquarters (like a purely Internet-based company), it should reside wherever the tax laws are most favorable.

If you don't go through a filing company to file the initial paperwork for your LLC, you can create your LLC yourself by drawing up a short document called the *articles of organization.* Your articles contain such basic information as the name of the company, how long the company will exist, the initial members or managers, and the name and address of the company's registered agent. In Chapter 6, I show you how to put together your articles of organization. After you're satisfied with your articles, you file them with your local secretary of state's office (or comparable state agency).

In most states, the document that you use to file your LLC is called the articles of organization. However, some states refer to it as the *articles of formation* or *certificate of formation.*

Operating Your LLC

After you form your LLC, you're ready to start business operations, right? Not even close. Actually, your work has just begun. After you're registered, you still have to complete the *formation* of your LLC by creating your operating agreement and making some very important decisions. Luckily, you can handle most of these things while you're waiting for your filed documents to come back from the state, saving you time.

Operating your LLC is meant to be easy. For the most part, if you forget something or fail to document something in writing, the courts will go easy on you. LLCs aren't like corporations, where a single misstep in following formalities can cost you your limited liability protection. Although this paperwork isn't nitpicked by the state statutes like corporation paperwork is, you still need it to maintain separation. Also, you can save yourself a lot of time, hassle, and potential legal battles by getting it out of the way and making your agreements as tight as a drum.

Creating your operating agreement

Think of your *operating agreement* as a sort of partnership agreement, except with much more power. Your operating agreement is the blueprint for your company. In it, you state your company's policies on important matters, including

- How the company will be managed and by whom
- How important decisions are to be made
- How profits are to be distributed among the owners
- The responsibilities and authority of managers of the company
- The membership information, including who is a member, what that person contributed, and what membership interest she has been assigned

Operating agreements are the best thing to have happened to the business world since the Internet. They make the LLC great because you can virtually put anything you want in your operating agreement. With the exception of some state requirements here and there, you can structure your LLC in any way you can imagine. *You* make the rules, not the government or the IRS. *You* say how you want your business to run, and then you structure it accordingly. This all happens in the operating agreement.

Creating an operating agreement takes some time and planning, but it's vital to the formation of your LLC. With the wealth of information and provisions that I provide throughout this book, you'll be able to draft an ironclad document. However, deciding what you want to put in it may take you and your partners a while. After all, you're creating an infrastructure that needs to serve you for many, many years to come.

After you create your operating agreement, make sure that all the members and managers of the LLC sign it. Distribute a copy to everyone, and put the original in your company records kit, which brings me to the next point.

Keeping books and records

Every company needs to have a records kit. In this kit, all the crucial company documents and information are stored and remain accessible to all interested parties. In the old days, a company records kit was normally a big leather binder with the company name emblazoned on the side. Nowadays, the corporate kit is usually housed online, always accessible to all the owners, wherever they are.

Whether your corporate records kit lives in the physical world or the virtual world, it serves the same purpose: to house your important company records, such as your filed articles of organization and company charter, your operating agreement, resolutions and minutes from any meetings or votes that take place, your membership roll, and your unissued membership certificates. In Chapter 13, I detail how to create and store your company's records.

Although strict formalities aren't required for LLCs, documenting decisions in at least a semi-formal way maintains that your LLC is a business separate from you as an individual. Otherwise, the courts could claim that your LLC is an *alter ego,* and you could still lose your liability protection. In Chapter 13, I go over how to incorporate quick, easy documentation into your business processes to make your liability protection ironclad.

Paying taxes

One of the most beautiful features of an LLC is that it can elect any form of taxation it wants (assuming that it's not a single-member LLC). This means that your LLC can choose partnership taxation, corporation taxation, or S corporation taxation. What flexibility! I dedicate Chapter 8 to helping you understand these different forms of taxation. You should read it thoroughly before making this hugely important decision.

The default taxation for LLCs with more than one member is partnership taxation, so this form is what you'll be subject to if you don't elect otherwise. With partnership taxation, the business's profits and losses get passed on to the owners, who report their share on their personal tax returns. These portions of profits and losses that get passed on to the members are called *allocations.* This type of taxation is commonly referred to as *pass-through taxation.*

Because the LLC itself doesn't have to pay taxes, the IRS only requires you to file an information statement (IRS **Form 1065**) that states how the company's profits and losses are allocated among the members. Additionally, the company issues each member an IRS form called a **Schedule K-1** that includes the information they need to determine how much tax they must pay on their share of the company's profits.

An LLC isn't required to distribute cash to its members. However, the members *are* required to pay taxes on the profits (allocations) whether or not they receive distributions. When the company doesn't distribute profits to the members, the members still have to pay taxes on them out of their own pockets. This sort of "profit" is often referred to as *phantom income.* In other words, the profits the members receive are about as tangible as a ghost.

Chapter 2

LLCs: More Handy Than Duct Tape!

In This Chapter

- Harnessing the power of LLCs
- Understanding LLC limitations
- Recognizing the different LLC types

Years ago, in the first edition of this book, this chapter was broken down into two parts: advantages and disadvantages of LLCs. Since then, everything has changed. LLC has become a household name, and legal precedents have been set — you no longer have to be the "test dummy" (pun intended) should your LLC get dragged into court, unsure of how your case will be decided. Also, state governments and the Internal Revenue Service have loosened the restrictions that LLCs used to be burdened with, now making it by far the most flexible of all business structures.

Long story short, whereas the "disadvantages" section used to take up a full five pages, it is now reduced to a measly few paragraphs. Now, an LLC is *not* the best option in only a very few circumstances. In this chapter, I give you a rundown on all the major qualities of limited liability companies — the good and the bad.

Because everyone's needs differ drastically, I'll let you decide for yourself which facets are benefits and which are drawbacks for your situation. (In Chapter 3, I help you explore whether an LLC is right for you.) Secondly, I give you an overview of the other types of LLCs that you may hear about in your endeavors.

Understanding Why LLCs Are Awesome

Everyone seems to be going crazy over LLCs, and for good reason. The LLC is one of the most flexible entities — you can choose how to distribute the profits, who manages the business's day-to-day affairs, and how the profits are taxed. The LLC also offers a lot in terms of liability protection (hence the name *limited liability* company).

Overall advantages of the LLC include

- **Personal liability protection:** Any creditor who comes knocking or lawsuit filed against your business can't affect you personally. You can rest assured that no matter what happens to your business, your family's assets are safe.
- **Business liability protection:** An LLC is one of the only entities that prevents personal lawsuits and creditors from liquidating your business to satisfy a judgment (in most instances).
- **No ownership restrictions:** You can have as many owners as you need. Even other entities can be owners!
- **Flexible management structure:** Owners can manage and managers can own — you decide. You can also outline the scope of each manager's power to handle important issues.
- **Flexible tax status:** You can choose from a multitude of ways to be taxed, depending on what works best for your situation. Structured as an LLC but want to be taxed like a corporation? No problem!
- **No separate tax returns:** With a standard LLC electing partnership taxation, the business's profits and losses are reported on your personal tax returns. Your LLC simply files IRS **Form 1065,** an information statement. I show you how to do this in Chapter 14.
- **Flexible profit distribution:** *You* decide what percentage of the profits to give to whom — no matter how much of the company each person actually owns.

In the following sections, I provide you with a more detailed overview of the advantages that LLCs offer.

Protecting your personal assets

As the adage goes, "You aren't in business until you've been sued." As litigious as society is these days, you don't even need to be one of the bad guys to be dragged into court. By simply transacting business with the general public, you open yourself up to myriad potential lawsuits, and no matter how arbitrary the complaint is, the destruction (and legal fees) it leaves in its wake can be crippling.

The states know that if entrepreneurs were forced to put their livelihoods at stake every time they started a new venture, significantly fewer businesses would be started. Therefore, certain entity types are afforded *limited liability,* which protect the owners and managers of the business from being held personally responsible for the debts, obligations, and misdeeds of the business. Out of all the entities, LLCs offer the most comprehensive form of this protection.

An LLC protects you from the liabilities that you inevitably come across during the normal, everyday course of business. If your business gets sued or goes bankrupt, your *personal assets* (home, car, investments, and so on) and other businesses (if they are placed in different LLCs) *cannot* be taken away. Only the assets included in the LLC that got sued are at risk.

An LLC's veil of liability protection is not infallible. If you don't take certain measures to establish and maintain that your LLC is not simply an extension of yourself (your *alter ego*), then a court can disregard the LLC and allow a plaintiff or creditor access to your personal assets. This is referred to as *piercing the veil* of liability protection. I discuss this situation — and how to avoid it — in Chapter 17.

Forming an LLC to protect your personal assets must be done in advance, not after you've already been sued. Too many victims of lawsuits have shown up at my office wondering what they can do to get out of them — asking how they can save their home and bank accounts that are about to be taken away. Unfortunately, at this point, it's always too late. If only they had spent some time planning, such as reading this book or working with an advisor, they could have saved everything. Luckily, you're off to a good start.

The one exception to the normal protection of LLCs is professional limited liability companies (PLLCs), because personal responsibility is essential to being a licensed professional. I discuss this unique entity type at length later in this chapter.

By establishing your new business or placing your existing business in an LLC, you sign your company up for the most cost-effective, ironclad insurance policy around. A business insurance policy may still have a role in keeping the business itself from having to pay for its own misdeeds. However, they're effective only in lawsuits arising from product or service liability and usually don't pay out to unsatisfied creditors if the company can't meet its debt obligations. Also, whereas insurance companies can be wishy-washy about paying out, the LLC is pretty fail-safe.

Here's the clincher: LLCs are so foolproof that attorneys often opt to negotiate a settlement or, better yet, avoid the time and cost of suing LLCs in the first place! Now, that's what I call protection!

Although an LLC shields you from being held personally responsible for minor negligent acts, it does nothing for egregious criminal acts or willful misconduct. Also, the LLC does offer some protection against certain government creditors, such as the IRS, with one main exception: As a member or manager of an LLC, you can be held *personally* responsible for the failure to pay payroll taxes. Therefore, if you withhold taxes from your employees' checks and for some reason fail to submit that money to the tax man, you put your personal assets at risk.

Taking charge of charging order protection

So now you know that an LLC protects your personal assets if the business gets sued or goes bankrupt. Pretty great, eh? Well, it gets even better. Unlike corporations, LLCs have a dual layer of liability protection called *charging order protection.* Many moons ago, when a creditor obtained a judgment against a partner of a partnership, the creditor could simply take the partner's interest in the business (and, proportionally, all related assets) and liquidate them in order to get paid, often leaving a ravaged business in his wake. Clearly, this wasn't fair to the other, innocent partner(s), who was just going about her business when suddenly everything she'd worked for was destroyed!

To remedy this unfairness, the courts amended the laws so that the creditor of a member (the partner) cannot go after that member's individual interest, but only the *economic right* to that interest. Read on to find out how this arrangement works.

How charging orders work

One day, finally getting a break from the constant demands of the restaurant you started and built, you drive to the supermarket and accidently hit someone with your car. Sure, the woman mindlessly walked in front of you and you only barely bruised her, but that means nothing when she shows up to court in a neck brace. The jury, sympathetic to the woman's plight, finds in her favor, and you now owe this woman more than your insurance covers and more than you can afford. After wiping out your family's savings, your equity in your home, and your kid's college funds, you still come up short.

But the bad news gets worse if the restaurant you've spent the past four years building is structured as a corporation. Your ownership interest *(stock)* in that corporation is considered a personal asset of yours, and the judgment creditor is therefore allowed to foreclose on it. Before you know it, your corporate account's been frozen, and you're holding a fire sale of your kitchen equipment to satisfy the debt. Your company is toast.

Now imagine a different scenario: Instead of forming your restaurant as a corporation, you formed it as a limited liability company. When you are sued, the plaintiff can't foreclose on your business, but instead can only obtain a charging order against your LLC. This means that she has no say in the day-to-day operation of the business and can only wait patiently with her hand out, should you decide to issue her profit distributions. And why would you ever do that?

Economic rights versus other rights

To better understand charging order protection, you should know that a member can have two rights in an LLC: *economic rights,* or the right to receive profit allocations and distributions from the company; and *other rights,* which include the right to vote on important matters or be involved in the day-to-day management of the business. Assuming that your operating agreement allows for it, charging order protection grants *only* economic rights to the assignee under most state laws. In other words, the creditor has no choice but to shut her trap, sit back, and receive whatever distributions you decide to grant her. You could stop profit distributions altogether, and the creditor would have no say in the matter.

This is the worst possible situation for your judgment creditor, because while you are withholding profit distributions from her, she is still required to pay taxes on that allocated share of the profits. This is called *phantom income,* which I dive into in Chapter 14, and it usually isn't a good thing. In this case, however, it works in your favor, and you can easily force your creditor to end up with nothing except the pleasure of paying down your tax bill. It's funny how this arrangement can make even the most bull-headed creditors call up, ready to negotiate an extremely favorable settlement!

Of course, considering that her attorney would know that trying to seize membership interests in an LLC is a losing proposition, it's unlikely that she would risk suing you at all. But who knows? Maybe that fake neck brace cut off circulation to her brain. I discuss charging order protection and this strategy in more detail in Chapter 17.

When formed and maintained properly, LLCs always hold up in court. When creditors see that you have shielded your assets with an LLC, they very rarely go through the hassle of taking you to court. And avoiding a lawsuit is always better than winning one, or, as legendary Chinese strategist Sun Tzu wrote, "The best battle is the battle that is won without being fought."

Enjoying the flexibility of management and ownership rules

All states have guidelines that dictate the management and ownership structure of an LLC, and they may seem a bit rigid. Unfortunately, if more people read their state statutes, they would realize how lax these statutes really are. Although the default laws can be undesirable, the states allow the majority of them to be overridden by custom rules built into the company's operating agreement, thus (again) making the LLC the most flexible entity around.

No ownership restrictions

Back in the day, if you wanted liability protection *and* a form of pass-through taxation, you were resigned to forming an S corporation. As I describe at length in Chapter 3, S corporations are just basic corporations with a special tax election that you can file with the IRS. Unfortunately, they also come with severe limitations as to the number and types of owners the business may have. For example, S corporations are limited to 100 or fewer owners *(shareholders),* and these owners cannot be other companies or non–U.S. citizens. Additionally, they can have only one class of ownership — meaning that all owners must be treated equally.

LLCs, on the other hand, have no such problems. You can issue as many shares as you want to any other entity or individual of any nationality. (However, as *individual* as your pets may be, they don't count!) You can also structure the ownership however you like using *membership classes.* You can give preference to certain owners when it comes to profit distributions, or you can allow some owners certain voting rights that others don't get.

LLCs also offer a lot of leeway as to how *individual* ownership is structured. For example, each member can be subject to his own buy-sell agreement that dictates the rules and restrictions on his individual membership interest, including what should happen to that member's interest should he pass away or get a divorce. Trust me, the last thing you want is to wake up one day with a dearly departed member's crazy son as your new partner. These rules can vary from member to member if you so choose. I discuss buy-sell agreements in Chapter 12.

No management restrictions

When it comes to the management of the business, an LLC can be managed by

- **Its members:** When you select *member management* for your LLC, all of the business's members have an equal say in the day-to-day operations, no matter their ownership percentage (unless you state otherwise in the operating agreement). They all have an equal right to sign contracts and enter into debts on behalf of the business. If you don't want one of your members to have this sort of power, then member management is definitely not for you.
- **Separate managers:** These folks may or may not hold a stake in the company. Most companies that have more than two or three operating members choose manager management. When you elect manager management, you can have as many of your members be managers as you want; however, not all of them have to be managers if you don't want them to be.

For example, say you are raising money for your new enterprise. Although you want your investors to profit from the business's success, you don't want them to have a say in the day-to-day operations. To achieve this, you form a manager-managed LLC and elect yourself as the only manager. As members without management authority, the investors have limited say in the day-to-day operations of the business. This is a really good strategy for creative projects like movies as a way to keep the investors from running wild on the set.

When establishing your LLC, you state in your articles of organization whether your company will be designated member-managed or manager-managed. I discuss the ins and outs of selecting the members and managers of your LLC in Chapter 10.

Most states give you heaps of leeway in prescribing exactly how your company is managed. You can create multiple management groups and multiple management roles. You can also restrict some nonmanaging members from voting or having *any* say whatsoever, including who is chosen to manage the company. All these types of details are up to your discretion and simply need to be laid out in the LLC's operating agreement.

The fact that you can specify separate managers is a trademark of LLCs that helps separate them from other entities, such as sole proprietorships and general partnerships. In a general partnership, all the members are owners, and all are equally (and personally!) liable for the business. A limited partnership can have members who also manage the business; however, it doesn't have any sort of limited liability protection. I indulge your curiosity on these (in my opinion) inferior entity types in Chapter 3.

The management aspect is one reason LLCs work well in estate planning. You can place your assets in an LLC with the kids as the full owners *(members)* and yourself as the manager. This way, you still control the company, while your kids can receive profit distributions. Upon your death, the assets are still in their name, and a new manager is elected.

LLCs are definitely *not* one size fits all; they need to be customized to your particular business needs. All this customization happens in the operating agreement, making it the most important document you'll ever write in regard to your business. I cannot emphasize that fact enough. If you don't have an operating agreement, your state's default rules apply, and I promise you that they won't give you much more than a headache. This doesn't mean that you should pull up a shoddy fill-in-the-blank operating agreement on the Internet and use that, either. Those generic forms are mostly antiquated, are not state specific, and likely won't address all your needs. In Part III of this book, I go into detail on how to create a custom operating agreement for your LLC.

Choosing your own tax status

As the owner of an LLC, you have the unique ability to choose how you want to pay taxes on your business. LLCs can be taxed as partnerships (with pass-through taxation) or as sole proprietorships (if the LLC has only one member); or they can even choose to be taxed as a corporation or an S corporation (which I explain in detail in Chapter 8). Although you can't easily flip back and forth from one type of taxation to another, this sort of flexibility is unique to LLCs. For example, corporations can't choose to be taxed like partnerships, and general partnerships can't choose to be taxed like corporations. LLCs have a choice, and in the business world, flexibility can determine success or failure.

Making your selection

The default tax status for LLCs with more than one member is partnership tax status. If you want to elect any other form, you must file a **Form 8832: Entity Classification Election** with the IRS. You can download a copy of the IRS form (including instructions) at `www.irs.gov/uac/Form-8832,-Entity-Classification-Election`.

When filing **Form 8832,** you can elect the new form of taxation retroactively up to 75 days. Under certain circumstances, the IRS may even allow you to elect a different form of taxation retroactively up to three years and 75 days, however it's best to make your election on time.

After you file **Form 8832** and elect a different form of taxation for your LLC, you are stuck with that chosen method of taxation for five years (called the *60-month rule*). In Chapter 14, I discuss potential ways to get around this rule, but because changing may not be possible, I suggest that you take some time to choose your form of taxation wisely. Turn to Chapter 8 for assistance in choosing your form of taxation.

Single-member LLCs and the IRS

A single-member LLC (an LLC with only one member) is automatically considered by the IRS to be a *disregarded entity* and, by default, is taxed exactly as it would be if it were simply a sole proprietorship. This doesn't affect the basic liability protection of the LLC, but it does change the tax rules.

A single-member LLC has fewer options when it comes to electing a form of taxation. Because it's not technically a partnership, the IRS restricts it from electing partnership taxation. In this case, you have three options:

- You can do nothing and be taxed as a disregarded entity.
- You can elect to be taxed as a corporation by filing a **Form 8832: Entity Classification Election** with the IRS.

- You can elect S corporation taxation by filing **Form 2553: Election by a Small Business Corporation.** Keep in mind that if you choose to be taxed as an S corporation, you'll be subject to the same membership limitations as S corporations.

If you are a single-member LLC and want to be taxed as a partnership, you can always issue a small percentage of your company to a trusted friend or family member and avoid this situation entirely. Or, as an alternative to bringing friends or family on board, you have the option of forming a corporation — with you as the sole shareholder — and having the corporation be your partner in the LLC. If you live in a state in which forming a corporation is a costly endeavor, you can always form your corporation in a less-expensive, tax-free state, such as Nevada. You pay about $125 per year in registration fees; however, your LLC gets the benefit of partnership taxation.

Nevada is a great state for forming a "partner" corporation because of the privacy it offers. You see, Nevada doesn't require you to disclose who the shareholders of a corporation are. This privacy is beneficial if for some reason you don't want anyone to know that the partner in your LLC is actually, well, *you.*

If you are a single-member LLC, you are not eligible to elect partnership taxation on **Form 8832.**

Distributing profits at your whim

With most entities, if a shareholder owns 10 percent of the company, he can receive only 10 percent of the profits that are distributed, no more and no less. With an LLC, you have freedom to choose! You don't have to split the profits in accordance with the percentage of ownership. If all the members agree, and you have a legitimate reason for doing so (the IRS won't accept tax evasion as a legitimate reason!), you can give 40 percent of the profits to someone who owns 20 percent of the business, or give 10 percent to someone who owns 50 percent.

For example, say you and John decide to partner together to create a web design company. You choose to partner 50/50, and you alone are putting in the initial $20,000 needed to get the venture started. You'll both be sharing the workload. But do you think that splitting the profits 50/50 is fair when you're the only one putting up capital? You know better than that (I hope).

So being the smart cookie that you are, you and John decide to form an LLC. You distribute 50 percent of the company to John and 50 percent to yourself. In the LLC's operating agreement, you agree that you get first dibs on the profits until they reach $22,000 (giving you 10 percent interest on your initial investment). After you're paid off, you and John will split the profits equally.

Taking a Look at a Few Wrinkles

As I describe in the preceding section, LLCs offer numerous advantages over other business structures. But they're not perfect. Nothing is, after all. You have to be careful about the rules regarding transferring membership, and you have be aware that the laws governing LLCs vary from state to state.

Membership can be a bit tricky

Many LLCs restrict the transfer of ownership. Although this restriction used to be a requirement of LLCs, it is now more customary than anything else. Basically, if a member wants to sell or transfer her shares, she can only assign the *economic rights* to the ownership, not actually transfer it. So the person purchasing the membership only has rights to the profits that are distributed; he has no voting rights and no control over the business's operations. Sometimes this restriction is firm, and sometimes it can be overruled by a vote of the other members. Regardless, you and your partners decide it all in your LLC's operating agreement.

Don't fret too much over this limitation — it can be more of a positive than anything else! An *assignee* (the person or company purchasing the membership) can become a full member upon the approval of the majority of the other members. All it takes is a quick vote. But keep in mind that to fully transfer your membership shares, the other members must approve the transfer; otherwise, the assignee may end up as a silent partner with no voting rights or control. (See Chapter 12 for more on transferring ownership.)

Most states allow you to make your own rules regarding the transference of membership interest by stating them in your operating agreement (the über-important document that I discuss at length in Chapter 9). But keep in mind that just because you *can* allow for free transference of ownership (rather than the default limitations I just discussed) doesn't mean that you *should.* A lot of the power of charging order protection (which I discuss in the section "Taking charge of charging order protection," earlier in this chapter) stems from the shares not being freely transferable. All this may seem vague and cryptic to you right now; read Chapter 12, where I dive into transferring membership, and you'll catch my drift.

If you intend to take your company public, bear in mind that you'll probably get a lot of pressure to convert to a corporation, which could result in a hurricane-sized taxable event. You see, Wall Street doesn't favor putting LLCs on the ticker — not when, by default, ownership in an LLC is not freely transferable and thousands (if not millions) of laws governing public companies have been written with corporations in mind. This is why you need to know your exit strategy before choosing your entity type. I guide you through the process of figuring out which entity type is right for you in Chapter 3.

Rules governing LLCs vary among states

Like all business structures, LLCs are governed by the individual states. Some states are progressive and comprehensive in their laws governing LLCs, whereas others have laws that seem to be last updated in the 1990s. In contrast, corporations have been around for centuries, and after so many years of working out the kinks, the basic structure is pretty much the same no matter where they're domiciled. The disparity in LLC law from one state to another isn't necessarily a drawback, but it does mean that you must do your homework every step of the way to make sure that you don't inadvertently structure your LLC in a way that your state doesn't allow.

I can't stress enough how important it is to review your state's laws concerning LLCs. You'd be surprised how many attorneys and national incorporating companies fail to take individual state laws into account. Whatever is in the state's statutes will pervade all aspects of how your company is structured, from what is contained in your articles of organization to how you can issue membership shares to what you can and can't dictate in your operating agreement.

Never use fill-in-the-blank forms or contracts for your company that you download off the Internet — it's a rarity to find one that is *legitimately* state specific and current.

Not only should you know the laws for the state in which you wish to form your LLC, but you should also familiarize yourself with the laws of any state in which you intend to register your LLC to transact business. To make your life easier, I set up a site containing all state laws regarding business entities, real estate, and taxation at www.docrun.com/dummies. Enter the password **onesmartdummy**. Here, you can view your specific state's laws, organized by topic.

Discovering the LLC's Many Variations

With all the hoopla about LLCs, a lot of the more progressive states are hurdling each other to find the newest and greatest form of the LLC. It's as if the states have embraced the flexibility of the LLC — especially all the leeway allowed by the IRS — and are amending their laws to fit the business needs of their populace. In some cases, the states are making slight variations to the standard LLC; in others, they're creating whole new entity types.

In this section, I go through all the different forms of LLCs and address whether they may be applicable to your situation.

The professional LLC

In all states except California, licensed professionals are allowed to operate under an LLC. In some states, you can actually form a specific entity called a *professional limited liability company* (*professional LLC* or *PLLC* for short), and in other states, you just file a regular ol' LLC and then abide by some best practices to make sure that you remain in compliance. The best way to do so is to look up the laws for a professional corporation (a separate entity in most states) and apply as many of those rules and constraints as you can to your LLC.

If you're a licensed professional in the state of California, you cannot operate under a limited liability company. You have to structure your practice as a *professional corporation,* a sole proprietorship, or a general partnership.

Simply wearing a suit doesn't make you a professional

Now, just because you are a professional at something and happen to be licensed doesn't mean that this legal "professional" designation applies to you. For instance, in some states, architects are considered professionals, but in other states they are not. To give you an idea of which types of services typically fall into this category, here is an excerpt from the Connecticut statute (Sec. 33-182a) governing the definition:

> *"Professional service" means any type of service to the public that requires that members of a profession rendering such service obtain a license or other legal authorization as a condition precedent to the rendition thereof, limited to the professional services rendered by dentists, naturopaths, chiropractors, physicians and surgeons, physician assistants, doctors of dentistry, physical therapists, occupational therapists, podiatrists, optometrists, nurses, nurse-midwives, veterinarians, pharmacists, architects, professional engineers, or jointly by architects and professional engineers, landscape architects, real estate brokers, insurance producers, certified public accountants and public accountants, land surveyors, psychologists, attorneys-at-law, licensed marital and family therapists, licensed professional counselors and licensed clinical social workers.*

The states differ so widely on which professions are required to be licensed that you could be required to operate as a PLLC in one state while being a standard LLC in another state. Therefore, if you think that professional licensing rules may apply to you, it's important to check your state's laws on the issue *before* filing your limited liability company. To make this research as easy as possible for you, I aggregated all the state laws governing licensed professionals on a private site especially for Dummies readers. Check it out at `www.docrun.com/dummies`. The password is **onesmartdummy**.

Different liability protection

A licensed professional generally has a much bigger impact on his individual clients than, say, the manufacturer of a mundane household product. The effects of an accountant failing to do his job properly are much more profound than the outcome of your bath soap not delivering on its promise. Because personal responsibility is a mainstay of being a licensed professional, the states want to make sure that these professionals don't shirk responsibility for their negligent acts by hiding themselves — and their assets — behind the liability protection of a corporation or an LLC.

Just like regular LLCs, a professional LLC protects you personally from debts and lawsuits against the business, with one major exception: Most states do not allow liability protection to extend to malpractice claims. Before you balk, think for a minute: Can you imagine what would happen if an irresponsible doctor were able to operate without malpractice insurance without fear of consequences? Assuming that she had the forethought to protect her business assets in another entity, nothing substantial would be at stake. She'd simply form another entity and continue on her way, leaving hurt patients in her wake.

If you're a licensed professional, this sort of liability is a serious concern, so professional liability insurance is a must. Often referred to as *malpractice insurance,* it indemnifies professionals from their mistakes. If you are a licensed professional, you'd be crazy not to have it.

Also, when one of the partners in a PLLC is liable for negligent acts while practicing her profession, the rest of the partners usually do not share in her personal liability. Assuming that they took no part in the negligence, their assets should remain safe. This provision not only protects your personal assets should your partner accidentally slip up during surgery, but it also keeps your malpractice claims separate so that your premiums don't rise if your partner screws up. This protection is a huge benefit over operating as a general partnership, in which you are jointly, personally responsible for your partners' mistakes.

Although the personal liability protection of professional LLCs is somewhat different from that of standard LLCs, charging order protection (the second layer of liability protection unique to LLCs) remains intact. I discuss charging order protection in more detail in Chapter 17.

Restrictions on ownership

All states have pretty strict restrictions on who can own and operate a professional LLC. Many states restrict membership in professional LLCs to individuals in the licensed profession. For instance, if a legal practice decides to operate as a professional LLC, then non-lawyers cannot hold an interest in that practice. Some states require only a 50 percent majority of licensed professionals. Others allow previously licensed and retired practitioners to be members, and some allow heirs and/or beneficiaries to inherit membership interests upon the death of a licensed practitioner member.

For example, here is an excerpt from Florida Statute 621.09 (2) governing ownership restrictions for professional LLCs:

> *No person shall be admitted as a member of a limited liability company organized under this act, unless such person is a professional corporation, a professional limited liability company, or an individual, each of which must be duly licensed or otherwise legally authorized to render the same specific professional services as those for which the limited liability company is organized. No member of a limited liability company organized under this act shall enter into any type of agreement vesting another person with the authority to exercise any of that member's voting power in the limited liability company.*

Some states also restrict who can and cannot be managers of a PLLC. Make sure to check your state's laws for restrictions pertaining to your business. To make your life a tad bit easier, you can read the most current laws for each state at `www.docrun.com/dummies`. The password is **onesmartdummy**.

Restrictions on business activities

Like the ownership restrictions described in the preceding section, professional LLCs are statutorily confined to transacting only the sort of business or service for which the licensed professionals who own it are licensed. I'm not sure why the states set this restriction. Perhaps they don't want things to get too muddy, so the sightline of personal responsibility remains clear.

I, for one, don't like cages. Anything that restricts me drives me crazy. If you're like me, then you're probably thinking, "Nobody's going to tell me what business I can and cannot engage in!" (***Note:*** This does not apply to drug-runners or those who club baby seals for a living.) If you're the entrepreneurial sort and, say, want to develop a software solution for your client base, you can't do it through your professional LLC. Luckily, I can offer you an easy solution: Simply form another, nonprofessional entity to manage your other business objectives.

Forming a professional LLC

Forming a professional LLC isn't difficult. The process is roughly the same as forming a standard LLC (which I outline in detail in Chapter 6), with a few major exceptions:

- You may need to show that you and your other members have been approved by your industry's licensing board before being able to operate under your professional LLC. In most states, you have to attach to your articles of organization a copy of the members' professional licenses and/or include in the articles the members' license numbers obtained from the state licensing board.
- One or more of the licensed professionals usually has to sign the articles of organization. Unless you are preparing and filing your articles of organization yourself, getting the articles to a qualified member may cause significant lag time compared with forming a standard LLC, for which a third party can usually file the documents by signing as the organizer.
- You may have to add a special designation at the end of your business name that identifies your company as a professional LLC. While the options vary somewhat from state to state, the required designation is usually a *Professional Limited Liability Company,* a *PLLC, P.L.L.C.,* or *PLLC.* Some states also allow such designations as *Limited, Ltd.,* or *Chartered.*
- Your business name cannot make reference to any services other than the services for which your PLLC's members are licensed. In some states, such as Nevada, the law is even more strict: Your business name must contain the last name of one or more of the PLLC's current or former members.

In states where the last name of a professionally licensed member is required, you can often still operate under a different name. You simply file a fictitious firm name statement (also called a *DBA*) with your local country clerk. I show you how to do so in Chapter 4.

The differences don't end after you finally have your professional LLC filed. Throughout this book, I advocate the importance of the LLC operating agreement. A PLLC is just as much, if not more, in need of a comprehensive and ironclad operating agreement to govern it. Your personal assets depend on it!

Due to the nature of the PLLC, your operating agreement will vary substantially from the operating agreement of a standard LLC. Because operating agreements for professional LLCs are very customized to your specific circumstances and state laws, you may want to work with a lawyer (make sure that she is proficient in and *experienced* with PLLCs!), or you can contact my office at DocRun (`www.docrun.com`), and I'll get you going in the right direction.

The series LLC

In certain states, a limited liability company can be comprised of numerous *series* (or *cells*), each with its own separate veil of liability protection. This is called a *series LLC,* and it's often used as an asset protection device that, in some states, saves the formation fees and the hassle of creating multiple LLCs for each asset. Think of a cell as a protective barrier — whatever is contained inside it (usually a valuable asset of some sort) has its own veil of liability protection. Nothing can touch it. It's as if each cell is its own LLC.

Series LLCs were created several years ago under Delaware state law for the purpose of simplifying structured financial transactions and collective investments such as mutual funds. Since that time, series LLCs migrated to other investments and business ventures, such as real estate. More states started offering them and/or recognizing them, and within a few years, they became the talk of the town. Personally, I'm not a huge fan of the series LLC, but let's examine this mysterious new business structure in more detail and you can judge for yourself.

Segregating your assets in a series LLC

I'm a big believer in forming a different entity for each of your assets (real estate, intellectual property, and so on) so that you can segregate each asset from the lawsuits and liabilities of the others. For example, if you own a taxi company, a common practice is to place each vehicle or two in its own limited liability company. That way, if an accident occurs, the liability is confined to the one or two vehicles in that LLC, and the rest of the business and its assets remain secure. Same goes for real estate investments: If all your property is in only one LLC, then if a renter sues you and a judgment is awarded, *all* your properties are at risk of seizure. This isn't the case if you segregate each property.

I get hammered with questions daily from clients who have heard of the series LLC and are interested in using this hot new entity type for their asset protection so that they don't have to form and manage a bunch of separate LLCs. This is a common misconception. You see, you *want* each cell to be treated as a separate entity from the others — each one should have its own operating agreement and bank accounts, should prepare separate financial statements, and should file separate tax returns. Otherwise, you run the risk of the liability protection failing between one cell and another.

So if you want each cell to be treated as a completely separate LLC, then why not just form completely separate LLCs? What's the benefit of a series LLC, anyway? Well, the answer is . . . not much. In some states, in which series LLCs are recognized, you can get away with paying only one filing fee (for the umbrella LLC) instead of the many fees you would have to pay if you went the traditional route of forming multiple LLCs.

But this is a benefit only if your LLC exists in one of these few states and doesn't transact business in one of the many states with less favorable laws. Let me give you an example: Say you have a couple of rental properties in California and you want to place each property in its own cell of a series LLC. You form the series LLC in Delaware (because California doesn't allow for the formation of series LLCs). Then, when you go to register in California, you learn that these states' laws are different — California requires each cell to be registered separately. This means that you're still paying the $800 annual minimum franchise tax for *each cell,* and all of that savings you were betting on goes out the window.

Only in rare situations do the benefits of series LLCs outweigh the risks. After all, the series LLC is a new type of business structure, and most states don't quite know what to do with it. Series LLCs lack legal precedent (which means that their effectiveness hasn't been tested in a court of law), and although the states that allow for their formation provide for that special barrier of liability protection between the different cells in their statutes, you have no guarantee that other states will agree. And if you form your series LLC in Delaware and register it to transact business in California for the purpose of holding California real estate, then your court case will probably be subject to California law — which, in this case, isn't a good thing!

Some states might recognize series LLCs, but this doesn't mean that they need to recognize the liability protection between the cells. Having a series LLC in a state that doesn't have specific laws clearly stating that each cell is treated separately is a pretty big risk.

So, is saving a few hundred bucks really worth it? Without the liability protection of a series LLC being tried and verified by a court of law, you are signing yourself up to be the test dummy if you are ever dragged into court. The irony is that, in the end, using an entity that's meant to save you fees may be the very thing that ends up costing you everything!

Forming a series LLC

If you're really set on going with a series LLC, it's much easier to form than you may realize. The process is very similar to forming a regular LLC. In most states, you simply file the same articles of organization as you would for a regular LLC and add a provision that allows for the formation of *series* or *cells* within the company.

From there, the series LLC essentially exists in your company operating agreement. As you can imagine, series LLCs require much different operating agreements than standard LLCs, and because the rules governing your LLC can vary from cell to cell, the length of your operating agreement will probably closely correspond to the number of cells you have in your LLC. Delaware state law does not cap the number of cells (series) that an LLC may have, which means that you could end up with one exorbitantly long operating agreement.

As of the publishing of this book, you can form a series LLC in the following states:

Delaware
Illinois
Iowa
Kansas
Nevada
Oklahoma
Tennessee
Texas
Utah

Additionally, Minnesota, North Dakota, and Wisconsin allow for the creation of series LLCs but don't offer a liability shield among cells.

Maintaining a series LLC

Series LLCs aren't bad for the businesses they were intended for — structured investments — but relying on liability protection holding up *among* the cells concerns me, especially for high-liability ventures such as real estate. But if you're absolutely intent on using a series LLC for your assets or operating business and are willing to take the risk, this section shows you how to maintain it in order to maximize your chances in court.

The first thing you need to understand is that series LLCs exist primarily in the operating agreement, and, given the flexible nature of the LLC, you have tremendous leeway as to how you structure each cell/series. If you want to add or remove cells, you simply amend your operating agreement. Your original filing (your articles of organization) remains unchanged.

If your series LLC ever ends up being scrutinized by a court of law, what you have written in your operating agreement is all that will uphold the insular nature of the liability protection among the various cells. Therefore, however you choose to structure your operating agreement, make sure that it's rock solid.

When you've established that your operating agreement is as comprehensive and cohesive as it possibly can be, you need to simply *be* a series LLC. If the cells of your series LLC are intended to replace separate LLCs, then you need to act in accordance with that plan. For all intents and purposes, each cell should be treated as a separate entity, complete with a separate set of books, records, and financials; a separate bank account; individual contracts; and so on. This includes having an additional, separate operating agreement for each cell.

Most, if not all, states allow you to elect whether your entire LLC is treated as a single taxpayer or each cell is treated as a separate taxpayer. As an example, here is the statute from Illinois that addresses the topic of taxation:

> *Series of members, managers or limited liability company interests. (b) . . . A series with limited liability shall be treated as a separate entity to the extent set forth in the articles of organization. Each series with limited liability may, in its own name, contract, hold title to assets, grant security interests, sue and be sued and otherwise conduct business and exercise the powers of a limited liability company under this Act. The limited liability company and any of its series may elect to consolidate their operations as a single taxpayer to the extent permitted under applicable law, elect to work cooperatively, elect to contract jointly or elect to be treated as a single business for purposes of qualification to do business in this or any other state.*

Since the last edition of this book was published, the IRS has ruled that each cell in a series LLC is treated as a separate entity for tax purposes. Each cell can have a separate tax ID number, elect a different form of taxation, and file a separate tax return. If the series LLC cell has elected partnership taxation, you should also file separate **Form 1065s** and issue separate Schedule K-1s to that cell's members at the end of each fiscal year. Doing so helps to further establish the segregation of the cells in your series LLC.

The family LLC

If you've ever heard of a family limited partnership, then you may think that you have an idea of what a family limited liability company is all about. Ironically, there is no such legal entity as a family limited partnership or a family LLC. If you were to call up your secretary of state and ask how to go about forming one, you'd hear a long pause at the end of the line. In short, these entities are just regular limited partnerships and limited liability companies that are specifically structured for holding family assets for asset protection and estate planning purposes. Even though it isn't *technically* an entity type, I include it here so you'll know the real deal if you hear people talking about it.

The limited partnership used to be the entity of choice for estate planning purposes; however, because the LLC is so flexible and has since developed enough case law to make it relatively reliable and predictable if you are taken to court, the LLC is quickly encroaching on the limited partnership's domain.

The strength of the LLC for estate planning purposes is its capability to create a firm separation between the operating members and the silent members of the business. Unlike in a corporation, an ownership interest in an LLC does not entitle the interest holder (the *member*) to any management of the affairs and day-to-day operations of the company. This separation enables you to substantially reduce estate taxes by discounting the value of the membership interests in order to increase the amount of the assets allowed to be transferred tax free during your lifetime. I go over using your LLC for estate planning in more detail at Dummies.com: `www.dummies.com/extras/limitedliabilitycompanies`.

The low-profit LLC

The *low-profit limited liability company* (*L3C* for short), the newest form of LLC, is a hybrid entity that sets out to bridge the gap between the for-profit and nonprofit business structures. L3Cs are a product of the social-consciousness movement and are still for-profit businesses, with the exception that profit motives take a backseat to the primary objective of public and social benefit. In other words, the first goal of an L3C is to make the world a better place.

L3Cs can only be formed in a handful of states. However, they are quickly gaining in popularity and every year, more and more states are jumping on board. As of the printing of this book, here are the states in which you can form an L3C:

Illinois
Kansas
Louisiana
Maine
Michigan
North Carolina
North Dakota
Rhode Island
Utah
Vermont
Wyoming

Here is the Vermont statute that defines the L3C and its requirements for compliance:

> *(27) "L3C" or "low-profit limited liability company" means a person organized under this chapter that is organized for a business purpose that satisfies and is at all times operated to satisfy each of the following requirements:*
>
> *(A) The company:*
>
> *(i) significantly furthers the accomplishment of one or more charitable or educational purposes within the meaning of Section 170(c)(2)(B) of the Internal Revenue Code of 1986, 26 U.S.C. Section 170(c)(2)(B); and*
>
> *(ii) would not have been formed but for the company's relationship to the accomplishment of charitable or educational purposes.*
>
> *(B) No significant purpose of the company is the production of income or the appreciation of property; provided, however, that the fact that a person produces significant income or capital appreciation shall not, in the absence of other factors, be conclusive evidence of a significant purpose involving the production of income or the appreciation of property.*
>
> *(C) No purpose of the company is to accomplish one or more political or legislative purposes within the meaning of Section 170(c)(2)(D) of the Internal Revenue Code of 1986, 26 U.S.C. Section 170(c)(2)(D).*

The L3C is the first entity to be created with the IRS primarily in mind. The IRS offers tax relief for private foundation *program-related investments,* which promote socially conscious efforts, and the L3C was created to enable entrepreneurs to attract private foundation investment more easily. Private foundations are typically penalized by the IRS if they make investments in certain for-profit entities. This can be frustrating for entrepreneurs looking for investment. With an L3C, entrepreneurs give up their tax benefits in exchange for the opportunity to have private foundations as investors who otherwise would not be able to invest.

Nonprofits are pretty restrictive in nature, but LLCs allow pass-through taxation, flexible membership and management, and freedom in how profits are distributed among the members. The L3C serves to take advantage of these benefits while allowing some of the tax advantages afforded to nonprofits. However, unlike 501(c)(3) nonprofit organizations, donations and investments in L3Cs are not tax deductible. Likewise, L3Cs are not exempt from federal and state taxes. They are subject to pass-through taxation, similar to that of a partnership or sole proprietorship, and are *not* allowed to elect a special form of taxation like a regular LLC has the right to do. On a brighter note, the IRS has yet to rule on whether the profit allocations of an L3C are subject to less taxation than the allocations from a regular LLC. We can only hope!

L3Cs are a powerful vehicle for various types of investors (from private foundations to individuals to government agencies) to take a risk on companies that offer a smaller chance of a fiscal return but possibly huge social benefits. The capital structure of the L3C allows for *tranching* by offering multiple tiers of membership interests, with each tier offering a different balance of social rewards and fiscal returns. This system enables a socially conscious organization to obtain financing from foundations, which usually donate money only to nonprofit organizations, and more profit-minded individuals, who, while being socially conscious themselves, are still interested in getting a return on their investment.

The single-member LLC

A single-member LLC isn't actually a different type of LLC. It's just a normal, regular LLC with one exception: there is only one member. Because LLCs were originally intended to be *partnerships*, a single-member LLC is still subject to some slightly different rules. Unlike an LLC with multiple members, a single member LLC is not allowed to elect the partnership form of taxation with the IRS. I discuss this in more detail in Chapter 8.

Additionally, in some states, a single-member LLC doesn't have the same level of *charging order protection* as a multiple-member LLC. This is because charging order protection was meant to protect the innocent partners from a member who has been subject to a judgment.

Aside from these few limitations, a single-member LLC is not much different than a multi-member one. Even though there is only one member, it's still required to have a detailed operating agreement in place. It's also still a good idea to document all company decisions in writing and retain them in the company kit, even though there is only one person deciding. Single-member LLCs *are* generally easy to run; however, don't get fooled into thinking that you're exempt from all of the documentation required of other, multi-member LLCs.

Chapter 3

Determining Whether an LLC Is Right for You

In This Chapter

- Comparing different entity types
- Deciding which entity is right for your situation

As a corporate consultant, the most common question I get is "Which entity is right for me?" That's also the question that's hardest to answer. After all, the entity type that's right for you depends wholly on your individual circumstances. You have to take into account all aspects of your business, such as the income you anticipate bringing in, the number of employees you intend to have, the amount of recordkeeping you're comfortable with, the state(s) in which you will be operating, how you intend to obtain financing, your exit strategy, and other personal preferences.

The majority of the time, I can safely refer clients to the limited liability company simply because it's so flexible that it can work for most business needs. However, that's not always the case, and the worst time to find out you chose the wrong business structure is after the fact. As you find out in Chapter 7, where I deal with converting to and from different entity types, rectifying this mistake can result in a monstrous taxable event.

So this is where I help you avoid all that drama and get started in the right direction. This chapter compares LLCs with other business structures and shows you how LLCs can help you achieve a variety of business goals.

Knowing Your Options: Other Business Structures

If you read Chapter 2, you're probably sold on the limited liability company as the entity type for you — and you're probably right! However, an LLC simply isn't the right match in a few situations. Before you can know for sure, you need to be aware of all the options. The following sections give you an overview of the different types of entities you have to choose from.

Going it alone: Sole proprietorships

Your kid's school bake sale . . . your stall at the local flea market . . . the consulting job you did when you weren't on the payroll — all perfect examples of sole proprietorships. A *sole proprietorship* automatically exists whenever you engage in business by and for yourself, without partners and without the protection of an LLC, corporation, or limited partnership. Although it sounds fancy and complicated, forming a sole proprietorship is about as easy as it gets.

Forming a sole proprietorship

When asked how one goes about forming a sole proprietorship, the simplest answer I can give is: You don't. When you begin transacting business, be it selling crafts at the local art fair or doing web design work in your spare time, you become a sole proprietor. Your state, city, and/or county may impose some business license requirements and fees on you in order for you to be allowed to do business in your current location, but aside from those few formalities, you're in business.

To do business under a name other than your own, you can file a fictitious firm name statement (also called a *DBA*) with your county clerk. A DBA enables you to market your services under the name "Super-Duper Fantastic Web Design" rather than simply "John Smith."

I know this sounds incredibly easy — and, for the most part, it is — but there are a few drawbacks. Namely, even if you file a DBA, you're still a sole proprietorship. So, although you may be operating under a name other than your own, don't get any lofty ideas that your business is anything other than just you. A DBA offers no barrier of legal separation between your business and yourself, and that fact should scare you. Keep reading to find out more about the considerations you have to take into account before settling on a sole proprietorship.

Shouldering full liability: The buck stops with you

Even though a sole proprietorship is simple to set up, it has many disadvantages. When you operate as a sole proprietorship, your personal assets are unconditionally at risk from being seized by an angry creditor or a lawsuit gone bad. There is an old saying, "You aren't in business until you've been sued," and as a sole proprietorship, you're handing over all your hard-earned assets (your home, your car, everything) on a silver platter. So if you're out selling cookies and somebody chokes on the oatmeal specials, you may be cashing out your kid's college fund sooner than you think.

Sole proprietorships are popular because they are super cheap and easy to form. I mean, they're sort of formed by default. You start selling a product or service and generate your first dollar of revenue and boom — you're a sole proprietorship. However, if the business you're pondering involves any interaction with the public, the costs you could find yourself facing can quickly eclipse whatever start-up fees you were trying to avoid in the first place. You won't think that they're so cheap and easy if you lose everything you own.

Exploring some more disadvantages

If I haven't scared you away from sole proprietorships yet, here are a few other drawbacks to ponder:

- **Limited financing options.** Unlike LLCs, which have membership interests, sole proprietorships don't have interests or any other form of ownership in the company. Your business is *you,* and you can't sell little pieces of yourself. This setup creates quite the conundrum if you want to raise money for your new venture by selling ownership interests.
- **No separate credit.** As an unincorporated entity, you cannot obtain credit in the name of the business. You're stuck using your own personal credit for things such as business loans and leases.
- **Limited life span.** With no legal separation between you and your business, your business is subject to the same limitations that you are: namely, your lack of immortality. In other words, your business dies when you do. After you pass away, instead of carrying on in one piece, your business goes through probate, and your business assets are ripped apart and possibly even liquidated.

All these disadvantages don't change the fact that sole proprietorships are *easy.* You don't have to do anything to form one, and you don't have to worry about recordkeeping requirements, keeping separate accounts, or accidently commingling funds like you would with a limited liability company or corporation. In a sole proprietorship, you get the benefit of being autonomous. You *are* the business; therefore, you answer to nobody. Well, except your customers.

At the end of the day, you need to decide whether going through the trouble and expense of forming your business as an LLC is worth your while. I can't give you a set answer to this question because it really depends on your individual situation, taking into account the value of your personal assets and how much exposure your entity has to the general public.

Not too long ago, I was teaching a class of MBA students at the University of Southern California, and a woman starting up a T-shirt business asked whether she should form an LLC right away. My answer to her was this: When you go into business, you need to be under the protection of an LLC or a corporation; however, before undertaking the formation process, operating as a sole proprietor for a bit to test your market is okay. This testing period includes such tasks as printing up samples and meeting with retailers to see what sort of reception your T-shirts get. This way, if you find that you don't have a viable market, the only investment you've lost is what you've paid to the local screen printer.

Losing LLC benefits with disregarded entity taxation

Like the courts, the IRS doesn't consider a sole proprietorship to be separate from its owner, which is why the IRS treats it as a *disregarded entity.* Disregarded entities have a form of taxation often referred to as *pass-through taxation,* because the business isn't taxed directly. Instead, the revenues and expenses of the business pass through and are taxed directly to the owner.

To calculate business profits and losses, you add a Schedule C to your 1040. On one side of the Schedule C, you list your business revenue; on the other side, you list your business expenses. Subtract one from the other and — voilà! — you get your net profit or net loss. You transfer this number to your 1040 and incorporate the income (or loss) into your normal tax burden.

Before applying your normal income tax rate to your business profits, you need to factor in a 15.3 percent self-employment tax. This tax serves as a substitute for Social Security and Medicare taxes that would normally be taken out of your paycheck. Shocked by the amount? Well, you may not realize it, but when you pay the 6.2 percent Social Security tax and the 1.45 percent Medicare tax out of your salary each week, your employer has to match it. Now that you are working for yourself, you get the full burden: 12.4 percent Social Security plus 2.9 percent Medicare equals a whopping 15.3 percent! Make more than most? At higher income levels, you pay an additional 0.9 percent Medicare tax! Luckily, to ease the burden a bit, the IRS allows you to deduct half the total amount of the self-employment tax.

Adding a partner: General partnerships

When a sole proprietor takes on one or more partners, a general partnership is born. Because a sole proprietorship by its very nature can be owned by only one person, there is no exception to this rule. Occasionally, smart entrepreneurs create a general partnership agreement among the partners. Like a sole proprietorship, no other paperwork is completed, and no filings need to be made for the formation to take place. All you have to do is start transacting business!

Even verbal agreements hold up in most states, so just because you don't have the terms of your partnership in writing doesn't mean that you aren't held to them. Considering that the person most likely to sue you is your partner (or wannabe partner), the fate of your business depends on you keeping accurate written agreements with everyone you do business with from day one. After all, if that person is willing to take you to court (you'd be surprised!), then he is likely also willing to embellish on any verbal "agreements" you may have made.

Even a *non-membership-related agreement,* which states that your business is taking on another individual for services but doesn't make her a partner, should be executed in writing so that the ownership (or lack thereof) can't be put up for interpretation later. Even better, don't take favors early on, and make sure to compensate those people who do work for you — especially when they don't own any of the business. Otherwise, they can either claim that they were employees (and sue you for minimum wage and so on) or, even worse, try to claim ownership of your business — no matter what you've agreed to verbally or in writing!

Doubling the trouble by doubling the partners

As easy as a general partnership is to form, it's equally easy to get into trouble. In a lot of ways, a general partnership is even *more* dangerous than a sole proprietorship. In a business organized as a general partnership, all the partners are *jointly* responsible for all the debts, judgments, negligent acts, obligations, and taxes of the business. Not only are you held personally responsible for those things that you had a hand in, but you also are personally responsible for the acts of your partners! This holds true even for silent partners who aren't aware of or involved in the day-to-day operation of the business.

All partners in a general partnership are held *jointly and equally liable* for the debts and obligations of the business. For example, say a partner at the deli you own wants to save a buck or two and, without your approval or knowledge, orders the weekly delivery of prosciutto from a shady supplier. A few days later, a customer calls to tell you that his 5-year-old got a severe bout of food poisoning, landing her in the hospital. The angry parent sues your partnership. He not only has full recourse against the personal assets of the offending partner, but he also can seize *your* house, car, and other assets in order to satisfy the judgment.

Finding out other disadvantages

In addition to this added exposure to liability, general partnerships share all the disadvantages that sole proprietorships do. Like a sole proprietorship, a general partnership isn't in any way separate from its owners. This means that your business cannot sell ownership interests in exchange for capital contributions and other forms of investment. This restriction makes raising any sort of formal financing close to impossible.

Another disadvantage to keep in mind is that the durability of the partnership is only as great as its weakest link. If one of the partners becomes disabled, goes bankrupt, or passes away, then the partnership goes with her.

Filing taxes with partnership taxation

General partnerships are subject to *partnership taxation.* This is a form of *pass-through taxation,* in which the profits and losses of the business flow through directly to the owners to be claimed on their personal tax returns. The partnership itself is not taxed. Instead, the partners are taxed on their share of the partnership income.

At the end of the business's fiscal year, you simply file an information statement with the IRS, **Form 1065,** which lists all the income and expenses that the business incurred during that time frame. After you total the amount of profit (or loss) that the partnership accrued, you issue each member a **Form K-1,** which lists the member's share of the profits that he must pay taxes on (or losses that he can use to offset income from other ventures). You can generally divide the profits and losses among the partners however you want, as long as all the profit gets allocated. If you're interested in learning more about partnership taxation, I go over it in more detail in Chapters 8 and 14.

General partnerships are subject to the same form of taxation that is the default for limited liability companies. However, the similarities end there. A general partnership is *not* considered an *incorporated entity* and offers zero liability protection for its owners.

Throwing in a little legal protection: Limited partnerships

Think of a *limited partnership* as a general partnership with a little bit of protection against lawsuits thrown in. Whereas a general partnership doesn't protect any of the owners against the business's lawsuits and creditors, a limited partnership protects the silent partners of the business (also called the *limited partners*). Limited partners can receive profit from the company, but they don't manage the business's day-to-day operations. If the business goes south, the limited partners risk losing only the money that they've invested in the company, while the managers (called *general partners*) put all their personal assets at risk.

As far as the general partners are concerned, the business may as well be a general partnership. They are jointly and equally liable for the debts and obligations of the business, even those entered into by the other general partner(s). Also like a general partnership, a limited partnership is subject to partnership taxation.

Limited partnerships can have any number of general and limited partners, as long as there's at least one general partner to take the blame if something goes wrong.

I'm often asked why anyone bothers to use limited partnerships, especially considering that they're somewhat complicated to set up and they lack basic liability protection for the general partners. These reasons alone make the limited partnership a bad choice for business owners; however, because of the limits they place on the decision-making power of the limited partners, limited partnerships are great for use in estate planning (for example, the kids can receive money from, but not manage, the assets of the limited partnership). If you are interested in estate planning, I discuss it at greater length at `www.dummies.com/extras/limitedliabilitycompanies`.

Meeting the black sheep of the partnership family: LLPs and LLLPs

Before the limited liability company was born, a few enterprising states decided to create variations on the limited partnership. The two main variations are the *limited liability partnership* (*LLP* for short) and the *limited liability limited partnership* (or *LLLP*). You probably won't see a lot of these entities in practice nowadays because the LLC has trumped all their benefits. However, they still have some roles to play in professional partnerships and real estate transactions.

These entity types aren't available in all states, so if you're thinking of forming one, check your state's laws to see whether they are recognized in your jurisdiction.

Limited liability partnership (LLP)

A limited liability partnership is like a limited partnership without limited partners. An LLP has only general partners who are held personally responsible for the debts and obligations of the business. So how is this entity different from a general partnership, you ask? Well, an LLP has an added layer of liability protection that insulates the partners from the wrongful acts of the other partners. In other words, if you're a partner in an LLP, then you're responsible only for your own misdeeds, not for those of a shady business partner.

LLPs emerged in the early 1990s in response to the real estate crash in the previous years. After a wave of bank failures, there was a rush to recover assets by targeting the accountants and lawyers who had advised the failed banks. LLPs were created to help shield the personal assets of the innocent lawyers and accountants from the massive claims made on their partnerships. The new partnership structure caught on quickly, and by 1996, more than 40 states had adopted rules on the formation and governance of an LLP entity type.

LLPs are still used to this day; the structure is common for professionals such as lawyers, accountants, doctors, and architects. This entity makes sense for them because licensed professionals aren't allowed the same levels of personal liability protection as those provided by regular LLCs and corporations. Some states allow LLPs to be used *only* in this manner.

Limited liability limited partnership (LLLP)

A limited liability limited partnership (try saying that ten times fast!) is sort of a hybrid between a limited partnership and a limited liability partnership. Like a limited partnership, an LLLP has both *limited partners,* who have limited liability and risk losing only whatever amount they invested in the business, and *general partners,* who are personally liable for the debts and obligations of the business. As in a limited partnership, only the general partners are allowed to engage in the day-to-day management of the business.

From a silent investor's perspective, this sort of arrangement can help keep the general partners honest. After all, they're a lot less apt to let the business flounder if their personal assets are at stake. Because of this feature, LLLPs are common in real estate ventures, with the financial backers acting as silent limited partners.

LLLPs have yet to really catch on and still are allowed in only about half the states. They are usually formed by converting an existing limited partnership.

Separating yourself from your business: Corporations

If this is your first venture, you may think of all corporations as massive multinational conglomerates, but that isn't the case. Corporations have been around for centuries and, until the recent introduction of the LLC, were the only business structure that allowed entrepreneurs to start ventures without opening themselves up to heaps of personal liability. Contrary to popular belief, a corporation isn't much more difficult to form and maintain than a limited liability company.

You'll notice that the vast majority of publicly traded companies are structured as corporations. This is because, unlike limited liability companies, corporations have automatic free transferability of ownership interests (called *stock*). They are also backed by hundreds of years of case law that removes questions as to the outcomes of lawsuits. This is especially true in Delaware, where a court of chancery takes lawsuits involving corporations incredibly seriously and has worked hard to develop fair and accurate case law that directly supports and benefits the shareholders of the business. This is why most publicly traded corporations are Delaware corporations.

Creating a legal "person"

A corporation is different from a sole proprietorship or partnership in that it's considered a legal entity unto itself, completely separate from its owners (called *shareholders*). In the eyes of the law, corporations are treated as if they were people, with distinct identities. Corporations are able to sue and be sued, and lawsuits must be brought against the corporation rather than the individual shareholders. (A limited liability company has a lot of similar characteristics.)

Maintaining a separation between you and your business becomes a big concern when you're operating as a corporation. If this legal separation fails, a creditor could *pierce the corporate veil* and go after your personal assets to settle the debts and obligations of the business.

In order to maintain your corporation's liability protection, you must be diligent about recordkeeping. This task includes drafting minutes that document the annual and special meetings of the shareholders and directors. Even if you're the sole shareholder, you still need to follow these formalities, and all major decisions affecting the operation of the business need to be made by formal resolution and properly documented. In addition, you must keep accurate financial records and refrain from commingling personal funds with those of your business.

Taking these steps to protect yourself may seem like a lot of work, but it's worth it in the long run. Limited liability companies have fewer recordkeeping requirements but also less case law that substantiates that recordkeeping *isn't* required. If you decide that a corporation is the route for you, then you'll want to sign up for an online service that automates and stores your company recordkeeping. This service enables you to relax, knowing that you're one important step closer to your corporate veil holding up in court. You'll also have fewer intercompany disputes because all major decisions will be made according to procedure and accurately documented.

A corporation protects its owners from lawsuits and creditors; however, it doesn't protect *the business* from the liabilities of the owners like an LLC does. So if a shareholder of a corporation is sued for personal reasons, her ownership *(stock)* of the corporation is considered a personal asset of hers and can be seized by the judgment creditor. Depending on the level of your personal exposure to liability, the fact that a corporation lacks this *dual protection* (which is inherent in a limited liability company) may end up being a huge prohibiting factor for you.

Dealing with the blow of double taxation

Like the courts, the Internal Revenue Service considers corporations to be entities separate from their owners. Corporations are the only entities that are subject to their own taxation. The company's profit (or loss) does not flow through to the owners of the business, but instead remains in the corporation and is subject to corporate income tax.

From there, you can distribute the profits to the shareholders in the form of *dividends.* This is where things can get a bit tricky. After the profit is distributed to the shareholders, it's taxed again at the shareholder level. Because the same profits are taxed twice — both at the corporate level and at the individual shareholder level — this is commonly referred to as *double taxation.*

As scary as it sounds, double taxation doesn't have to be a bad thing. If you wish to retain the profits in the company rather than distribute them, then only the company will pay taxes, and you'll actually pay less in taxes than if your business was subject to the pass-through taxation of a partnership or sole proprietorship. LLCs can elect corporate taxation, and in some cases, this is the right thing to do. In Chapter 14, I go into more detail on ways you can curtail the double-taxation problem.

When a corporation issues dividends to its shareholders, it doesn't have the same flexibility that a limited liability company enjoys, as I explain in Chapter 2. Dividends in a corporation must be issued in proportion to the shareholders' ownership interests.

Unfortunately, the corporation's losses cannot be passed on to the individual shareholders to help offset their other income. Even though the losses do need to stay in the corporation, this isn't such a bad deal for small businesses that intend to turn a profit soon. Corporate losses can be used to offset corporate profits in other years (so you don't pay taxes on that portion of profits), up to 2 years retroactively and up to 20 years in the future.

The IRS recognizes corporations as separate taxable entities. So, unlike in partnerships and sole proprietorships, you can't transfer assets into and out of a corporation as easily without creating a taxable event.

Easing the tax burden: S corporations

All *S corporations* start out as regular corporations. An S corporation is formed only when a regular corporation elects a special small-business tax status with the IRS. This is done by filing an S Election, **Form 2553,** with the IRS within a few months of the corporation's formation.

Obtaining pass-through taxation, corporation style

S corporation tax status is a pass-through tax status. Like sole proprietorship or partnership taxation, the revenues and expenses of the business "pass through" to the shareholders' individual tax returns. The similarities end there, however. S corporation tax status requires that the business file its own tax return, the 1120S (instead of the **Form 1120** return that regular corporations are required to file); however, the company is still required to issue K-1s to the shareholders as it would if it were a partnership.

The main difference between S corporation taxation and that of other entities is that the owners/shareholders can be employed by the business, paying themselves a salary that is subject to the same sort of payroll taxes deducted from all paychecks. If you've been paying attention, you're probably wondering what the big deal is — after all, as I mention earlier in the chapter, self-employment tax is equal to the Social Security and Medicare tax that gets deducted for each employee. So where are the savings?

Here's the kicker: Any profit allocated to the shareholders above and beyond the "reasonable salary" they've already paid themselves is not subject to the 15.3 percent self-employment tax. If your business generates more than the salary you pay yourself, the resulting savings can be substantial. What constitutes a "reasonable salary" in the eyes of the IRS? Well, the amount isn't really set in stone, but if you were ever audited, the IRS would want to make sure that it is consistent with the standard for a professional in your industry with your job title and responsibilities. If you aren't sure of the amount, you may want to do a quick search on `www.salary.com`, a site that lists average salaries for various job titles.

Complicating matters with IRS restrictions

The IRS seems to live by the maxim that all roses have thorns, and if a rose doesn't have thorns, then gosh darn it, they'll give it some! So the IRS gave the S corporation ownership restrictions. Lots of them. If your corporation (or even your LLC) has elected S corporation tax status, then you are required to abide by a few little rules:

- Your corporation must not have more than 100 shareholders.
- Shareholders can consist of only natural persons, individual trusts (for estate planning purposes), and tax-exempt nonprofit organizations. This specifically excludes any other entity or business structure, such as a limited liability company or corporation.
- Shareholders must be citizens or resident aliens of the United States.
- The corporation is allowed to issue only one class of stock.
- Banks and insurance companies are barred from being shareholders.
- All shareholders must unanimously consent to the S corporation tax designation. In other words, a majority vote won't do the trick.

If you're truly a small business, then an S corporation may suit you. Just make sure that you intend to stay small for the time being, because when you elect to be an S corporation, you're stuck with the decision for five years. (Don't even think about going public or raising institutional capital!) At least that much time needs to pass before the IRS will allow you to make another tax election.

Getting Personal: Using an LLC to Achieve Your Goals

I've noticed that a lot of books about LLCs and corporations dive into the advantages and disadvantages of the various entity types but never help you bridge that gap between understanding these business structures and applying them to your real-world situation. It's a tough endeavor, indeed, especially because no two entrepreneurs' issues or circumstances are exactly alike.

If you haven't already, read Chapter 2 regarding the ins and outs of limited liability companies. The background information there can help you make sense of what I tell you in this section. After skimming that chapter, you should have a pretty good idea of the various entity types you can choose from. In this section, I show you many of the benefits that forming an LLC can bring not only to your business ventures but also to your personal financial plans.

Keep in mind that if I promote one entity over another, it's not because I'm biased on the matter. The truth is that, due to the tremendous amount of flexibility a limited liability company offers, there is a good chance that the LLC will end up being your entity of choice.

Running a small business

Tens of millions of Americans operate small businesses. They range from small, home-based side businesses to fully operational companies with many employees. For the most part, these individuals operate without protection. Granted, they may not take what they do too seriously. They may consider themselves independent contractors or consultants, but in today's litigious society, operating without even a basic level of liability protection is a bad move. Not to mention that establishing your (albeit "small") business as an LLC helps others take it more seriously. If it's clear to the world that you're serious about your business, others will be serious about it as well.

If you're operating as a sole proprietorship, you're probably used to a specific way of being taxed and the liberty of not having to keep records or officially document decisions. And, unless you're a full-fledged operation, you may think that this is worth the risks. Spending a lot of time and money to form a corporation or an LLC is overkill for a simple, at-home web designer, plumber, or dog walker, right? Well, consider this: What if one of the dogs you're walking bites someone? Or the pipes you installed burst, causing tens of thousands of dollars in water damage? When you're sued, you risk losing everything — not just your business, but all your personal assets as well.

Very few businesses wouldn't benefit from the protection of an LLC or a corporation. If you're still operating as a sole proprietor, my guess is that your accountant or CPA has advised you to remain so. What a lot of tax professionals don't understand is that even if a particular business may not derive tax benefits from forming an LLC or a corporation, operating as a sole proprietorship is still a dangerous proposition because of the risk of losing all your personal assets in a lawsuit. In this section, I present the options that small-business owners have for protecting their companies and personal assets.

Relying on insurance — to a point

Business liability insurance is a good way to help protect yourself. I am a big proponent of these insurance policies because they add an extra layer of protection . . . the key word being *extra.* Most insurance policies have disclaimers a mile long and aren't too keen about paying out in a timely manner. Also, over the years, I've found that having insurance tends to *encourage* lawsuits rather than deter them. After all, if someone knows that you have insurance that will pay out, he will have *much* more incentive to file that lawsuit.

Your best bet is to keep the policy as your second line of defense rather than your *only* defense. This is especially true for small-time independent contractors such as babysitters and pet-sitters. Following are the only two exceptions to the rule of using an LLC with business liability insurance as a second form of protection:

- **Making gift baskets for your friends as a side business?** If your company isn't exposed to a lot of liability and is so small that forming a corporation or LLC would be cost prohibitive (for example, you have a business operating in California, where the fees can be pretty gnarly), then you may want to look into getting a good insurance policy and saving the LLC for later when you're more established and have more dough.
- **Is your company professionally licensed and required to operate under a professional LLC or corporation?** You probably don't have much choice for having insurance as your first line of defense. For instance, if you're a doctor, malpractice insurance isn't just smart, it's legally required. Want to know if this applies to you? Read Chapter 2, where I go over professional LLCs in detail.

Taking your business seriously so that others will too

If you don't take your business seriously, neither will your customers. One of the easiest ways to show that you're serious about what you do is to form a corporation or limited liability company. Adding *Inc.* or *LLC* after your name helps reassure your customers that you're official, not some fly-by-night operation. You'd be surprised how beneficial this designation can be to a small business — so much so that the added business may far exceed the formation costs.

Considering S corporations

S corporations have pass-through taxation similar to LLCs, the difference being that the owner is allowed to hire herself. As I discuss earlier in this chapter, as long as she pays herself a salary that is commensurate with those of her peers, all additional profits are *not* subject to self-employment tax.

In a nutshell, if the total annual income you personally derive from your business is more than the average salary of others with a similar job description, then, from a tax savings perspective, you should elect to be taxed as an S corporation over any other form of pass-through taxation. The benefit of being able to hire yourself does favor the S corporation pretty heavily in certain circumstances. I explain S corporation taxation in more detail in Chapter 8.

Electing S corporation taxation comes with a slew of ownership restrictions, which I address earlier in this chapter in the section "Complicating matters with IRS restrictions." If you aren't prepared to abide by them, you shouldn't elect this form of taxation. Otherwise, you'll automatically revert to corporation tax status, which can bring about some pretty large tax burdens if you aren't prepared for them.

Taking it to the next level with C corporations

Corporations (that haven't elected S corporation tax status) are often referred to as *C corporations,* simply to differentiate them from S corporations. C corporations are subject to double taxation of profits, which tends to scare a lot of entrepreneurs away. In some situations, it doesn't necessarily have to. Because a corporation is taxed as its own entity, taxable income on a federal level, if under $50,000, is subject to a corporate tax rate of only 15 percent. The tax rate is tiered, and after about $75,000 of profit, it jumps to around 35 percent.

This high rate can seem daunting at first, but keep in mind that most upstarts and growing enterprises operate at a pretty modest profit (which is the majority of your "taxable income"). This is especially true for corporations, which are allowed to deduct a lot of business expenses that S corporations and LLCs cannot. Although the extra paperwork and recordkeeping required for a corporation, as well as the tax structure, may be a bit much for a simple independent contractor trying to feed a family, they're well suited to businesses that place a high priority on growth and want to retain company profits. I discuss corporate taxation in more detail in Chapter 8.

Another scenario in which a corporation is a better option is if your company is operating in multiple states. Multistate taxation is often much more favorable at the corporate level than any other form of taxation, especially that of the S corporation. I discuss multistate taxation issues in more detail in Chapter 15.

Combining all the perks in one entity: LLCs

Although I discuss the merits of S corporations and C corporations for small businesses in the preceding sections, everything I've said thus far is applicable to LLCs as well because the LLC is the only entity type that can choose how it wants to be taxed. By default, multiple member LLCs are subject to partnership taxation; however, they can also elect corporate taxation or S corporation taxation. Although you're stuck with the form of taxation you choose for five years, there are a few ways you can get out of it if you're an LLC, which I discuss in more detail in Chapter 8. This sort of flexibility is one of the reasons LLCs are perfect for almost all small businesses.

The LLC being the only entity able to elect pretty much *any* form of taxation is a huge bonus. In so many situations regarding small businesses, LLCs are superior to S corporations and C corporations — I could go on all day. But I'll keep this point short and sweet: I strongly recommend that you form your small business as a limited liability company if

- **You and your partners require varied distributions of profit.** With a corporation, unless you create a whole new class of stock (in other words, jump through quite a few hoops), you are required to issue dividends in proportion to the ownership percentages. With LLCs, this is easy!
- **You want to allow your business to grow a bit before electing corporate taxation.** Because LLCs are automatically subject to partnership taxation, you can enjoy the pass-through taxation for a few years until you're ready to elect corporate taxation.
- **You and your partners have a lot of personal liability.** Remember, an LLC has *dual liability protection,* which protects the integrity of the business if one of the partners *personally* faces bankruptcy, divorce, or the wrath of a judgment creditor.
- **You want a flexible ownership/management structure.** With an LLC, you have a lot of flexibility in regard to who can and cannot engage in the day-to-day acts of the business, whereas with a corporation, you're stuck with the traditional structure of officers managing day-to-day operations, directors managing the officers, and shareholders managing the directors.
- **You want pass-through taxation yet cannot abide by the restrictions that come with operating as an S corporation.** If you have an institutional investor or a business partner who is not a U.S. citizen, you automatically fall into this category.

- **You have substantial assets that you want to transfer into (or out of) the business.** Only with an LLC can assets be transferred in and out without creating a taxable event.
- **Partners of the business are personally guaranteeing business loans and debts.** Only with an LLC is recourse debt allowed to be calculated as a loss to the responsible member. This is one reason LLCs are so popular for holding real estate — so the mortgage interest deduction can be passed to the guaranteeing member.
- **Investors want capital contributions to be immediately deductible.** If the business does not make a profit in that year, the partner theoretically is able to take whatever he contributed last year as a loss. With an S corporation, that loss can be taken only after the business has folded. With a C corporation, that loss never flows back to the individual and instead remains in the business, allowed to be carried forward up to 20 years.

If you are set on S corporation taxation, your best bet may be to make that tax election through a limited liability company rather than a traditional corporation. LLCs, by statute, require a lot less strict recordkeeping formalities than corporations.

Even if you opt for a corporation, if your business has substantial assets, you should do your best to insulate each asset in its own limited liability company. That way, each asset is safe from the liabilities of the operating business and the liabilities of the individual shareholders. I show you how to do so in Chapter 17.

If your small business involves professionally licensed services, you may be required to operate as a *professional corporation* or *professional LLC.* You may also be subject to certain restrictions on whom your partners can be and what liability you are personally protected against. If you think this requirement applies to you, flip to the section about professional LLCs in Chapter 2.

Raising capital for your business

The majority of the questions I get from readers relate to raising capital for a new venture or idea. My answer depends on whether the person is looking to create the next Google, wants to find a cure for cancer, or is interested in putting food on the table and nothing more. If the latter applies to you, then I wrote the previous section "Running a small business" with you in mind. If you want to start a company with the potential to be huge, however, keep reading.

Forming your business as a corporation to attract investors

One of the primary concerns of starting a new venture is acquiring capital. This need for cash can be a game-changer when it comes to selecting an entity type for your new business. If you seriously intend to go after private equity (venture capital, institutional investors, and so on) or raise money through an *initial public offering (IPO),* then there's a chance that you'll want to form your business as a corporation rather than a limited liability company. In this section, I tell you some of the big reasons why.

If you're raising venture capital, your first round of financing is either your *seed round* or your *Series A round* (if you don't raise a seed round first). When you get your first term sheet, one of the things you'll notice is that the venture capital firm or institutional investor isn't issued plain ol' common stock. Instead, the investor gets *preferred shares,* usually titled Series A, that offers special privileges, such as

- Liquidity (the shares can be converted to common stock).
- First dibs at dividends and the proceeds of any liquidation that occurs.
- Anti-dilution protection, which allows the investor to maintain fractional (for example, 15 percent) ownership of the company even when more stock is issued in the future.
- Mandatory or optional redemption schedules (indicating when the investor can sell out). This keeps the investor in the game until the company has had a chance to prove itself.
- Special voting rights and preferences giving the investor special abilities to exercise control over the management.
- A fixed return on investment.

Any future financing rounds are titled Series B, Series C, and so on, with the most recent taking priority and first position. If you want more information about securities issues, such as registrations and exemptions, turn to Chapter 11.

Venture capitalists have investors, too! Because some of the larger venture capital firms have investors of a certain type (such as pension funds or other pseudo nonprofit or public interest companies) for tax purposes, they cannot invest in a pass-through entity like an LLC with partnership taxation. This is one of the reasons why, if you are operating as an LLC, you'll likely be required to convert to a regular (C) corporation before a venture capital firm will invest capital.

Corporation shares were made to be liquid and freely transferable. Although a limited liability company can be structured to have similar flexibility, LLCs aren't designed for it. Also, although the formalities required for corporations may be a drag for a small business owner, sophisticated investors have grown to appreciate them. With the law on their side, they can be sure to get their regular financial statements and know that all corporate decisions are properly documented, which helps prevent intercompany disputes later on.

The fixed structure of shareholders, board of directors, and officers of a corporation also offers an established set of roles that have been tried and tested over the years. Usually, larger investors request to sit on the board of directors, while you and your founders — the entrepreneurs — take the officer roles.

Because corporations have been around for so long, a lot of case law has developed around them, which significantly limits the chance of courtroom surprises down the road. This is especially true in Delaware, where a special chancery court handles all business issues and is backed by hundreds of years of case law. LLCs, on the other hand, don't have the benefit of a long history. They are the new kid on the block, and when an investment firm is handing over millions of dollars, the last thing it wants is another unknown.

Knowing when an LLC will work

Small-time angel investors, friends, family members, and other investors who don't require a complex capital structure in order to invest money in your business or idea may actually prefer a limited liability company over a corporation. Most companies don't operate at a profit in their first year, and due to the pass-through taxation of LLCs, the company's losses flow to its owners. These losses can be used as a fat write-off to offset an investor's other income. With all other things being equal, the investor gets to write off the value of her investment immediately.

When you are raising money for your LLC, you must make sure that you have an ironclad operating agreement and buy-sell agreements in place. I show you how to draft these agreements throughout Part III of this book.

Maximizing real estate investments

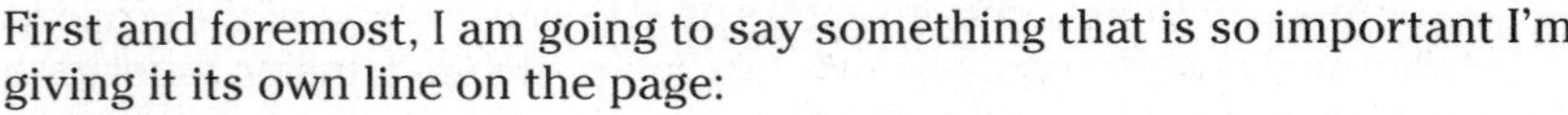

First and foremost, I am going to say something that is so important I'm giving it its own line on the page:

You can do nothing worse than hold investment property in your own name.

Please read that statement again and again until it's a mantra that keeps repeating in your head. Of course, this statement is not 100 percent factual. Technically, you could do worse things, such as look down a mortar tube after lighting a firework to see why it didn't go off, profess to the IRS that income taxes are not legal and you don't have to pay them, point a gun at the police, and so on. However, holding investment property in your own name really is a terrible idea. You see, if your tenant slips and falls on the front porch, not only could your property be dust, but also your savings, your other properties, and even your kid's college fund (and possibly even your dog, if he is valuable enough!). Once they know that you have assets, attorneys and claimants can be vicious beyond belief. Get it? Got it? Good.

So now that you know you need some kind of entity to protect your investment real estate, the following sections help you compare corporations to LLCs.

Knowing when corps can kill

This is by far the easiest section for me to write because the limited liability company has an acute advantage over all other entities when it comes to holding real estate. With all the characteristics of LLCs — flexibility, pass-through taxation, dual-layer liability protection — it's almost as if they were made for real estate.

If you're using an entity to hold real estate assets, you're most likely looking to gain passive income from the investment. If you were to place that rental property into a corporation, all the passive income you earn would be subject to double taxation — first at the corporate level and then individually when you remove the profits. What's worse is that because assets cannot be freely transferred into and out of a corporation, you'll face a pretty severe taxable event when you decide to sell. Oh yeah, and you'll face double taxation on that income as well.

To get around double taxation, real estate investors used to use S corporations for holding property. If you remember, S corporations are just like regular corporations but have a pass-through tax status. They also come burdened with a slew of ownership restrictions. But the big thorn in your side comes when you want to transfer the property out of the corporation. Unlike an LLC, an S corporation cannot do so tax free.

You may remember the one big advantage of S corporations is that profits aren't subject to self-employment tax. Well, that perk doesn't apply here. Because real estate isn't an active trade or business and generally involves only the passive holding of property, the income derived from it isn't subject to self-employment tax anyway. Only regular income tax applies. So the S corp's one claim to fame doesn't even apply in this scenario. The only time to consider using an S corporation with real estate is if you're so active in your real estate endeavors (rehabbing, flipping properties, and so on) that the IRS considers it a business. In this case, you have some number crunching to do before selecting your entity type.

Protecting real estate with LLCs

An LLC, when used to hold passive real estate investments, rocks your tax bill. First, when purchasing a property, it can usually be transferred into an LLC without creating a taxable event. Second, whatever profits you acquire from the property are considered passive and subject only to regular income tax. And third, as you get older, your limited liability companies fit perfectly into your estate planning strategy. I devote Chapter 18 to the ins and outs of real estate investing, but I'm warning you, you may find a teeny-weeny bit of preaching on the merits of the LLC.

With an LLC, profits do not need to be allocated and distributed according to the ownership percentages. You can choose to dole them out however you want. For example, if you own only 10 percent of the limited liability company but want 90 percent of the profits (and the other members are okay with that setup), then that's what you get. This is just one more advantage that LLCs have over C corporations and S corporations. (By the way, if you're lucky enough to find partners who are okay with this arrangement, then please send 'em my way!)

Because an LLC's losses are passed on to the owners, if you own multiple real estate properties, each within its own LLC, and one of the properties encounters a hefty loss, you can deduct that loss at tax time against the income from your other properties. Typically, this sort of loss is deductible only against *passive income,* such as real estate. However, if you work with your accountant or corporate consultant and structure it correctly, you may be able to deduct the loss against *active income* (such as dividends). You can do so by becoming an active real estate investor who spends a certain amount of time each year handling the day-to-day management of the properties.

If you are a silent investor and you want your operating partner(s) to add some skin to the game, you may want to consider using a *limited liability limited partnership* to hold your property — assuming that your state allows them, of course (not all states do!). I discuss these entity types earlier in this chapter.

Planning your estate

Note: If you are immortal, you may skip this section.

LLCs are becoming more and more popular in estate planning. Trusts are still king, but now they're generally used in conjunction with LLCs so that your assets are protected while you're still alive. A trust usually doesn't provide any asset protection whatsoever, whereas an LLC provides *dual liability protection,* as I discuss in Chapter 2.

Within every family looms the perfect LLC

Dan and Denise Sager have two children, Michael, 17, and Mary, 16. One night at the dinner table, Michael has one of his crazy business ideas, but this time it's actually a good one! He suggests that they all go into business together with a company that will buy old, sad-looking homes, fix them up, and sell them at a profit. They would start locally — in their own neighborhood — and then branch out from there. Their background: Dan is a builder with dozens of industry connections; Denise is a part-time accountant; Mary has an eye for design; and Michael is a born handyman, a jack-of-all-trades with the passion and excitement to keep the project moving.

For this highly motivated, entrepreneurial family, an LLC for each project works best — but not just any LLC. They know that LLCs are extremely flexible in their organization and operation, so the Sager family discusses each partner's role to decide how to structure their first entity.

The company will be divided into four equal parts, with each family member owning an equal percentage (they're all members) and handling different aspects of the business. Dan will line up the financing and hire the necessary subcontractors, while Denise will take care of the budgeting and accounting. Mary will be the design master, picking out the materials and colors for the renovation; and Michael will spearhead the actual labor, along with marketing the property once the renovation has been completed. Because of their children's ages, Denise and Dan don't want to empower their kids with a lot of management decisions until they turn 18. So Ma and Pa create a manager-managed LLC in which they are the sole managers and the kids are hired as employees and take a draw. This way, the kids get their profit distributions, but they can still be fired (should their grades drop).

With estate taxes as they are, if you have a large estate worth more than $1 million, you may want to start gifting your assets to your heirs while you are alive. LLCs are especially useful for this purpose because they allow you to gift small portions of large assets (such as real estate) by gifting membership shares. They also enable you to maintain control of the assets while you are alive, even if your heir is the majority owner of the LLC. You do so by making yourself a manager of the LLC until your death, at which point your heir takes over.

When you actively plan your estate by using trusts and LLCs, you have much more control over what happens to your assets after your passing. An LLC can keep your estate out of probate and avoid the accompanying (often astronomical) *probate fees* (costs that are incurred when the court system has to distribute an estate).

A word on probate: If the Spanish Inquisitors had been just a little bit more vicious, they probably would have just subjected their victims to the bureaucratic nightmare that is probate. In probate, you leave the major decisions up to a judge, and you never know how things could turn out.

With an LLC, you can ensure that your assets go to the right people and don't get dwindled away with legal fees until they turn to dust. For more information on estate planning, check out `www.dummies.com/extras/limitedliabilitycompanies`.

Protecting your personal assets

In the section "Running a small business" earlier in this chapter, I go over the importance of segregating business assets out of the operating company and protecting them in their own separate entities. Well, the same thing applies to individuals. Business aside, if you want to protect certain personal assets from personal lawsuits, then you'll want to follow the same formula.

Without a doubt, the limited liability company is the best entity type for asset protection. Without the *charging order protection* inherent in LLCs, whatever assets you're trying to protect are open to any personal creditors or lawsuits you may have. In other words, if you place an asset in a corporation and are sued personally, then the judgment creditor would be able to attach your stock in that corporation and seize the underlying asset in order to pay the judgment. If this lack of protection offered by a corporation doesn't automatically disqualify it, then here's something else for you to chew on: You cannot transfer assets into and out of a corporation without creating a taxable event. Not so with LLCs.

There are myriad ways to use LLCs to protect your assets. If asset protection is your primary goal, then flip to Chapter 17, where I discuss the different strategies in detail.

Part II

Your First Steps: Forming Your LLC

Five Characteristics of the Perfect Name for your LLC

- **It's distinct.** Naming your brand-new and improved social media site FaceSpace or MyBook won't give the impression that it is either "new" or "improved." Quite the opposite, actually.
- **It's meaningful.** This doesn't mean to be descriptive; save the description for your taglines and slogans. Make your LLC's name evocative and allude to the heart and soul of your business.
- **It's expansive.** Be careful that your name doesn't restrain your business to a specific location, product, or service.
- **It's global.** Make sure that your name is internationally friendly. Otherwise, you may be ready to expand abroad one day only to find out that the name you chose has a negative connotation in certain cultures!
- **It's searchable.** In this day and age, there's a good chance that most of your customers will find you on the Internet, even if your LLC is not a web company. When entering your company name into a search engine, you don't want a potential customer to be flooded with irrelevant results.

Visit `www.dummies.com/extras/limitedliabilitycompanies` for advice on changing the name of your LLC.

In this part . . .

- Decide what state in which to form your LLC.
- Find out what decisions you and your partners need to make before creating your articles of organization.
- Create and file your articles of organization.
- Discover how to transfer the assets and business operations of your current business to your newly formed LLC.

Chapter 4

Playing — and Winning — the Name Game

In This Chapter

- Deciding on a company name
- Finding out whether the name you want is available
- Securing your intellectual property
- Thinking about a logo
- Switching to a new name

Compared to other decisions you have to make, selecting a name for your LLC may seem simple. However, after you get started on the process, you may soon realize that settling on a name can be one of the most agonizing and time-consuming aspects of starting a business. Don't believe me? Well, after a few rare and cherished "aha!" moments followed by the discovery that your chosen name is already in use, you'll be able to relate.

In this chapter, I help you get started in the hunt for a good (and available!) name and tell you the precautions to take so that no one else can nab it. I also give you the scoop on changing the name of your LLC should you ever have the need to do so.

Establishing the Best Name for Your LLC

An inescapable fact of human nature is that we are inclined to imitate one another. Imitation is a good thing for all those fashion-challenged folks out there; however, that collective intelligence doesn't do you much good when you're naming your LLC. Without anything to guide you, the "name-storming" sessions you hold may result only in the regurgitation of everyone else's (already considered and rejected) bad ideas. So let's go over some quick guidelines that may help you through the process.

If your LLC happens to be a real estate development project and you're happy with a name like 543 Winnetaka Street, LLC, you can happily skip this section. Otherwise, keep reading for some tips that I've picked up over the years along my entrepreneurial journey.

Considering naming guidelines

You may think that having boundless options gives you a better chance of coming up with a great name, but think again. After all, creativity is better served when it's subject to a few (helpful) restrictions. Before you let the ideas fly, check out a few naming "rules" that I've gathered from industry experts:

- **Be distinct.** Naming your brand-new and improved social media site FaceSpace or MyBook won't give the impression that it is either "new" or "improved." Quite the opposite, actually.
- **Be memorable.** Avoid acronyms like the plague. Unless you have a huge annual marketing budget to waste, don't attempt to grab anyone's attention with a few letters. If you're serious about shortening your name, condense it into an amalgam, like FedEx for Federal Express or Nabisco for National Biscuit Company.

  That said, long names are often more memorable than short names, contrary to what you may hear elsewhere — think TGI Friday's versus Joe's. An added plus: You'll have better luck finding a domain name for a longer name than a shorter one.
- **Be approachable.** Make sure that your LLC's name is easy to pronounce. You don't want people to avoid saying the name because they're afraid of mispronouncing it. Try out potential names on a first-grader. If he can't pronounce it, ditch it and have him help you find an alternative. Hey, you'd be surprised at the good ideas kids can have!
- **Be meaningful.** This doesn't mean to be descriptive; save the description for your taglines and slogans. Make your LLC's name evocative and allude to the heart and soul of your business. For example, Netflix is a great name for an online video rental site, whereas FilmsOnline.com is literal rather than meaningful.

- **Be vivid.** What image and feeling do you want your customers to associate with your brand? Try to paint a picture. For example, the name Stonyfield Farm makes you think of green cow pastures, which gives the impression of wholesomeness.
- **Be bold.** With so many names already taken, you can't be afraid of taking risks. As long as your name is evocative (see "Be meaningful" earlier in this list), don't worry about being too unusual — just look at Yahoo! and Google.
- **Be eternal.** LLCs are now made to exist in perpetuity, so why restrict the life span of your business with its name? Choose a name that will sound good for decades or even centuries to come, or you may face the same conundrum as *Twentieth Century* Fox.
- **Be expansive.** Be careful that your name doesn't restrain your business to a specific location, product, or service. For instance, Los Angeles Rentals would have to spend a pretty penny on rebranding if it ever expanded to another market. No matter how small your LLC is now, you don't want your name to hold you back as your business moves forward.
- **Be global.** Make sure that your name is internationally friendly. Otherwise, you may be ready to expand abroad one day only to find out that the name you chose has a negative connotation in certain cultures! It's only funny when it happens to other people (like when Chevrolet learned that Nova translates to "no go" in Spanish).

  Think this rule doesn't apply to you because you don't intend to go global anytime soon? Take a walking tour of a major city and you'll see how many people speak foreign languages. To avoid having entire market segments laugh at you when they pass your booth at a convention or spot your ad in a magazine, get a third-party assessment done to verify that your LLC's name has universal appeal!
- **Be searchable.** In this day and age, there's a good chance that most of your customers will find you on the Internet, even if your LLC is not a web company. When entering your company name into a search engine, you don't want a potential customer to be flooded with irrelevant results.

  For example, say you want to name your new cold-weather clothing company Arctic Ice. If you do an Internet search for "Arctic Ice," you get so many search results referencing global warming and glaciers that you'd never be able to compete!

Before choosing a name, do a quick Internet search and see what comes up.

Letting the ideas fly

Now's the fun part — you get to hold a brainstorming session (otherwise known as a "name-storming" session). Lock yourself away in a quiet room with a pad of paper and write down every name you can think of. This is the part where you can let loose. Keep the naming rules in mind while you create your list of possible names, but don't limit yourself too much. This is a time for creativity; you can be critical later.

Try to come up with 50 or 100 names. Even if you think that you've found "the one," don't stop. As a matter of fact, don't leave your name-storming session until you're completely depleted and can't come up with even one more name. Or until your family calls in a missing persons report, whichever happens first.

After you finish your name-storming session, cross out the names that you don't like. Check that the remaining names comply with the restrictions listed in the earlier section "Considering naming guidelines," and cross out any that don't. Rewrite the list with the names that make the cut, putting them in order of preference, with the ones you absolutely love at the top of the list. Now you're a big step closer to finding your perfect match, and you're ready to play with the names and see which ones are available.

Not absolutely thrilled with the names you came up with? Don't worry! Either hold another name-storming session tomorrow, when your mind is fresh, or just stick with what you have. Remember, with the right marketing, a good brand (comprised of your name, logo, marketing materials, company values, and so on) transcends its name and inspires an overall feeling that creates a strong and lasting relationship with its customers.

Following naming law

Yes, such a thing exists! Although you do have autonomy in choosing your business name, the state has some requirements that you'll have to keep in mind, namely (no pun intended) that you must designate your business as a limited liability company. You do so by adding the designator *limited liability company, limited company,* or an abbreviation such as *L.L.C. or LLC* to the end of the name in uppercase or lowercase letters.

If the addition of *LLC* at the end of your name doesn't seem catchy, don't fret. You must use the designation at the end of your company name when forming your articles of organization, but you can operate your business without it by filing a fictitious firm name application with your county clerk. I tell you how in the section "Getting the name you want with a DBA," later in this chapter.

Even if you intend to request corporation or S corporation tax status with the IRS, you still need to add the LLC designation at the end of your company name when filing your articles of organization with the secretary of state.

The state also restricts the use of certain words that may imply that your business is part of a regulated industry. This policy varies from state to state but typically restricts the use of words that could give the idea that the LLC is in the banking or insurance industry, such as *bank, credit union, trust,* and *insurance*. I have published a list of all state laws on naming requirements (current at the time of publication), on a special site especially for Dummies readers at `www.docrun.com/dummies/naming`. Password is **onesmartdummy**.

Determining the Availability of a Name

Finding out whether the name you want is available is difficult, mostly due to the level of fortitude it takes to scratch a beloved name or two off your list when you find that it's unavailable for use. As difficult as parting with some of your favorites may be, you must do so if they're already in use. Otherwise, not only could you be forced to change your company name down the road after you've gained a considerable following, but there's a good chance that you'll have to pay for a pricey legal battle in the process.

Checking names in your state

If the name you choose conflicts with a name already in use in your state, the secretary of state will reject your articles of organization, and you'll be required to select a different name before resubmitting. This change can be costly (some states don't return filing fees for rejected filings!) and time-consuming.

When checking to see whether a name is conflicting, most states take into account only the businesses that are in good standing. So if a corporation or an LLC is using the name you want but is in "revoked" status, then you have a very good chance of being able to use the name.

The term *conflicting* is pretty subjective, and the decision whether to allow your name often depends on how conservative the state employee who files your articles is in her evaluations. However, you can get a relatively good idea of whether your name conflicts with others by conducting a name search in your state. Go to the appropriate section of your secretary of state's website (you can find the address in the State Information Listing on `www.docrun.com/dummies`; password is **onesmartdummy**) and enter the name you want to use — leaving off all identifiers, such as LLC or limited company. Read through the search results. If any name is very similar to yours, regardless of whether the business is an LLC, you may have to choose a new name. You can also request a free name search at `www.myllc.com/namecheck.aspx`. This option is especially valuable if your state doesn't allow you to search company records online.

If the name you want isn't available, you may have a work-around. Assuming that the name doesn't conflict with any existing trademarks (which I get into later in this section), you may be able to file the LLC under a different name and then file for a fictitious firm name (a DBA) with your county clerk. Check out the following section for details.

Getting the name you want with a DBA

Also referred to as a *fictitious firm name, trade name,* or *assumed name,* a *DBA* (short for "doing business as") is a name that is secondary to the name your company uses to identify itself in its articles of organization. A DBA filing is normally done with the clerk's office of the county in which your business is located and gives your LLC authorization to transact business under that name, including opening a bank account, advertising to potential customers, entering into lease agreements, and taking on debt. Having a DBA does not change the name of the business; rather, it creates a secondary name under which the business is permitted to operate. Just keep in mind that the official name of your company — the name that's listed on the articles of organization — is the name you put on your tax returns, your membership certifications, and any government or official documents.

A business can register an unlimited number of DBAs. Having multiple DBAs can be useful if you're looking to operate certain segments of your business or market certain products under distinct business names while keeping everything under the same LLC. This is very common. For example, Crest (the toothpaste manufacturer) has multiple toothpastes, all operating under different names. Just keep in mind that although DBAs may offer you separate names for different segments of your business, they don't offer separate liability protection. Meaning that if one product gets sued for being faulty, all products under the LLC and *everything* the LLC owns is up for grabs.

Keep in mind, though, that a DBA does not give your company an exclusive right to use that name. As far as I know, no local clerk's office checks DBA filings for conflicting names, which means that the name you want to use theoretically could be used by dozens of other companies in your county alone! The only way to obtain exclusivity for a DBA is to file a trademark, which I tell you how to do later in this chapter. Likewise, a DBA doesn't guarantee that someone hasn't already trademarked the name in your particular industry, thereby making it unavailable for use. Therefore, doing a trademark search before committing your company to using this secondary name is imperative. (Check out the following section for info on conducting this search.)

DBAs are often required to be filed in person and over the counter, and the fee is usually around $50, depending on the rules of the particular county in which the DBA is being filed. Some states require that a notice of the filing be published in a local newspaper, which can add substantially to the cost. If you want to avoid the hassle of obtaining the DBA yourself, many formation companies offer this service.

Conducting a trademark search

When a company wants to protect its name from being used by other companies in similar industries, it obtains a state or federal trademark. A *state trademark* gives the trademark holder exclusive rights to use the name in that particular state. A *federal trademark,* filed at the U.S. Patent and Trademark Office, gives exclusive rights to use the name throughout the entire United States. This means that, for the most part, the company that has trademarked that name or set of words is the only company that has the right to use those words in that business sector.

Before committing to a business name, you must do a comprehensive trademark search for the name that you want to use. You, an experienced law firm, or a trademarking company can do this search. If the name you're interested in is available, I recommend registering it as a trademark immediately, before anyone else does, so that you have the exclusive right to use the name. Better safe than sorry.

You can conduct a trademark search online at the U.S. Patent and Trademarks Office's website by searching its TESS (Trademark Electronic Search System) database. Go to `www.uspto.gov` and do a search for Trademarks.

When reviewing the search results, be sure to pay attention to which *IC class* the word was trademarked in. This information is incredibly important when determining whether a name is available for use.

Because trademarks are exclusive only by industry, if you find some trademarked words that are similar to the name you want, you may still be okay. To see if your business and the business that holds a potentially conflicting trademark are in the same industry, find your company's International Classification (IC) code by searching the USPTO (United States Patent and Trademark Office) list at `tess2.uspto.gov/netahtml/tidm.html`. You can find the IC next to the Goods and Services heading in the trademark's TESS listing. After you have your company's IC code, compare your code to those of the trademarked names that are similar to what you want to use. If those IC codes match yours, there's a good chance that the name you've chosen is not available. If you find a conflicting name, the next step is to see whether the record is marked as "live" or "dead." If the record is dead (which means that the trademark wasn't completed or maintained over the years), you can use the name. Otherwise, you'll probably have to cross that one off your list.

Going global

As I discuss in the section "Considering naming guidelines," earlier in this chapter, it is important to do a linguistic assessment of your name to make sure that it doesn't have a negative connotation in another language, but that's not your only concern when going global. When you're ready to take your business to the next level, you need to make sure that your chosen name is available for use in the countries in which you want to operate.

The United States isn't the only country that offers federal trademark protection to businesses. Almost every country has some sort of system in place or is part of an international consortium that provides a legal infrastructure for such matters. Other countries don't care if you have legal authority for your name in the United States. If a conflicting trademark is already filed in another country's jurisdiction, that trademark prevails, and you have to choose a unique name in order to legally operate in that country.

If expanding outside the U.S. borders is a core component of your business's strategy, you need to take foreign trademarks into account immediately, preferably before you file your articles of organization. You may even want to preemptively file trademarks in the countries in which you intend to operate.

Many governmental bodies regulate trademarks, and some jurisdictions overlap. Before you settle on a name, I suggest that you do a quick search of some of the major international organizations to verify that you aren't facing any major conflicts, such as with a large, international organization that hasn't penetrated the U.S. market yet.

Protecting Your Name

Congratulations! If you're reading this section, you must have found a name that not only encapsulates the purpose and essence of your company and brand but also is so unique that no other business — possibly even in the farthest reaches of the world — is using it. Whew! I know it was hard work, but you probably feel great right now.

You worked hard to choose your name, and now all you have to do is keep it. The following sections outline a few tricks of the trade when it comes to retaining and protecting your LLC's name.

Registering your domain

When you finally choose a great, available name, first things first: Register your Internet domain name. And do it immediately. The world of domains is incredibly competitive, and good domains can be snatched away within hours.

Finding a good domain name isn't easy. If your business is Internet based and having a short, catchy, relevant domain name is *crucial,* then you may have to pay a premium to purchase a domain name on the aftermarket. Resale prices can be astronomical, so first check to see if you can get an unregistered variation or a comparable domain name for as little as $5.

Registering a domain name is simple — just go to `NameCheap.com`, 1&1, or any other domain registrar and type in the name you wish to register. Most registrars use the same central database of names, so no matter which registrar you use, you can find out whether the name you want is available.

If you aren't familiar with registering domains, then it'll probably be a shock to see how few good domain names are available. You may do fifty searches until you find one you like. In this case, consider purchasing a premium domain on the aftermarket. Some of the more popular domain brokerage firms are `www.sedo.com`, `www.afternic.com`, and `www.greatdomains.com`. Fair warning — this option can get pricey.

Domain names are generally entered in all lowercase letters, so double-check how your domain name *looks.* For example, you may be thrilled that your start-up Therapist Finder has the option to purchase its domain name, only to realize later that that domain can easily be misconstrued as `www.TheRapistFinder.com`.

Search for your domain name only when you're willing to register the name, should it be available. Otherwise, you're giving these companies exclusive information about which names may be of value to you. Many common registrars (such as `NetworkSolutions.com` and `GoDaddy.com`) have been accused of, or have even openly admitted to, *front-running* domain names, which means that they find valuable domains you've searched for and register them immediately in order to sell them to you later at a premium. If you search for a domain and go back a few hours later to register it, only to be told that it's available only at a premium price, well . . . you get the picture.

Reserving your name

Imagine this: You go through the painstaking process of selecting a name, checking to see whether it's available, and filing a trademark. Then, after the care and expense of preparing and submitting your articles of organization, you get a letter from the secretary of state that says that your filing has been rejected due to a conflict of name. Someone has taken it in those few weeks between your checking the name and submitting your filing! As unbelievable as it may seem, this scenario happens on occasion, and it can force you to start the process all over again, wasting time and money.

The best way to avoid having your name taken is to file a name reservation with your secretary of state, thereby reserving your chosen name while you take the time to prepare your articles of organization. You can do so as soon as you see that the name you want is available.

Unless you have chosen a very popular name or you'll be waiting for some time before filing your articles, you may not need a name reservation. If you'll be filing your articles of organization in just a few days and the process of reserving a name happens to be costly and/or time-consuming in your state, then you may want to consider whether it's worth the hassle.

The process and fees for name reservations vary from state to state, but in most states, you can reserve your company name by going to your secretary of state's website and downloading the appropriate form. Complete this form and mail it to the secretary of state. (If you don't want to do so yourself, ask your incorporating company to do it for you.) Some states allow you to reserve the name online but may charge more for the convenience. You can usually reserve a name for 60 to 90 days.

The person or organization filing your LLC's articles of organization must be the same person who is listed on the name reservation; otherwise, you may have a problem getting the secretary of state to release the name. For instance, if the reservation is in your name but your incorporating company is filing the articles, the articles probably will be rejected until you sign off on the use of the name.

If you foresee your LLC transacting business and foreign-filing in other states (I discuss multistate operations at length in Chapter 5), you may want to consider doing a *name registration* in each of those states. A name registration is the equivalent of a name reservation but is specifically geared toward a foreign entity (an entity formed in another state) that wishes to reserve its name for later use.

Getting a trademark for your name

After you register and reserve your LLC name, you need to block anyone who tries to follow in your stead. The only official way to do so is to file a trademark to prevent the competition from mimicking your company or brand elements in order to snatch market share or mislead consumers. A trademark can also prevent foreign companies from importing products or services that may conflict with yours, and it can get deceptive or even simply ambiguous domain names taken down.

When you trademark your company name, logo, and/or brand elements (such as packaging), you create something of inherent value. As you invest in the brand and develop brand loyalty, that value increases. Take the necessary steps to protect this investment for as long as your company is operational.

The irony of trademark protection is that your business name (also called a *trade name*) is not in itself qualified to be legally protected under federal trademark laws, because it doesn't specifically identify the source of a

The different types of trademarks

Trademarks, by definition, can be anything — words, symbols, phrases, shapes, colors, and so on — that identifies a product with its source. If the mark identifies the source of a service, such as accounting or dry cleaning, it is called a *service mark.* A *design mark* refers to the specific shape or color of a product package that defines the product. For example, the yellow/black cover of this book may be protected under a federal trademark so that competitors can't make look-alike products. Another example is the trademarked color Tiffany Blue that designates the Tiffany brand. Design marks can even include architectural details, such as the distinctive red brick–like roof at Pizza Hut.

product or service. After all, trademarks were born to serve products and services, not necessarily the businesses that own them. So unless your business name is the same as your product (or service) name, you have to take a few steps if you want to keep it for yourself.

First and foremost, make sure that you trademark after you have your logo created — you don't want to go through the costly effort of updating your trademark later if you don't have to. (See the section, "Completing Your Identity with a Logo" later in this chapter, for more on creating your logo.) Then tweak your actual business name a bit in order to make it look less, well, like a "business":

- Remove words like *Company, Associates, Group,* and all entity-type identifiers such as *Inc., Incorporated, Limited, Limited Liability Company, LLC,* and so on.
- Remove all descriptors, such as *Services.*
- Remove identifiers that name the product or service. (For example, remove *Automotive Repair* from the business name *Red Rock Automotive Repair* and simply register the moniker *Red Rock.*)

You are now ready to register your trademark — assuming it's any good, that is. Read on to find out what makes the cut.

Much ado about marks

There are two other federally protected trademarks that probably don't apply to you, but you may want to know about them anyway: *certification marks* and *membership marks.*

A certification mark is comprised of an image, usually a seal of some sort, and is used by a national accreditation organization to indicate the quality or standardization of a product or service. A common example of this is the "Good Housekeeping Seal," which reassures customers about their product purchase decision. The owner of a certification mark cannot use it to create a consumer assurance on his own services, only others'. This is a rare instance in which a mark benefits someone other than its owner.

A membership mark is used by an association to show that an individual or entity is a member of that association, such as the patch used by the Boy Scouts of America.

Knowing what constitutes a good trademark

Now that you've tossed all the filler out of your name, what's left? If you end up with something mundane, such as *Vino* for your wine store, you may have a problem, because in order for a name to be trademarked, it must be distinct. Generic words that name a product, such as *lamp,* hold no legal protection at all — can you imagine if the courts allowed people to own parts of the English language? For example, in order for Toys"R"Us to trademark its name, it had to add *"R"Us.* On its own, *Toys* is generic and simply describes the products offered in its stores.

The same goes for names that simply describe the product or service that a company offers. For example, if this book series were titled *Easy to Understand Books* instead of *For Dummies,* the publisher would be unable to acquire legal protection for the name. (Not to mention that you probably wouldn't be reading this book right now, considering that very few people would want to read, much less write, a bland book series called *Easy to Understand Books.*)

Also, the name you're registering shouldn't be primarily a surname. You can't register *Smith's Bakery* in the baked goods category and then block anyone with the surname Smith from using her name in connection with her bakery.

How distinct a trademark is is exactly proportional to how well that trademark will hold up if it is ever challenged in court. Running a business named BookSellers? You'd be laughed out of court if you tried to defend a trademark like that (assuming that you were granted a trademark in the first place, which is unlikely). However, add a word like "Amazon" to your name and you're golden.

Registering your trademark

After you determine that no conflicting names or marks are federally trademarked (refer to "Determining the Availability of a Name" earlier in the chapter), you're ready to file your trademark. Remember, you can't simply file your business name (sans logo or any other type of visual ornament) and be done with it. You must create a logo containing the major elements of your business name and trademark that logo instead.

You file your trademark with the United States Patent and Trademark Office (USPTO). You can do so online at `www.uspto.gov/trademarks` for a fee of $325 per category of goods or services in which you wish to register. If you're willing to do everything online and keep things simple for the USPTO by doing your own search for your company's IC (International Classification), you can use the TEAS Plus form and pay only $275 per category. You can find your company's IC by searching the USPTO list at `tess2.uspto.gov/netahtml/tidm.html`. Remember that filing a trademark protects your trademark in only those specific categories that you choose and pay for.

Keep in mind that the trademark filing fee is nonrefundable and that you may have to wait as long as four months to find out from the USPTO whether your trademark was successfully filed. This lag time makes it imperative to get your filing right the first time. If you hit any snags on the way or don't feel confident that you know exactly what you're doing, consider hiring an intellectual property law firm or a compliance company, which can give you a much better shot at success.

After you file the online application, you must prove that you've used the trademark *in commerce* in order to finalize the registration. You can submit an *intent-to-use application* for the trademark before you use it in business, thereby blocking any subsequent party from obtaining the trademark, but it isn't actually issued until you prove that you've used the trademark in commerce.

After you have the trademark, you've got it forever — or for as long as you maintain it. You can keep the marketplace from using your name, but now you have to use it and build it into a strong and ubiquitous brand. Keep in mind that you must renew your registration every ten years by filing a Section 8 affidavit with the USPTO showing that your mark is still being used in commerce and hasn't been abandoned.

After you register your trademark, you need to take action against anyone who infringes upon it. Otherwise, the courts could invalidate your mark. On the flip side, if your mark becomes popular enough to be associated with a particular product class (such as Vaseline for petroleum jelly or Kleenex for facial tissue), you can lose trademark protection for being generic (regardless of how distinct the name was to begin with).

Completing Your Identity with a Logo

Humans aren't just vocal and aural beings; we're visual, too. So, unless your target demographic is of the nonhuman variety (not likely!), you also need to take into account the visual element of your brand: your logo.

Logo designs come in four basic forms:

- **Word mark:** Your company name in a specialized typography is your logo. Think of the Coca-Cola logo, for example.
- **Combination mark:** Partner your stylized name with an icon of some sort, and you have a combination mark. Think of AT&T and its iconic globe.
- **Emblem:** Some companies go for the more artistic approach and put the company name inside an emblem. Think of the Starbucks round seal or the Porsche coat of arms. This approach can reap big rewards by giving you more creative license to reflect the tone of your brand in the logo.
- **Symbol:** Some companies are so well known that they can get by with just a symbol. Everyone knows the Nike swoosh, the McDonald's golden arches, and Apple's . . . well, apple. Usually only extremely well-known brands can pull this off, and even then it can backfire. Remember when Prince changed his name to a symbol? A bad move. Think hard before going down this road.

When deciding which type of logo you want, carefully consider how you want your business to be perceived. I suggest that you first take the time to educate yourself by figuring out your complete brand — the image and feeling you want to convey, the demographic to which you want to convey it, and the mark of your personal creativity with which you wish to endow it. Then draw up a few ideas and take them to an experienced logo artist and/or graphic designer to assist you in creating a final logo.

When you hire a designer to create your logo, keep in mind that just because you paid her doesn't mean that you own the final product! Make sure that you have a concrete, state-specific work-for-hire agreement with the designer that explicitly states that you own the final work.

Before you put too much time and money into your logo, make sure that both the name you want to use and the image you want to convey are available for use. Otherwise, you may go through great expense only to throw it all away and start from scratch. Read on to find out how to determine name availability.

Changing Your Name

After you find a good name and go through all the steps to protect it, you probably can't fathom ever wanting to change it. But it does happen, and other than having to go through the processes of vetting and securing the new name that I describe in this chapter, changing your LLC's name usually isn't difficult.

A common misconception is that after you file your articles of organization, you're forever stuck with the name you chose, and the company's name is inextricably linked with the company itself as its sole identifier. Not true. Legally, an LLC can change its name an unlimited number of times. Of course, if the name changes too often, your customers may not approve!

Changing the name of your LLC is relatively easy depending on the state: You simply amend your articles of organization by filing a name-change amendment with the secretary of state in the state in which your LLC is domiciled. If you're foreign-filed in multiple states, you also need to contact those particular state agencies with the updated business name.

Chapter 5

Choosing the Best State for Your LLC

In This Chapter

- Deciding between your home state and another state
- Looking at states with the best tax and privacy laws
- Understanding what a registered agent can do for you

Say you've lived in California your entire life, and now you want to create an LLC all the way across the country in Miami. That's where you believe your retirement community real estate project will have its greatest chance to flourish, but you worry that because you don't live in Florida, you'll have trouble establishing your LLC. Not to fret: Many LLCs have different home states than their owners.

It's a common myth that you need to form your LLC in the state in which you live. LLCs are considered *incorporated entities,* which means that if you maintain them properly, a layer of separation exists between the business and the owners. Think of an LLC as an individual over which you have full control. Like an individual, your LLC can live in whichever state benefits it the most. Sandy beaches and nice weather may be the appealing qualities of the state you choose to call home, but your LLC will benefit from other qualities, such as low taxes, privacy, and favorable laws. The state in which your LLC is formed is called its *domicile.*

In this chapter I give you an overview of some of your options when it comes to deciding where to form your LLC. I help clear up some of the confusion that comes with the term *tax haven,* and I also point all you multistate moguls in the right direction when it comes to forming your LLC in a state other than the one in which you currently reside.

Your State or Not Your State, That Is the Question

When choosing a state to live in, your LLC cares little about the weather and even less about the school districts. Your LLC is pretty easy to please: Give it favorable laws, privacy, and low taxes, and you'll have one happy camper! You can choose any state (and maybe even country!) that you want for your LLC — the world is your oyster! But this leads us to the main problem you're facing: LLCs in different states are not all created equal. Some states have more favorable laws than others. So how do you choose?

LLCs bring with them fantastically flexible options that make them suitable for any industry, any location, any dream. If you've read this far, you probably already know that an LLC is right for you. But which LLC? Each state makes its own laws regarding LLCs. For this reason, LLCs tend to look, feel, and act differently depending on where they are formed.

Forming your LLC in a state other than the one in which you reside may not be right for you. And if it is a viable option, you still have to decide which state. Before you can answer any of these questions, you must answer this one: *What's your business?*

In order to know your options, you must have a clear picture of what sort of business you'll be transacting and where you'll be transacting it. You need to know what your future plans are — for instance, do you want to go public, or would you prefer to stay small? Is your business ingrained in your community, or does it exist in the Internet realm and have no real territory? What are your priorities? Is it important that you save on your tax bill? And what about privacy?

Considering another state for your LLC

It's true that some states offer much better conditions for LLCs than others. If you're lucky enough to live in a state that has low taxes and the privacy you desire, then why form out of state? Before writing off your territory in favor of one of the more popular ones, you need to do a little research. Your state may not be the best, but it may be good enough. For instance, Montana has no sales tax and very low corporate income tax (6.75 percent), and its personal income tax is nominal as well. The state works hard to be pro-business and has created a tax structure that encourages business start-ups and growth by offering millions of dollars in tax credits to certain emerging industries and allowing a myriad of corporate deductions that many other states don't recognize.

Although business-friendly states like Montana aren't commonly referred to as *tax havens,* they do offer very amicable tax climates and corporate laws. If you live in one of these states, then the benefit of doing business close to home is hard to beat! So before you decide to go out of state with your business venture, be sure to check your own state's laws. You can find your state's current tax tables and tax analysis on the special *For Dummies* site at www.docrun.com/dummies (password is **onesmartdummy**).

Forming your LLC in your home state

An LLC can be formed in any state you wish, but if your LLC conducts business elsewhere, it must register to transact business in those states.

When I say "conducting business," I mean serious business, such as hiring employees and leasing office space. Simply selling your products or services to folks in a certain state doesn't count.

Registering your company to transact business in a state other than its domicile is often referred to as *qualifying* or *foreign filing.* When an LLC foreign files in another state, it becomes subject to the laws, taxes, and disclosure requirements of that state. For instance, if you form your LLC in Nevada in order to keep the ownership of the company completely private and then register to transact business in Arizona, then you would most likely need to disclose the membership of your LLC, just as local companies are required to do. Problems such as these can reduce or eliminate many of the benefits that motivated you to form your LLC out of state in the first place!

Determining whether you are transacting business

So what *exactly* constitutes "transacting business"? Well, the states purposefully remain vague in their definitions. Case law and attorney general opinions hold a lot of weight, but you can't be expected to sift through all those stacks of legal history, now can you? To make your life easier, I have aggregated all the laws addressing each state's legal definition of *transacting business* (if any) on a special *For Dummies* site at www.docrun.com/dummies/transacting_business (password is **onesmartdummy**).

Regardless, if you're in any way confused about whether your company is considered to be "transacting business" in a particular state, don't bother calling the secretary of state's office and asking. If the administrator you speak to *does* venture to guess, the answer will almost invariably be yes. So take an hour or so and read up on your state's laws.

If you're opening up a brick-and-mortar business that operates in only one state — for example, a local shop that deals heavily in a particular community — make it easy on yourself and keep your LLC close to home. Sometimes a business is viable only if it's in close proximity to interested customers, resources, and/or land, such as your local dry cleaner or an oil well. Running this type of hands-on, locally based company means that you have to register to transact business in the state in which your business (and you!) resides and abide by its laws. You may as well save on filing fees and paperwork hassles by keeping everything local from the get-go.

Sticking with pass-through taxation

If you want to take advantage of the favorable tax laws of a specific state, you won't be able to do so and be taxed as a partnership. With partnership taxation, the revenue and expenses (and the resulting profit or loss) of the business *flow through* to you and the other owners, to be reported on your individual personal tax returns, and you pay personal income taxes on that profit in whatever state(s) you reside in. This process eliminates any tax savings you may have gotten by forming your LLC in a low-tax or no-tax state (often referred to as a *tax haven*). Same goes for other forms of pass-through taxation, such as being taxed as a sole proprietor (which the IRS refers to as a *disregarded entity*) or an S corporation.

A corporation, on the other hand, is considered a legal entity unto itself and is taxed separately. Unless a company is legally transacting business in another state and is required to register there, whatever profit the company makes remains in the corporation, and thus in the state in which the corporation was formed. This profit is subject to any corporate income tax that its home state — its *domicile* — levies on it. In short, any LLC formed in another state for the specific purpose of reducing state income tax must elect corporate taxation in order for the strategy to be feasible.

If you are considering electing corporate taxation for your LLC, I suggest that you read Chapter 8, where I discuss at length the differences between the tax structures and what they mean for you.

All LLCs are *not* created equal

Wherever you decide to form your LLC, you must abide by that state's LLC and tax laws. Some states have more favorable laws than others. Keep the following facts in mind:

- Some states have lower taxes than others.
- Some states charge fewer fees than others.
- Some states have laws regarding LLCs that better protect the managers and members.
- Some states allow the members to remain completely anonymous.
- Some states encourage new business by offering tax breaks and other incentives.

Looking for LLCs out of state

If you don't have a brick-and-mortar business — maybe you're running an Internet company or a consulting or service business that isn't restricted to a particular state — and you live in a high-tax state, then you may want to consider forming your LLC in a more business-friendly jurisdiction. Some states have worked very hard to structure their laws and corporate taxation for the specific purpose of encouraging businesses to form or move their operations there. Now that's the sort of government action I can stand behind!

The entire idea of forming your LLC in a faraway place can be somewhat daunting at first, but don't let the perceived difficulties overwhelm you. For guidance, go to `www.docrun.com/dummies` and pull up an up-to-date tax table for your state. Use it to compare the tax structure of the state you live in to the tax structures of other states. If it looks like you can do much better (eh, Californians?) and forming in another state seems like a feasible option for you, then strongly consider doing so.

Exploring Tax and Privacy Havens

For years, when people heard the term *tax haven,* they would think of some shady money-laundering operation in the Caribbean. Thankfully, that's not necessarily the case! A tax and/or privacy *haven,* as I define it, is any jurisdiction that has structured its laws in such a way to attract businesses and individuals seeking privacy and tax relief.

What most people fail to realize is that, internationally speaking, the largest global tax haven happens to be the United States! Foreign companies form LLCs here in droves due to our favorable federal tax rates (especially concerning foreign investment) and incredible privacy protection. So you can forget about going offshore because you'll probably find what you're looking for right in your own backyard (or a few states over).

But what about your individual state? If your state imposes heavy personal and corporate income taxes and forces you to disclose private information about your business, then you lose out on the benefits of starting a small business in one of the most small business–oriented economies in the world. If this is the case for you, then read on because in this section I discuss a few of the major states that are serious about attracting business — *your business* — their way.

Nevada: Clinging to its heyday

Nevada has been notorious for being the ultimate state for small businesses, but this reputation is changing. Don't get me wrong — there's still a lot to rave about. Nevada technically has no taxes — no franchise taxes, no corporate taxes, and no personal income taxes. How can Nevada afford to do this? Well, let's just put it this way: The next time your buddy loses $200 at a craps table, make sure to thank him!

But here's the catch: After the influx of new business formations that came during Nevada's heyday, lawmakers got greedy. They started imposing fees. Lots and lots of fees. Which really is just another form of taxation, right? The biggest fee is the $200 business license fee that must be paid every year. Only film production companies and IRS-approved 501(c)(3) nonprofit companies are exempt. This fee comes on top of the $125 annual fee paid to the Secretary of State for renewing your annual list of managers.

Luckily, one thing that Nevada still has going for it is privacy. In Nevada, only the managers of the LLC appear on public records. This means that if your LLC is manager-managed and you're not a manager, you can't be easily tied to the company. This protection is pretty powerful — if a lawyer doesn't think that you own anything, she probably won't want to sue you!

If you form your LLC in a state where LLC members aren't on public record, you may want to elect a nominee manager. See Chapter 17 for more information on nominees.

In addition to the powerful benefits already mentioned, Nevada is the *only* state that has consistently refused to enter into an information-sharing agreement with the IRS. Whereas the other states give the IRS information about bank accounts and corporate records, Nevada tells them to butt out. In other words, if the IRS wants to target your Nevada bank accounts in order to settle a debt, they can get the information only via a court order or if you voluntarily let them in the loop. If that's not fighting for small businesses, I don't know what is.

Wyoming: The birthplace of LLCs

If it wasn't for the pioneering nature of the state of Wyoming, I wouldn't have written this book. No, I wasn't born there. But LLCs were! Wyoming was the first state to enact laws governing the creation and management of limited liability companies. And you thought Wyoming was just for skiing.

Wyoming, a notoriously pro-business state, has managed to curb the desire to raise taxes and fees on businesses over the years. It's one of the few states to realize that, as tempting as it is to take money from businesses, tax increases eventually drive them out, leaving the state worse off in the long run. Wyoming offers a lot of the same benefits for LLCs as Nevada, such as no corporate or personal income tax, but the fees tend to be much lower.

Wyoming may be a good choice for you if you want to form your LLC out of state. It's geared heavily toward small businesses, not just big public companies. When I wrote the first edition of this book, I wasn't a huge fan of Wyoming because at the time it disallowed single-member LLCs. Luckily for all you singletons out there, Wyoming has loosened its restrictions and now allows the formation of small businesses in which only one person holds all management titles.

South Dakota: Getting serious

I'm not sure who's running things in South Dakota, but whoever it is, they're sure on a mission! In all the years I've been working with LLCs, I've never seen a state so serious about attracting small businesses. If you need proof, take a look at your bills sometime and check out the addresses to which you send payment. You'll probably find at least one or two billing services operating out of Sioux Falls or Rapid City, South Dakota's two main hubs.

South Dakota ranks #2 (after Wyoming) on the 2014 State Business Tax Climate Index, an independent report that ranks states by their level of business friendliness. South Dakota has zero personal income tax and zero corporate income tax. Its fees are minimal, and it offers ample privacy protection. So private, in fact, that only one manager and one organizer are required to be listed on your articles of organization. This means that, as long as they aren't also serving as managers, the members — the owners — of your LLC can remain private.

South Dakota doesn't aim to be simply a tax and privacy haven, though. The state wants your *business.* Yep, the whole thing. The state offers some pretty slick enticements in the form of substantial tax credits (who doesn't love free cash?) and other financial incentives to companies willing to base their entire operations there.

Delaware: The heavy hitter with the chancery court

Do you have great expectations for your venture? Are you designing an LLC that needs room to grow? Then Delaware is the state for you! Delaware is a perfect domicile if you intend to grow your LLC really large and do business in several states.

Most public companies want to be in Delaware because of its *chancery court* (a special court that makes decisions on business matters) and its long history of case law. Also, its laws (and boy, are there a lot of them!) are geared toward protecting the directors and shareholders — a must for larger businesses. Because of these two qualities, the majority of public companies listed on the stock exchange are domiciled in Delaware. That's a pretty big reputation for such a little state!

Delaware is the only state with a chancery court. Most states' courts are very backlogged, and you may wait years for a judge to hear and decide on a lawsuit. In contrast, Delaware can get cases resolved in weeks. That quality alone is appealing, but the chancery court goes a step further. When you go to court in other states, you never know how much the judge actually knows about business. ("You mean to tell me that his honor was just promoted from traffic court?") All judges in the chancery court, though, are experts in matters of business and are renowned for their fair and educated decision making. You can rest assured that the person deciding the fate of your company is more fluent in the laws of LLCs than petty larceny.

Another benefit of Delaware is its privacy. The state has earned this reputation by allowing a greater amount of financial secrecy for businesses than any other jurisdiction in the world. Yep, you got it — *in the world*. Delaware is more secretive than jurisdictions in the Caribbean and even Switzerland! Only a registered agent and an authorized signer need to be listed on the articles of organization. Now that's privacy!

Working with a State-Required Registered Agent

"We're suing you, but we can't drag you into court until we serve you in person, so where can we find you?" If this question were posed to most business owners over the phone or e-mail, they'd probably just reply, "Mars." For this reason, states require a business to have what is called a *registered agent* — a term that is interchangeable with *resident agent* and *statutory agent* — in the state in which you domicile or "home" your LLC and in every state in which you transact business.

A registered agent's primary duties are to have an in-state address that is not a P.O. Box and to be open during business hours in the event that the company is sued and paperwork needs to be served. Fun job, huh? This company or person is also legally required to be able to accept government documents, such as correspondence from the secretary of state's office, clerk's office, and state tax bureaus, on behalf of the company and then forward them on to you, the owner. In many cases, the agent's office can also serve as your corporate headquarters in the state where your LLC was formed if you don't have an office there.

Why you need a registered agent

In some states, you can serve as your own registered agent (provided that you have an office address in the state). However, I could fill about five pages with reasons why this is never a good idea. The following list touches on the big ones:

- **You can't ever leave.** Someone must be at the registered agent's office address at all times during business hours to sign for government papers. If the court service comes to drop off legal documents and you're not around, there's a chance that you could lose the lawsuit by default! Went to lunch? Too bad. Needless to say, that would be one *really* expensive lunch.
- **You look bad in front of employees and customers.** If lawsuits are served at your business address, imagine what your customers (and employees) will think when they see a couple of cops come into your place of business carrying a lawsuit and asking for you. Even if you've done nothing wrong, the talk among your employees and customers can be incalculably damaging.
- **You lose some of your privacy.** A lack of privacy makes you more vulnerable to lawsuits. For example, if you use your home address, someone considering suing you can instantly see online if your home is in an affluent area. This may be the deciding factor for an attorney considering whether to take a plaintiff's case without a retainer. Using your registered agent's address on your state filings gives you an additional level of privacy.
- **You lose safety.** Imagine if a disgruntled customer wanted a refund in the form of your landscaping, or an unlucky day trader came directly to your home to "discuss" his losses. You're better off avoiding these sorts of scenarios by concealing your personal address and using a registered agent instead.

What your agent should do for you

Due to the sad truth that a registered agent's primary function is to sit and wait for a lawsuit to arrive, most registered agents now provide extra services. After all, you're a well-behaved citizen and you probably aren't getting sued very often, so what's a registered agent to do all day?

A good registered agent warrants its nominal fee by taking on such important tasks as keeping your LLC in compliance with all the state-required filings, forwarding your government mail, and protecting your identity. Because of these extra tasks, registered agents have gone from being mere legal irritants to being important members of LLCs' teams. They have the following responsibilities:

- Have a separate business location at a commercial (not residential) address and stay open during normal business hours to accept lawsuits and filing documents, which they forward immediately to you.
- Protect your address by allowing you to use their address as your corporate headquarters.

- Forward your state and government mail and/or notices each business day.
- Remind you of any state filings that are due and make sure that you stay in compliance. Some registered agents even have online "compliance calendars" that keep you up to date with any upcoming filings you may have to make.
- File your documents (if necessary) with the requisite state and local bureaus.
- Assist you in finding state-specific tax and legal professionals.
- Keep copies of your corporate documents in case of theft, loss, or natural disaster (this is a legal requirement for certain documents). A *lot* of Louisiana businesses were happy that they had employed the services of legitimate registered agents after Hurricane Katrina!

How to find an agent

Finding a registered agent isn't too difficult. Finding a legitimate one that can and will do the job for a reasonable price is another story altogether. The best way to find an agent is to call your secretary of state's office and ask for a recommendation. Some state offices will give you some names; others try to remain impartial. Some states maintain lists of registered agents on their websites, but, like the referrals you get over the phone, these agents aren't vetted by anyone. In many cases, any motivated registered agent (or wannabe) can get on this list, regardless of legitimacy.

Summons served. Or was it?

You formed an LLC for your restaurant and found ways to keep customers coming back for more. The company is thriving, and your bank account is growing faster than you can plate the next meal. Life is good. Then one day you find out that last spring a customer got food poisoning from your shellfish, you were sued, the case went to trial, and, worst of all, you lost by "default judgment!"

Whoa! How does something like this happen? As your kitchen equipment is hauled away for auction, you curse your cousin Bob. Why? Because he was on file as your registered agent, and he never notified you of the summons to appear in court. You weren't even there to defend the restaurant against claims that you suspect weren't even true. Maybe it wasn't the shellfish (after all, you tried it yourself) but something else the customer ate earlier that day.

Of course, this scenario is a nightmare, but it demonstrates the importance of selecting a reliable registered agent. You can also face unfortunate outcomes if a summons is misplaced at your busy establishment or simply ignored by an ignorant employee. So how do you defend yourself from such a nightmare? Choose a qualified registered agent and keep the lines of communication open. Doing so may save your business from going under one day.

In this section, I give you detailed information on how to find and vet a reliable and legitimate registered-agent company in whatever state you wish to form your LLC in.

Calling in the Big Four

I recommend that you retain one of the "Big Four" national registered-agent firms:

- CT Corporation (`ct.wolterskluwer.com/`)
- Corporation Service Company (`www.incspot.com`)
- InCorp Services, Inc. (`www.incorp.com`)
- National Registered Agents, Inc. (`www.nrai.com`)

These four large national companies specialize in registered-agent service, for the most part. They're good at what they do, and they're generally more technologically advanced than local companies. Also, as your LLC expands to multiple states, you don't have to deal with a different company in each jurisdiction. Virtually all Fortune 500 companies use one of the Big Four as their registered agent.

Prices for these companies' services vary greatly, so shop around. Registered Agent Information (`www.registered-agent-information.com`), an independent comparison site, has pretty good up-to-date reviews of each company, as well as links to sites for the major registered agents doing business in each state (including the Big Four), along with their prices.

Evaluating agents

When interviewing a potential agent, first get a feel for its policies on dealing with lawsuits. You and your registered agent must agree that any legal paperwork it receives on your behalf will be brought to your attention immediately. Perhaps you decide that the agent will call you and summarize a document's contents and then have it delivered to you overnight. Or maybe the agent will e-mail you copies of the documents and then send the originals to you. Just be sure that both of you are clear on what procedure will be followed. Use the same method for state documents and tax notices as well.

Whatever the delivery method you and your agent agree on, make sure that you can track your packages.

One characteristic to look for when choosing a registered agent is how long that person or company has been working with the secretary of state's office. If your registered agent has close relationships with the administrators at the secretary of state's office, your filings are likely to be completed much faster and issues are likely to be resolved more easily. Also, it's a good sign of legitimacy. If the administrators at the secretary of state's office have never heard of your registered agent, that person or company probably isn't doing a lot of work there.

If you plan to do business in multiple states, choose a registered agent that's also located in those states. That way, your filings, invoices, and records can be consolidated, and you have one firm that knows the ins and outs of your business and can work for you in multiple jurisdictions. Also make sure that the agent can collect, complete, and file your state and local business licenses and permits for you. (See Chapter 13 for more on business licenses and permit filings.)

Although registered agents don't come free, their services usually cost only $100 to $200 per year. Most fees are billed annually, the same month in which your LLC was initially created. Think twice about hiring an agent that requests that you sign a multi-year contract. A lot of legitimate agents don't require contracts, so why lock yourself in if you don't have to?

Make sure that your agent always has your current contact information. If your agent can't find you, she'll have trouble forwarding Uncle Sam's letters to you. I have had numerous clients who used my company as their agent to maintain their privacy, and they were so private that they wouldn't even share their contact information with *me!* Needless to say, tracking them down to forward their legal paperwork wasn't always the easiest task.

I suggest choosing an individual within your LLC to maintain regular contact with your registered agent. Doing so helps you avoid confusion about whom the agent is supposed to contact in the face of a lawsuit. However, all members should feel comfortable contacting the agent at any time.

Attorneys will try to place themselves as your registered agent. Although many attorneys are qualified to be agents, be aware that they tend to be much more expensive than commercial registered agents. And if you have an attorney/agent and he isn't the most qualified attorney to handle a particular legal battle, you have to go through the fun of explaining to him that you don't want to use his services for a lawsuit that was served to him.

Chapter 6

Creating and Filing Your Articles of Organization

In This Chapter

- Answering a few important questions
- Knowing what you need to include in your articles
- Completing your state filing
- Deciding whether to use a formation company

The articles of organization is your LLC's most important document. Why? Because you can't even *be* an LLC until you create and file your articles of organization with your secretary of state's office. And because the filing of this document brings your LLC into existence, you need to initiate it before you can do much else, like assign ownership.

The articles of organization describes the basic structure and management of your LLC, as well as who your registered agent is and where your company's principal office is located. With so many uses for LLCs and all their flexibility, why on earth would you want your LLC to look and act the same way as someone else's? If you are raising money for a multimillion-dollar real estate venture and your Uncle Joe is running a paper route, do you really want both companies operating as carbon-copy LLCs? Heck, no! You need something that is customized to your specific needs.

Although most of the customization occurs in your company's operating agreement, which I cover in detail in Part III of this book, some states require you to list some of these specifics in your company's articles of organization. In addition, some states are nitpicky and want specific wording in the *provisions* (a fancy name for the sections of your articles of organization). But don't you worry — I go over all this stuff in this chapter.

Making a Few Big Decisions

The articles of organization is the document with which you officially notify the state of your intent to become an LLC. However, even if you're starting a business from scratch, you need to make some important decisions before you can prepare your articles. Most states require that the articles list at least the managers (as well as the members, if they are the ones managing the LLC), which means that you must figure out this crucial component of your business before you can file your articles with the state. But don't sweat it too much; your operating agreement enables you to modify the players and their roles later on (see Chapters 9 through 12).

At a minimum, you need to answer the following important questions before creating your articles of organization:

- **What is the name of your LLC? Is that name available for use in your state?** In Chapter 4, I go over in detail how to select, verify, and reserve your LLC name in your intended state.
- **What is the purpose of your LLC?** This can be a deep rabbit hole of a question. Luckily, the state doesn't need the lengthy, detailed answer that you would give to, say, someone looking to invest in your business. As a matter of fact, when it comes to your articles, the broader the better. I give some specific examples later in this chapter.
- **Who will be the initial members?** Some states require you to list your company's initial members in your articles of organization, especially if you specify that your company is member-managed (and you're forced to list the managers). Later in this chapter I address a few ways to get around this requirement, but you should still have an idea of who the initial members of the company will be before forming. Most states don't require you to list ownership percentages or other specifics of ownership — all that is done in your operating agreement and kept private to your company.
- **Who is going to manage your LLC?** Who is going to be involved in your new venture, their level of involvement, the compensation they receive, and the rules they need to abide by — these are the sorts of decisions that make or break your business. Luckily, most states require only bare-bones information in the articles, so I'm going to touch on this topic only briefly in this chapter. In Chapter 10, I discuss the ins and outs of deciding what role(s) each person should play and how to bring on outside managers (who aren't owners).
- **In which state(s) are you going to form your LLC?** LLC and tax laws vary from state to state — some states have no taxes, others have less paperwork, and others less disclosure. You should take these

differences into consideration when determining where to form your LLC. Chapter 5 helps you decide which state is the best home for your LLC and whether you're doing enough business in a particular state to be required to register there.

- **Who is going to act as your registered agent?** Every LLC needs to have a registered agent acting on its behalf in *every* state in which it does business. Have you chosen your registered agent for each state in which you are registering? Bear in mind that you must rely on this agent if your LLC is ever served with a lawsuit. See Chapter 5 for more on registered agents.
- **Where is your principal office going to be located?** Most states require you to have a principal office address located in the state in which you are filing. If you don't have a physical presence in a particular state, see if your registered agent offers a service that allows you to list its address as your principal place of business in that state.

Choosing the initial members

LLCs are like children — they need parents! No matter what, your LLC must have at least one owner and, in some states, preferably two or more. The owners of the LLC are called the *members.* One of the best characteristics of an LLC (assuming that you don't intend to elect to be taxed like an S corporation) is that anyone (or any *thing,* really) can be a member. In other words, any person or entity— an individual, other LLCs, corporations, trusts, limited partnerships, and so on — can be an owner of your LLC. Also, you aren't restricted in how many members you can have — you can have 1,000 members or more if you like! This is one of the main reasons why LLCs are becoming popular for raising private capital.

The amount of the business you own is called your *membership interest.* The percentage of your membership interest in relation to all the membership interests that the company has issued is called your *membership percentage* or *ownership percentage* (your individual piece of the pie).

The issuance of membership — including how much of the company each member actually owns — doesn't take place in your articles of organization, which is why I don't go into this topic further in this chapter. Instead, it's executed in either your operating agreement or, sometimes, in a separate buy-sell agreement. I recommend that you disclose as little as possible about membership in the articles of organization because that information ends up on public record (and is available to the prying eyes of ambitious litigators).

Dual liability protection doesn't always fly for single-member LLCs

For many years, professionals and consultants argued about whether single-member LLCs were allowed the same dual liability protection as regular multiple-member LLCs. Finally, in 2003, a case came up in the Colorado Bankruptcy Court, and the court decided that this dual protection (also called *charging order protection*) doesn't apply to single-member LLCs because there are no innocent partners to protect (the reason the charging order exists in the first place).

After this ruling, more states got on the bandwagon and restricted dual liability protection to LLCs with more than one member. Other states, however, decided to go against the grain and instead drafted charging order protection into their state laws — for *all* LLCs, even single-member ones.

On `www.docrun.com/dummies/charging_order_protection` (password is **onesmartdummy**), I have posted an analysis of charging order protection for each state. Our lawyers will make sure to keep it updated for you as the laws change.

If you want to protect your privacy but your company has only one or two members, you can always elect to be manager-managed. In that case, instead of listing your company's initial members, most states allow you to list one or more managers. You can then elect a corporation (that you control) or a *nominee* — a friend or paid professional to stand in your place on public records, thus preserving your privacy. Then use the operating agreement to direct specifically how the LLC is to be managed.

Your state may require only that an *authorized representative* — usually your registered agent or formation company — be listed in your articles of organization. In this case, none of these rules and work-arounds apply to you. You can see your state's laws defining what you are required to list on the articles of organization on the *For Dummies* resources site at `www.docrun.com/dummies` (password is **onesmartdummy**).

Deciding how you want your company to be managed

Businesses don't operate themselves — someone needs to manage them! You don't have to decide immediately exactly who will manage the day-to-day operations of your business and what their specific roles will be (which I go over in Chapter 10), but most states require that you give a basic idea of how your company will be managed in the articles of organization.

Luckily, you need to decide between only two management options for your LLC:

- **Member-managed:** The LLC's members (the owners) also deal in the business's day-to-day operations. If you select this option, *all* the members are also managers — you can't prevent one member from getting involved while allowing the rest to manage the business. However, you *can* limit the power of individual member-managers (or groups of member-managers) in the operating agreement.
- **Manager-managed:** A separate manager (or two or three or ten) handles the business's day-to-day operations. This is a good choice if not *all* members want to manage and/or an outside person would be a good candidate. The benefits of manager management include flexibility — you can assign certain outside individuals as managers, now or in the future — alleviated confusion, and a break-up of the workload.

Just as the number of members an LLC can have is unlimited, your LLC can also have an unlimited number of managers, but I would choose wisely if I were you. Unless specifically restricted in the operating agreement managers have absolute authority to obligate the business to contracts, loans, debts, and so on. It takes only one manager to do so, and he can act without the knowledge of the other managers. Therefore, unless you clearly limit that person's authority, all the members must absolutely trust whoever is chosen as a manager.

A manager doesn't have to be a person; it can also be another company or a trust. Sometimes there are benefits to setting up a separate company that acts as manager for your LLC. One such benefit of structuring your business this way is *privacy* — you can list the managing company's name as manager instead of your own.

In Minnesota and North Dakota, an LLC's managers are called *governors.*

When the members manage

When an LLC is member-managed, *all* the owners are responsible for the day-to-day operations of the business. If you're a small business without outside investors (who don't have an operational role), then chances are your LLC is managed by its members.

However, if you, like most entrepreneurs, put everything you have into your start-up, then a partner slipping up and getting your company embroiled in lawsuits could be devastating. If you're a small business and you want to exclude certain members who have a tendency to make bad decisions, like using company funds for personal, non-business-related exploits and adventures (we all know the type!), then you may want to severely limit that member's management powers in the operating agreement or isolate that member from all management activities by making your LLC manager-managed and not electing that individual as a manager.

If your LLC is a larger company with a lot of members, you may want to think twice about choosing member management. Think about it — if you have 25 members and each member has a say in the day-to-day operations of the business, it will be a total mess! That's like having 25 CEOs! Not only is this setup unrealistic, but it will also lack credibility if your LLC is ever taken to court. Members don't need to be managers in order to have basic voting powers over the company's *big* decisions, and the beauty of an LLC is that you're free to specify what qualifies as a big decision in the operating agreement. I show you how to do so in Chapter 9.

If you choose member management, you may lose the benefit of charging order protection if you don't take a few steps to protect it. If a creditor gets a charging order against your membership interests and those interests come with management rights, that creditor can use his management powers to distribute a good portion of the profits to himself to pay off the claim. Chapter 17 explains how to structure your operating agreement to protect against this action.

When separate managers manage

Your company is considered manager-managed if one of the following is true:

- One or more of the managers of the company is not a member.
- Not all members of the company manage the day-to-day details.

When you select manager management, you must choose at least one manager. The manager doesn't even have to be a he or a she! You can select an entity (an LLC, corporation, limited partnership, and so on) to manage your LLC.

Why would you have separate managers manage? Maybe one of the members wants to remain a silent partner. He's willing to risk his money but doesn't want to be bothered with the everyday business decisions that the managers are confronted with. Or say that none of the members has time to manage the business, so they want to hire an outside CEO who can do a better job than they ever could. In many situations, separate managers may make more sense for your LLC.

Manager-managed LLCs are commonly used in estate planning. You can give your children membership shares in the LLC every year while remaining the only manager of the LLC. While you're alive, your children can't make management decisions regarding the money but can receive profits from it (finally, a true gift that keeps on giving!). Then, when you pass away, they are elected as the new managers and have full rights over and use of the LLC's assets.

Managing her LLC means that she can have her cake and eat it, too

Jill's family and friends have been pressuring her to start a bakery for years now, and Jill finally relents. She is looking forward to the challenge and has even taken business classes to learn how to run a company. She puts together a business plan so that she can look for financing. Her credit isn't great, so that leaves her with the option of going to an investor.

Jill's cousin is a successful lawyer and offers to loan her the money. He trusts Jill's expertise and is willing to be a silent partner. He lives across the country, so he can't be active in the business's day-to-day operations anyway. With this structure in mind, Jill sets up an LLC. She issues 50 percent of the membership interests to herself and 50 percent to her cousin in exchange for the start-up capital. Jill then designates the LLC as being manager-managed with herself as the only manager. This gives her the full power she needs to run her business as she sees fit, while relieving her cousin from being hassled with the day-to-day hassles.

When you have a manager-managed LLC, the Securities and Exchange Commission or your state securities division may determine that you are involved in the sale of securities if your members are investing in an LLC that they have no say in managing. This isn't necessarily a bad thing. Just be sure to speak with a qualified securities lawyer before disallowing any of your investors decision-making power in the company's operations. I go into how to make these sorts of decisions in Chapter 11, where I address raising capital for your LLC.

Preparing Your Articles

Preparing your articles of organization can easily end up being overwhelming — especially if the state rejects your articles a number of times. But keep your chin up. If you stay organized and get helpful assistance, you should be able to get your articles submitted within a couple of days and be certain that they will be filed without incident. After you submit everything correctly, you can sit back and wait for your approved articles (sometimes referred to as your *corporate charter*) to arrive in the mail.

Meeting your state's requirements

The articles of organization are made up of *provisions*, which is just a fancy term for the sections of your document that address particular topics. Some provisions are required to be included in your articles, so I cover those first, and then I give you an overview of other provisions that you may want (or need) to include.

Each state has different requirements, but I cover the commonly shared provisions in this section. To find out specifically what your state requires, check out the fill-in-the-blank articles of organization that your state provides. This document tells you all the information your state requires and assists you in the planning process.

Provisions that your articles must have

In most states, your articles of organization must include the following provisions:

- **LLC name:** This is pretty straightforward — your articles need to identify the name of the company to which they apply! Keep in mind, though, that this name needs to be unique. I show you how to go about checking the LLC names already registered in your state in Chapter 4.
- **Company address:** Some states require that you put your company address in the articles of organization, and some even require that the address you give is located within that state. Because you will be receiving only state filings at this address, I recommend using your registered agent's address, but make sure that your agent is okay with this and can forward your mail every day. Also be aware that many states won't let you use a P.O. Box.
- **Powers and purpose of the company:** Here, you designate what sort of business you'll be engaging in. Although some states require you to be detailed, most states allow you to be really broad and say that the LLC isn't limited in its purpose and has the power to engage in any activity it wants. I feel that the broader you make this statement, the less you are limited should you decide to venture into other business areas in the future. Sometimes envisioning where your business will be at the ten-year mark is an impossible feat, so to be safe, always stick with the idea that broader is better.

  Here's an example of a broadly stated provision:

  The purpose for which this Company is organized is to transact any or all lawful business for which Limited Liability Companies may be organized for.
- **Registered agent and office:** Your registered agent can be your greatest asset — especially if you're organized in a state other than the one in which you live. First of all, the law requires you to have a registered agent, and second, a registered agent can handle much of the paperwork involved in maintaining compliance in your state(s). See Chapter 5 for instructions on finding and working with a registered agent.
- **Member-managed or manager-managed:** As I discuss earlier in this chapter, whether your LLC will be managed by its members or separate managers is a big decision that can really help or hinder your business operations. Carefully consider the implications before making a choice.

- **Names and addresses of managers and/or members:** Quite a few states require that you list the names and addresses of the managers and/or members (if your LLC is member-managed) in the articles. Because the articles of organization are public record, state as little as is legally allowed. As a matter of fact, if your registered agent allows it, try to use its office address in this section.
- **Organizer:** In most states, only an *organizer* (sometimes referred to as an *authorized signer* or *authorized party*) is required to sign the articles of organization. This practice is becoming more and more popular as formation companies do most of the LLC filings. The organizer has no true legal responsibility or further obligation to the LLC, so you can designate anybody, really. This arrangement is great if you're looking for extra privacy!

Some states require that you also state the amount of each member's initial contribution (money, services, equipment, whatever) and the percentage of profits that each member gets. If you don't yet know this information or don't want to disclose it, you can do one of two things:

- State what you *do* know or are willing to disclose, and then put the remaining information in the company's operating agreement. I show you how to do so in Chapter 10.
- Domicile your LLC in another state that doesn't require this disclosure, and then foreign-file in the state in which you're operating.

The antiquated duration provision

When LLCs first came about, the IRS placed a few restrictions on them in order to make them eligible for partnership taxation. One of these restrictions was that LLCs can't live forever. The states complied by giving LLCs a limited life span of 30, sometimes 50, years. Though this restriction is long gone, a couple of states have been slow to adapt and still require a duration to be declared in the articles of organization.

At this point, all states allow a "perpetual" duration; however, you have to state your intent in the articles. Just to be on the safe side, you may want to include the following statement in your articles:

> *"In accordance with all state statutes, the duration of the company shall be perpetual."*

Extra provisions you may want to include

You're allowed to include whatever extra provisions you want in your articles of organization; however, keep in mind that your articles are public record. Also, in order to amend them, you must go through a costly filing process.

When it comes to customizing your LLC, you get into a lot more specifics in the operating agreement (see Chapter 9) than you do in the articles of organization. If you don't see an important provision discussed in this chapter, it's probably because I believe that including it in the operating agreement instead is a better idea because the operating agreement isn't on public record and is easy to amend. Privacy is important, especially when it comes to protecting yourself against lawsuits. And if you want to amend customized provisions, you don't have to pay a dime to change your operating agreement.

An extra provision that you likely will want to include and never amend is the indemnification of managers and members. When you are *indemnified,* you can't be held personally responsible for the acts of the company or even for your acts on behalf of the company. This provision is normally provided in state law, but it's always good to publicly state in your articles of organization that each member is permitted the maximum indemnification available.

Following is a sample provision:

Article IX: Indemnification of Managers and Members

A. *Under the current law, including any amendments hereafter, each manager shall be entitled to the fullest indemnification available to them.*

B. *Each manager shall be liable to the Company for the following actions:*

   1. *The breach of the manager's or member's loyalty to the Company or its members.*

   2. *To be liable hereunder, the manager in question must have acted in a malicious or grossly negligent manner, as defined by law.*

   3. *A transaction in which the manager benefits to the detriment of the Company or its members.*

   4. *An action for which there is no indemnification provided by law.*

C. *This indemnification shall not deter or cancel out other rights to which each manager or member is entitled.*

Provisions for professional LLCs

In most states, if you are a licensed professional, you must have a special provision in your articles of organization designating you as a *professional LLC* (or PLLC for short). As I explain in Chapter 2, a PLLC is very similar to a standard LLC; however, professionals can't be exempt from personal responsibility and malpractice, so they have less liability protection. A PLLC's formation is the same, but the articles are slightly different and the filing fee may be slightly higher, depending on the state.

Before creating your articles of organization as a licensed professional, read Chapter 2 and make sure that you're well aware of your state's laws in regard to professional LLCs (or whether your state even allows a PLLC to be formed). Also keep in mind the following points:

- Typically, you have to abide by name restrictions and add the word *Professional* or the letter *P* to the designator. In some states, the name of the LLC must contain the professional's name. For example, if you're a doctor and your name is Jane Goodman, then your professional limited liability company can be called *Jane Goodman, MD, PLLC.*
- You can't state a broad purpose; it must be specific to the service you provide. You must use a purpose provision stating something like the following:

  The purpose for which the Company is organized is to engage in the professional service of ____________________.

  In some states, your licensing board may need to approve your articles of organization and sign them before the secretary of state will accept them for filing. Contact MyLLC.com (888-88MYLLC) or your secretary of state's office to see if this step is required. If it is, you may need a good dose of patience — these things can take time!
- The fees may be slightly higher if you are forming a professional LLC.
- If you are using the generic, state-provided articles of organization, check to see if you need to use a different one for a PLLC.

Putting it all together

After you figure out what provisions you're going to include in your articles of organization, you need to wrap up everything into a professional-looking document. One option is just to amend the state's generic form with your extra provisions, but do you really want to walk into a bank, ask for a million-dollar business loan, and then hand over articles that look like a patchwork quilt of legalese? Not likely.

If your state allows it (most states do), retype the articles into your own document so that it looks more professional. A lot of people who can make important decisions affecting your LLC will be looking at these articles — bankers determining your eligibility for a business loan, investors looking to buy in, and so on. You want to demonstrate that you take pride in your company documents.

Different states require different formats, so contact your secretary of state's office to make sure that it doesn't have any special requirements as to how the articles of organization are laid out. However, most states have the basics in common, and with that in mind, here are a few tips:

- Print your articles of organization on regular 8½-x-11-inch white paper. Use black ink and print on only one side of the paper (no double-sided copies). Make sure that the articles are clean and legible.
- Spell your company name exactly as you want it to look on your checks, letterhead, and other official documents. This is where spell check definitely comes in handy!
- Structure the document into articles, sections, and subsections. Doing so makes referencing provisions a breeze — for example, "Article A, Section 4," or "Article II, Section B, Subsection 4." You can find this structure in any professionally drafted contract.

Articles of organization are pretty simple, and for the most part, you can draft them yourself. However, your time may be better spent doing other important tasks, so if you don't feel like researching laws and typing out provisions, consider hiring a formation company. These companies are generally well versed in creating articles of organization (after all, they do it every day!) and charge a heck of a lot less than attorneys.

Choosing who signs

So you put all this work into forming your articles of organization, and now you need to sign it, right? Probably not. Believe it or not, in most states, a manager or member doesn't even need to sign the articles before filing them.

Most states assume that when an LLC is organized, it hasn't had its first member meeting. At that meeting, managers are traditionally elected. If the LLC doesn't have any managers, they can't sign the articles. Most states also assume that you're forming your LLC through an attorney or a formation company, and to make it easy for everyone, states allow someone at the law firm or formation company to sign the articles instead of the client. That is why most states allow an *organizer* to sign and file the articles of organization.

The organizer doesn't have to be associated with your company and isn't a manager or member (unless you want her to be). She is simply the person who creates the LLC. After the LLC is formed and the managers and members are assigned, the organizer fades away — she has no future position of power in the company.

Although most states allow an organizer to sign the articles of organization, some states require a manager and/or member to sign. Also, some states require the articles to be notarized. A quick way to determine who must sign the articles of organization in your state is to look at the filing form for your state.

Getting the necessary signature sounds fairly simple, but there's a catch. In most states, the LLC's registered agent is required to sign the articles of organization before it can be filed. The agent normally signs an acceptance of appointment document that is appended to the articles. This can be a bit of a headache for most people, especially if you live in a different state than the one in which you're filing. In that case, I recommend that you make sure your formation company and the registered agent for your entity are one and the same.

Filing Your Articles

Filing your articles of organization with the secretary of state can be an exciting process — especially when you receive your file-stamped articles in the mail! After that, you can *finally* get to the important stuff that you need to do to get your business up and running: opening bank accounts, printing marketing materials, hiring employees, renting office space, and so on.

If you're interested in the how-tos of filing, then you've probably created your articles of organization by now, and there's no point in waiting to do the filing. After all, your LLC can't come into existence until the secretary of state has approved it. Think of the date that your articles of organization are stamped as your company's official birth date. If you're ever asked what your date of organization is, you'll refer to this date (called the *formation date*) — not the date on which you drafted the articles or the date on which you received the filed articles in the mail. Along with your filed articles, you'll receive a company charter that shows the date of formation.

In the following sections, I go over the step-by-step process of filing your articles of organization.

Dotting your i's and crossing your t's

Before you file your articles of organization, *please* take the time to do a bit of research to make sure that you file them properly. Following the filing steps to the letter saves you a lot of time and headaches later, because your filing won't be rejected. From my experience working with secretaries of states' offices, I can't tell you how often they have to reject filings for silly reasons: The fee amount is incorrect, the organizer sent only one copy, and so on.

To file your articles, the first thing you need to do is to go to your secretary of state's website and determine a few things, such as

- What fees are required?
- To whom do you make out the check?
- Can you pay with a credit card?
- Can the filing be done online?
- How many copies are required?
- To what address do you mail the documents?
- Are any cover sheets required to be submitted with the articles?

After you answer these questions and double-check your filing against the state's filing procedures, make a copy of the articles (for your own files), put a copy of the articles and anything else the state requires in an envelope (don't forget to include the fee), and mail them. I recommend sending your filing packet by a service that requires the recipient to sign for the package.

An alternative now available in most states is to file your articles of organization online. You may not end up with the prettiest corporate documents at the end of the day, but the sheer amount of time saved may be worth it. Most states offer an easy step-by-step process, and any mistakes that you make in the filing process can be corrected immediately online, whereas with a paper filing you may have to wait weeks to receive a rejection notice in your mailbox.

Sending it off

You're eager to put your business plan into action. You have planned out your first official day of work with your new company in your head. The one thing holding you up is the need for some file-stamped articles that prove to the world that your company exists.

After you send in your articles and payment, the secretary of state's office generally can take as long as it wants to file your articles of organization. Don't be alarmed if you still haven't heard back six weeks later. Some states, such as California, can take up to three months if you file by snail mail!

In some cases, you can file the articles of organization in person by walking them into the secretary of state's office and substantially reduce the turnaround time. If you can't file personally because you live in a different state or the secretary of state is in a city far-far away, you can always have a formation company do it for you. (See Chapter 5 for details about registered agents.) For other ways to speed up the approval process, see the following section.

When you don't want to hurry up and wait: Fast-forwarding your filing

Some states will — for a fee — put your filing at the top of the pile! Depending on the state, you may be able to expedite the processing of your articles of organization. Some states give you the option of getting your articles back within 48 hours, 24 hours, or even the same day.

When submitting expedited articles, label the outside of the envelope *Expedited Handling Required.* Putting a sticky note on your document that says the same thing is also a good idea.

Although this seems like a perfect scenario, beware that the fee for a quick turnaround can range from an extra $10 to hundreds of dollars. Call your secretary of state's office or visit its website listed at `www.docrun.com/dummies` (password is **onesmartdummy**) to find out the exact cost. Also, keep in mind that you're required to pay the expedited processing fee even if your articles of organization aren't perfect and are rejected as a result.

After the secretary of state's office approves your articles, you receive your file-stamped articles back in the mail. Attached to your filed articles, you normally receive a *company charter.* This one-page document shows the all-important date of formation. The charter and the file-stamped articles of organization are your proof that your business is formed as an LLC in your state.

Dealing with a rejected filing

If you receive a large envelope from the secretary of state's office and open it expecting to see your filed articles, but instead see a rejection-of-filing notice, your heart sinks. It's a bummer when your articles are rejected — especially when you can't wait to get your business up and running.

The worst part of a rejection is that a small error can be time-consuming to fix because you may need to go back and wait at the end of the line. For example, if it took three weeks for a clerk to review your documents the first time, then they may go to the bottom of the pile after you resubmit them, and you'll have to wait another three weeks to get them looked at again. (Of course, you can always take the expedited route if your state offers it. See the nearby sidebar "When you don't want to hurry up and wait: Fast-forwarding your filing" for the skinny on this option.)

The secretary of state may reject a filing for any number of reasons. Here are a few mistakes that applicants make and how you can avoid them:

- **The name you want to use conflicts with another LLC (or other entity) that is already formed in that state or a name that has been reserved.** In this case, you just need to choose a new name. If you don't want to do that, you can contact the competing firm and ask for a letter giving you permission to use the name, but this is usually a long shot.
- **The name is considered misleading.** The name may contain forbidden words, such as *banking, financial,* and so on. You can do two things in this situation:
  - Go to the department in your state that regulates your industry and get its approval for the wording. (You'll probably have to jump through a lot of hoops.)
  - Change your company's name.
- **The filing fee is incorrect.** In this case, just write a check for the additional amount and resubmit your documents. Or, if the state returns your old check to you, void it and send a new one for the correct amount.
- **A registered agent is not specified.** This is a common error. Often, when individuals form an LLC, they don't know what a registered agent is or does, so they leave this section blank. But you won't have this problem, because you can read Chapter 5 for more information about registered agents and then fill in the appropriate section on the form.
- **A provision is missing.** In this case, you most likely prepared the documents yourself and missed a *provision* (a section of the document that deals with a particular topic) that is legally required to be included in the articles of organization. Just add the provision to your articles (you can create a fresh draft so that they look nice) and resubmit them.
- **The cover sheet is missing.** Some states require a cover sheet to be submitted with the articles. In this case, obtain the cover sheet from the secretary of state's website, fill it out, and resubmit your articles with the cover sheet.

Although a rejection is a setback, don't get too down about it. Nothing bad will happen. You just need to fix the problem indicated in the rejection notice and resubmit your documents. If the notice isn't specific enough, call the number listed on the form for your secretary of state's office and ask for more information. Or better yet, consider using a formation company to set up your LLC. If you use a reputable company that deals with these sorts of formations all the time, there's very little chance that it will mess up in the first place.

Considering Formation Companies

Don't know exactly what a formation company is? Sure you do! Have you seen those ads offering to form your LLC for a few hundred dollars? Normally, those ads are placed by *formation companies* — companies whose sole business is forming corporations and LLCs. When I started in the formation business in 2001, there was very little competition, but now these companies seem to be popping up everywhere. With all the advertisements and hoopla, the real question is: Do you really need a formation company? And if so, how do you choose one?

First things first: Using a formation company to form your LLC makes sense if you

- **Want to save money:** Attorneys charge upwards of $1,000 for a basic LLC formation, but a good formation company may charge as little as $99. And because formation companies deal with a much larger quantity of LLCs than individual attorneys do, they have the process down to a science. So unless your articles of organization are über complex, you may want to keep the extra dough and save the legal fees for consulting work.
- **Want to save time:** When dealing with a large number of filings, formation companies are forced to work out the kinks and get the whole LLC formation process down pat. This prevents any lag time that you may encounter when attempting to file on your own. Plus, because formation companies deal so much with the various secretaries of state offices, they've developed relationships that can prove useful when you want to get your filing completed in a timely manner. With the right formation company, this nominal fee can save you weeks of tedious research and bureaucratic hassles.
- **Are forming multiple LLCs and want an expert to look over your structure:** Some brick-and-mortar formation companies (the ones that operate outside of the online realm) have consultants who can review your strategy with a skilled eye and set you up in the proper business structure.
- **Are forming an LLC in a different state than the one in which you live:** Different states come with different laws, and a good formation company located in all 50 states is well aware of how the various governments operate. It can also serve as your registered agent, hand-deliver your filings, and make sure that you stay in compliance while you're living hundreds of miles away.

If you decide that a formation company is right for you, make sure that you hire a quality firm. Screen prospects by asking the following questions:

- Do you have an attorney and an accountant on staff to advise me on legal and tax issues?
- Will you assign a consultant to work with me on an ongoing basis?
- Are you located in all 50 states? If not, do you have knowledge of and relations in all other states?
- Will you customize the company to suit my needs?
- Will you customize the articles of organization as opposed to just using state forms?

Shameless plug ahead: As one of the founders of MyLLC.com, a leading formation company, I'm offering you a $24.99 discount (the price of this book) on all formations. Just use coupon code **Dummies3** at checkout.

Chapter 7

Converting Your Current Business into an LLC

In This Chapter

- Determining whether a conversion is for you
- Understanding the tax implications
- Completing the conversion
- Dealing with the details of conversion

Chances are, if you're considering forming an LLC, you're not starting from scratch. LLCs are relatively new entities, and if you've been in business for a long time, you're probably operating your business or maintaining your assets as a sole proprietor, partnership, or corporation. You likely know the benefits of operating under an LLC, but you may not know how to convert your existing business into one.

When you're busy running a bustling enterprise, the last thing you want to do is cause any more chaos by changing your infrastructure and switching to a completely different type of entity. In most cases, you have to navigate a tax minefield and spend a lot of time changing contracts, business loans, and possibly even marketing materials (if you change your company name in the process) over to your new company. Although the conversion to an LLC can be time-consuming, the protection, freedom, and tax benefits offered by an LLC make it well worth it in the long run.

In this chapter, I show you how to convert your current business structure into an LLC, no matter what entity type you're currently using. I also show you how to avoid most of the fees and taxes that pop up and how to avoid falling into a tax trap that you can't get out of. Although this process may seem complicated, it isn't as difficult as it first appears. With proper planning and the help of a qualified accountant, you can be operating under your new LLC in no time!

Considering Conversion to an LLC

Life is good: Your business is flourishing. But you know that as you operate more and more with the public, your chances of being sued increase tenfold, so you've decided that you need the reassurance of liability protection. Or you may want to take on investors or acquire loans to help you grow. Or you may want the benefits of partnership taxation. For your business to have the best protection and advantages, you need a powerful and flexible entity, and, you've read that the LLC is your best bet. If you're still undecided, I suggest that you go back to Chapters 2 and 3, where I give you an overview of LLCs and all the other major forms of business — sole proprietorships, partnerships, and corporations.

When I use the term *conversion,* I'm not talking about converting only a corporation, limited partnership, or other *incorporated entity* (an entity that needs to be filed with the state to exist); I'm also referring to *nonincorporated* business structures, such as sole proprietorships and general partnerships. You may be surprised to know that even if you're simply operating under your own name, converting to an LLC is sometimes just as complicated as converting from a corporation. Of course, a few factors play into this process, which I discuss later in the chapter.

I can't possibly list all the reasons why you may want to convert your business to an LLC, but the following example situations give you a taste of why a conversion can be an incredibly powerful step on your path to success:

- You're operating as a sole proprietorship or general partnership, and you're afraid of being sued by a customer or an employee.
- You're operating as a corporation, and you're afraid that you may be sued personally or may someday face bankruptcy or divorce, and your ownership of the business will be taken away from you.
- Your small business — which is currently a corporation — is becoming more and more profitable, and your corporate tax rate is up to almost 35 percent. You want to minimize this tax burden by electing partnership taxation.
- You just purchased real estate in your own name and you want to protect the property from lawsuits, so you know that transferring your property into an LLC is your best bet. Luckily, unlike a corporation, you can usually transfer assets into and out of an LLC tax-free!
- You're currently operating as a sole proprietorship or general partnership, and you want to raise financing to get the business off the ground.

- Your business is formed as an S corporation, and you've outgrown the ownership limitations imposed on you (for instance, you want to take on a non–U.S. resident as an investor). By converting to an LLC, you can remove any ownership restrictions while maintaining pass-through taxation (see Chapter 8 for details on the differences between the two types of taxation).
- You're operating as a corporation, and you or a partner plan to invest a substantial amount of additional capital. You prefer the partnership taxation of the LLC so that you can immediately write off that contribution as a loss on your personal tax return (thereby offsetting other income).

The question often isn't whether a conversion is right for you — if you opened the book to this chapter, then you've probably already determined that an LLC is right for you. Instead, the question is how to make the conversion work. Depending on your current entity structure, a conversion may seem a bit daunting, especially if you believe that a conversion will bring a lot of tax consequences. But don't fret — if you've got the will, I can show you the way!

Navigating the Tax Minefield

Any drawbacks encountered while converting your business into an LLC are likely to be tax traps of some sort, but being informed can help you navigate the best path. LLCs can trick you! Because you can transfer money and property into them without creating a taxable event, you may think that any transactions you want to perform while converting to an LLC are good to go. Unfortunately, you need to take into account any taxes or fees you may encounter with your old entity (corporations are the worst when it comes to taxes and fees!) and any taxes incurred by changes in debt structure or ownership interest. Also, if you aren't on the lookout, you may be hit with a bunch of local and state taxes, such as sales tax, use tax, and transfer tax.

Although you can elect an alternative form of taxation for your new LLC, in this section I assume that you intend to go with the default form of LLC taxation: partnership taxation. After all, it is the most flexible and least restrictive form of taxation. (If you aren't sure of your options, turn to Chapter 8 to find out which form of taxation is right for you.) Be aware that electing some other form of taxation for your brand-new LLC (such as corporation or S corporation taxation) is a game-changer. The strategies and information outlined in the rest of this chapter may not apply to you. Same goes for single-member LLCs, which the IRS considers *disregarded entities* and taxes as if they were sole proprietorships. So if you think that you may be straying from the norm, you definitely want to get the advice of a qualified accountant before executing the conversion. Don't make assumptions when it comes to LLC taxation and conversions; way too much is at stake.

Converting from a sole proprietorship

Considering that the most common, albeit dangerous, method of operating a business is as a sole proprietorship, you may well be running a sole proprietorship currently. Although sole proprietorships are easy and cheap to start, they offer zero liability protection, and they give your customers and employees little confidence in your business acumen. Plus, due to the fact that sole proprietorships don't have shares you can sell, you'll never be able to raise capital or find investors.

If you're currently operating as a sole proprietorship, I strongly recommend that you form an LLC immediately. Luckily, converting from a sole proprietorship to an LLC can be a pretty effortless, tax-free process. Your business assets are currently in your name, so transferring them is easy. You simply contribute the business's assets to the LLC in exchange for your ownership interest.

If you convert your sole proprietorship to a single-member LLC simply by contributing your business assets to the LLC in exchange for membership interests — in other words, you use your business assets as the currency to purchase ownership in the new entity — then no taxable event occurs. With the IRS, exceptions always exist, but chances are that the transfer is tax-free.

However, if your company has outstanding debt, you may face one potential tax pitfall called a *deemed cash distribution.* In a business, the two kinds of debt are

- **Recourse debt:** Debt that one or more members is personally responsible for should the business default on the loan
- **Nonrecourse debt:** Debt that's secured only by the business; the owners have no personal stake.

A deemed cash distribution occurs when a member reduces his share of the business's recourse debt.

The IRS treats any reduction in a member's share of recourse liability as a cash distribution, and, like a cash distribution, the member must pay taxes on any amount that goes over his *tax basis* (I discuss tax bases in

Chapter 14). Luckily for LLCs, being the most flexible entities around, allocations and distributions of profit can be amended and handed out disproportionately (as long as a majority of the members agree).

Frankly, getting around the deemed cash distribution problem isn't too difficult if you have a qualified accountant to help you. If your company has substantial business loans and liabilities and you're bringing on a partner, speak with an accountant who has extensive experience with partnership taxation. If you don't currently have an accountant onboard, try to find other businesses with structures like yours and get a referral. The ins and outs of deemed cash distributions can get pretty complex, and you need to have a clear map through any potential tax minefield. A neighborhood bookkeeper simply won't cut it.

You know that old adage, "Don't change horses midstream"? Remember it if you're considering changing your accounting methods, and keep your accounting method the same when converting from a sole proprietorship to an LLC. For instance, if you're on a cash-based system, don't switch to an accrual-based system. In the IRS's eyes, this switch could "accelerate the income," which means taxes, taxes, and more taxes! If you really want to change your accounting method, wait until the conversion has been completed and then have your tax advisor assist you.

Converting from a general or limited partnership

The conversion to an LLC from a general or limited partnership is probably as straightforward a switch as you can get. No matter whether you're a general partnership, limited partnership, or limited liability company electing partnership taxation — you're all the same in the eyes of the IRS. The states may treat the entity types differently, especially when it comes to liability protection; however, they are all subject to partnership taxation.

Keep in mind that before you can convert your general partnership operation to an LLC, all the partners must unanimously agree to the decision. You can't convert without them knowing it! All the partners usually have to sign off on it in the company's operating agreement.

The big nontaxable event

Assuming that everything is straightforward, a conversion from a general or limited partnership to an LLC is a *nontaxable event,* so you won't get hit with a big tax bill at year's end. All you have to do is contribute the assets of your current business to the new LLC in exchange for membership shares. Most of this is done in your operating agreement, which I show you how to draft in Chapter 9.

This easy step makes converting from a general partnership or limited partnership to an LLC a relatively pain-free process. You simply execute the conversion with the state (I describe exactly how to do so later in the chapter). As long as nothing changes in regard to ownership percentages or business debt, nothing changes with the IRS. You can have the same tax year-end and continue to be taxed as a partnership with the same year-end filings due.

It gets even better: Under Section 721 of the Internal Revenue Code, you're allowed a friendly little exemption for any appreciation that your business property may have accrued. For instance, if your limited partnership purchased a piece of property five years ago for $100,000 and it is now worth $150,000, when you convert the limited partnership to an LLC, you don't have to recognize the new fair-market value of the property ($150,000) or pay taxes on the $50,000 appreciation that your property accrued over the past five years. The IRS allows you to put off that burden for later years, when you legitimately sell the property. To learn more about this and other partnership tax tricks, you may want to check out Chapter 14, where I discuss taxation at length.

The usual partnership tax trap

The entire conversion is absolutely, 100 percent tax-free? It sounds too good to be true! Well, yeah . . . about that . . . . As with sole proprietors who may be looking to bring on another partner, if your business adds or removes members or changes any percentage of ownership during the conversion process, you may end up with some pretty gnarly tax consequences.

The same problem occurs if you change who is personally responsible for the business debt. If an owner personally guarantees a business loan, that loan is considered *recourse debt,* and the owner can use it as a deduction of sorts against any income he derives from the partnership. If, when converting to an LLC, this partner changes the amount of debt he personally guarantees or writes it off entirely, the IRS likely will consider it to be income to the partner (since he's no longer responsible for the debt), and the total amount offloaded may end up being treated as a cash distribution from the company. Depending on the member's tax basis in the company (which I discuss in detail in Chapter 14), he may be taxed on this amount as if he were being paid in cash. Although this tax trap can occur in sole proprietorships, it's much more common with partnerships. After all, more hands in the pot usually means more issues popping up.

To illustrate this tax trap with an example: You own a piece of property worth $200,000, with a mortgage on it for $150,000. You've been a good customer, so your bank decides to release you from having to personally guarantee the $150,000 loan and instead puts it in the name of your LLC. At that point, depending on where your capital account stands with previous deductions and such, you may need to pay tax on the $150,000 simply because you're no longer responsible for the debt. Bet it ain't lookin' so bad on your credit report now, eh?

Keeping the ownership and distribution percentages the same is the only way to avoid a taxable event when changing an existing partnership into an LLC.

Converting from a corporation

If you're currently operating as a corporation, converting to a limited liability company is a clear good move unless you plan on going public or raising venture capital. The double taxation inherent in corporations is rarely helpful for a growing business. Unfortunately, as good a move as the conversion to an LLC is, especially where taxes are concerned, it can also be a pretty hairy process.

With a good accountant, and some in-depth brainstorming sessions, you can find multiple ways to accomplish your conversion with very little tax burden.

Navigating state taxes

Transferring assets from a corporation to an LLC without the help of a qualified accountant is like crossing a freeway wearing a blindfold. If you somehow manage to make it across the IRS obstacle course, you still need to take into account state and local taxes. First, know your enemy: Find out what sales tax and transfer tax your state may hit you with. In high-tax states such as California, they can be astronomical, so you need to be aware of the worst-case scenario.

Knowing your many options

When you have an idea of what you're dealing with, you and your accountant can structure the conversion in a way that minimizes (or even eliminates!) these taxes. If your state allows *statutory conversions* (converting a corporation into an LLC instead of dissolving the corporation and starting a new LLC), then this could be a viable option. (See "Executing the Conversion" later in this chapter for more on statutory conversions.) Or maybe you're better off doing a merger, with your LLC remaining as the surviving entity. Or perhaps your state provides a tax exemption that allows you to go the conventional route of forming a new LLC and transferring the business assets in exchange for membership interests.

If, after looking with your accountant at all the routes available to you, you still can't find a work-around, consider leaving your assets in your corporation. After all, no law says that a business's assets need to be maintained in its operating company. Actually, *not* having your business assets in your operating company is generally a good idea. Not only is isolating your assets from potential lawsuits a good asset-protection strategy, but it can also help you *save* taxes in the long run.

Converting smoothly with a merger

You may be able to save taxes when converting a corporation to an LLC by forming a brand-new LLC and doing a standard merger with it and your corporation. A *merger* is the combination of two existing entities into a single surviving one, and merging your corporation into an LLC is a great way to avoid sales and transfer taxes that are associated with moving assets from one entity to another.

All states have laws regarding mergers, so you have to research whether the laws of your state allow two different entity types (a corporation and an LLC) to merge into one with the LLC being the surviving entity. Some states provide no guidance at all; in this case, your attorney is the best person to direct you through the proper procedures.

Keeping the corporation

Sometimes the best thing to do is nothing at all. A *dual-entity strategy* is an arrangement in which a newly formed LLC serves as your operating company and leases assets from your corporation. I discuss this strategy at length in Chapter 17, but I give you a quick rundown here.

If your business assets are located in a corporation, separate from your operating company (in this case, a newly formed LLC), then you can lease those business assets to the operating company (the LLC) for a certain sum commensurate with the going rate in your industry. When your LLC operating company makes those lease payments (a fully deductible expense) to your corporation, that income (which would otherwise be deemed profit) is then shielded from whatever hefty state taxes would otherwise be imposed.

For example, if you own a local pizza company and you want to convert your corporation into an LLC, you set up your new LLC, transfer your contracts to the LLC, and convert your business operations over to it. However, you leave your stoves and other equipment in the ownership of the corporation. Your corporation becomes a leasing company and leases the equipment to your operating LLC. This arrangement has two benefits:

- If one of your customers gets food poisoning and sues your company (your LLC), your assets are protected in your old corporation.
- If you want to retain profits without having to pay personal income tax and self-employment tax on them, you have a legitimate way of transferring them to a corporation (thereby subjecting them only to corporate income tax — usually a much lower amount — until you use them).

A dual-entity strategy is effective at saving you some tax dough only if your corporation is in a state that has low enough corporate taxes to make it worth it. If it isn't, you can always relocate it to a more favorable state (called *redomiciling*), but check first with your accountant that this step wouldn't inadvertently create a taxable event on either the federal or the state level. (I tell you how to redomicile in Chapter 5.) Also, you have to make sure that you avoid what would be considered "transacting business" in your new state, otherwise you would be forced to register there, which would remove any tax benefit. In Chapter 5, I show you how to determine whether or not your'e technically "transacting business."

Creating a leasing arrangement between an existing corporation and a new LLC may be overkill if you aren't too concerned with avoiding state taxes. If this is the case, then don't worry so much about the state in which the corporation is located or about transferring profit. However, if you happen to be one of those folks who cannot transfer your assets from your corporation to your LLC tax-free, then this arrangement may be your best bet. And don't forget the added bonus of protecting your company by isolating your business assets from whatever entity is handling your company's day-to-day operations and is most likely to be sued.

If your corporation is in a tax-free state, such as Nevada or Wyoming, you may want to lease the assets to your operating LLC at a standard lease rate (so the lease is legitimate and you don't raise red flags). This way, that profit won't be distributed to you at the end of the year and be subject to your personal income and self-employment taxes; it will safely sit in a corporate bank account free from hefty state corporate taxes and franchise fees. What a great way to save up to buy more assets and equipment! I discuss using a tax haven for the dual-entity strategy in more detail in Chapter 17.

Executing the Conversion

Before you begin to convert your business into an LLC, be sure to do the following:

- Carefully consider whether converting your current entity to an LLC is the right thing to do. If you decide that it is, then . . .
- Scope out any tax issues that may arise; and
- Sit down with your accountant and work out a plan.

After you have done your homework and are ready to move forward, you need to decide what type of conversion to do. When I say *conversion,* you probably think of one of two things: Actually transforming your old entity into a limited liability company by changing its structure (often referred to as a *statutory conversion*), or what I call the *form and liquidate process,* which I discuss later in this section. These two methods are the most popular ways of executing a conversion, but other possible conversions, such as a merger or an acquisition, may end up being a better bet for your situation. These are advanced strategies to be used in complex situations and are best handled by a qualified tax attorney and/or a CPA. At the end of the day, all you really care about is getting assets from point A to point B without major tax ramifications and with as little legal paperwork as possible.

If your state allows statutory conversions

If your state is one of the few that allow a *statutory conversion,* consider yourself lucky! A statutory conversion is a means for entities such as corporations and partnerships to change their entity type simply by filing a certificate of conversion, along with the articles of organization of the new LLC, with the secretary of state. I've listed each state's rules regarding statutory conversions on a website only for *For Dummies* readers at `www.docrun.com/dummies/statutory_conversion` (password is **onesmart dummy**).

Statutory conversions are available only for *incorporated* entity types, which means that they don't apply to sole proprietorships and general partnerships. I show you how to convert to an LLC from a sole proprietorship or general partnership later in this section.

Note that a statutory conversion doesn't result in the dissolution of your old company and the formation of a new one. Instead, your company is simply *converted* to a new entity type. If done properly, the conversion qualifies as a reorganization under Section 368(a)(1)(F) of the Internal Revenue Code, which offers much more favorable tax treatment than simply transferring assets to a new LLC. A qualified CPA or tax attorney can further inform you as to whether this type of conversion is the best option for your particular situation.

With a statutory conversion, you keep your same tax identification number; you simply contact the IRS to change the entity type associated with that tax ID. Additionally, most states' conversion laws automatically transfer the rights of creditors and liens on property. Neither of these little tidbits may seem important, but they can save you a world of hassle when you go about amending your contracts with your lenders, creditors, and vendors with your new name with *LLC* at the end.

When executing a statutory conversion, keep the structure of the company — including percentages owned, voting rights, and so on — the same for tax purposes. And regardless of tax implications, most states require that no significant structural changes take place in order to complete a statutory conversion. Depending on the laws of your state, you may be required to structure the management in a similar manner.

Knowing what your state requires

Some states, such as Alaska, require simple articles of conversion to declare only the name of the entity before the conversion, the name of the entity after the conversion, and the date on which the conversion is to be effective. However, other states require a *lot* more detail. For instance, California requires a plan of conversion that rivals the page count of *War and Peace.* Most states also require that an *operating agreement* for the LLC be completed prior to the conversion taking place (which I address in detail throughout Part III of this book).

I can't overstate how dramatically the states' laws on conversions differ, so doing some research and learning exactly what your state law requires is very important. The easiest way to do so is to read the actual law. At `www.docrun.com/dummies` (password is **onesmartdummy**), you can find links to all of the state laws that address converting to a limited liability.

Here are a few documents that your state may require from you in order to execute a statutory conversion to a limited liability company:

- **Articles of conversion:** By far the simplest document of the bunch, the articles of conversion are normally just one or two pages containing some basic information, such as the name and entity type of the old and new entities, any updated company addresses, and the date on which the conversion is to be effective. The secretary of state usually provides a basic fill-in-the-blank document online.

- **Articles of organization:** All states that allow statutory conversions require you to file articles of organization for your new limited liability company. In Chapter 6, I give you details on how to create articles of organization for your LLC, but when converting, you may want to do things a little differently and list the date on which the company was first formed as the effective date of the LLC. Again, look to your state's laws for direction.
- **Plan of conversion:** Not all states require this document. For the ones that do, the specifications can vary dramatically. In a nutshell, this document lays out exactly how everything will be moved from one entity to another, what the new articles of organization are going to say, how the new entity is going to be structured, and so on.

  Keep in mind that your plan of conversion can be a tool for you and your partners that helps keep everyone on the same page. The information and decisions that you lay out in your plan don't have to be limited to what the state requires. As a matter of fact, even if your state *doesn't* require you to file a plan of conversion, I think that creating one anyway for your company's own internal use is a good idea. As I'm sure you know, business can get chaotic, and a plan of conversion keeps everything on track so that the conversion runs smoothly and without a glitch or, even worse, a day of missed work!

All the possible required filings are relatively simple and intuitive to fill out, but the plan of conversion requires a great amount of detail. To give you a taste of what you may be in for, the following are some items that California requires businesses to address in the plan of conversion:

- The terms and conditions of the conversion
- The jurisdiction of the original entity, the jurisdiction of the new entity, and the name of the new entity
- How shares will be converted into ownership of the new entity
- How the new entity will be run, including partnership agreement, articles of organization, and operating agreement
- Any other details that are required by law or that the entity wishes to include

As you can see, California requires a lot of information, yet it doesn't give businesses a lot of guidance on how to format it, what decisions to make, and so on. This is where the help of a qualified business attorney comes in handy, so be sure to talk with someone who can assist you with the details.

Documenting approval for the conversion

Some states require the plan of conversion to be approved by a specific majority or unanimous vote of the shareholders or partners of the original entity as well as the board of directors (if a corporation) or managers or general partners (if a partnership). Regardless of whether your state requires this proof, make sure that you wrap up your old entity type properly and document *everything*.

If your company is a corporation, this requirement means that you need to file a resolution of the board of directors and also of the shareholders that records the plan of conversion and the approval of all members. Just because you are converting to an LLC, which requires a lot less recordkeeping and fewer formalities, doesn't mean that you shouldn't respect your current entity type before the conversion takes place.

Filing the conversion

Typically, all the necessary documents are filed with the secretary of state in one complete package. As complex as organizing all these pieces may sound, the filing shouldn't be too expensive — probably the cost of filing the articles of organization plus a couple hundred dollars. That's probably even less than the cost of forming a new entity and dissolving your old one!

After the secretary of state approves the filing, some states require that you report the filing in a local newspaper or other publication. Be sure to check for this requirement, because failing to meet it could leave you in bad standing with the state.

If your state doesn't allow statutory conversions

You can find out whether your state allows statutory conversions by going to `www.docrun.com/dummies/llc_conversion` (password is **onesmartdummy**) and clicking on your state. If your state doesn't allow statutory conversions, then you'll probably want to opt for what I call the *form and liquidate process,* which entails forming a new limited liability company, transferring business assets from the old entity to the new LLC in exchange for an ownership interest in the new LLC, and finally dissolving your old entity.

You may face tax implications by doing a conversion this way, so clear things with a qualified accountant before proceeding. If you're currently *unincorporated,* namely operating as a sole proprietor or general partnership, then you want to follow this process with the exception of the *liquidate* part. After all, you need to *have* an official entity before you can dissolve, or *liquidate,* it.

Following is a broad view of the steps you need to take to convert your business to a limited liability company:

1. **Form a brand-new LLC.** When you form your LLC, do it just as I describe in Chapter 6. Nothing fancy required.
2. **Check all your loans for a *due on sale* clause that may become effective upon the conversion.** If you see this clause, you may be required to pay back your entire loan if you transfer it. This could force you to refinance, and if the interest rates aren't as good, it could cost you a lot of money in the long run. You can normally work with your bank to avoid this scenario.
3. **Revise any contracts that your current entity is party to so that the contracts reflect your new entity name.** In this case, you may want to work with your attorney, because some of the people with whom you are in contractual arrangements may see this as an opportunity to get you to renegotiate the contract before transferring it.
4. **If you are currently operating as a sole proprietorship or general partnership, check whether your business name is available to be registered in your state.** If it's taken, you may have to form your LLC under another name and then file a *fictitious firm name statement* (or *DBA,* which stands for "doing business as") at your county clerk's office. I go over these naming issues in Chapter 4.
5. **If you have any current fictitious firm names, transfer them to your new entity.** The same goes for other intellectual property, such as trademarks, copyrights, and patents. Some jurisdictions simply require you to refile your DBAs under your new entity.
6. **Check to see if your insurance carrier requires a new premium after the conversion takes place.** Often, insurance isn't transferable from one entity to another, so you may run into some snags if you don't find out ahead of time.
7. **Dissolve your old entity.** I go into the basics of dissolving your old entity later in this chapter, and I show you how to do a formal dissolution in Chapter 16. Obviously, if your business is a sole proprietorship or general partnership, you don't have any "official" entity to dissolve, so this step doesn't apply to you.

8. **Check to see whether you must publish a notice of dissolution or conversion in the local newspaper.** Some states require that you give notice to the public when you do a conversion. You can contact your secretary of state's office or your registered agent to find out whether this step is required in your state.

If your business is a party to a sizable number of contracts and/or agreements (such as mortgages, employment contracts, lease agreements, loan documents, and license agreements), collect them all and take them to your attorney. She can review each document, determine whether a conversion would result in any dire consequences, and, if necessary, renegotiate any contracts that need to be transferred to your new entity. (A word of caution: You may want to work out a flat fee in advance, because having your lawyer do this work can easily become relatively costly on a per-hour basis.)

Tying Up Loose Ends After the Conversion

It's official: Your business is a limited liability company. Congrats! So now what happens? First, you must amend all your official documents — your licenses, permits, and registrations — with your new name and entity type. Even if you're using the same name as before, you must be careful never to refer to your company without having *LLC, L.L.C.,* or *Limited Liability Company* after the name. Most states legally require it anyway; however, if you're ever taken to court, using the LLC designation ensures you'll be able to prove that you were operating as an LLC when transacting business.

Following are some of the common licenses and permits that you'll need to update or even refile (especially if you've gone the form and liquidate route):

- Your tax identification number
- Your state business registration/license
- Your sales tax permit
- Your DBA (fictitious firm name) filings
- Your city and/or county business license
- Any professional licenses or permits

Also, don't forget that you're now an LLC! This means that you need a comprehensive operating agreement that governs the structure, ownership, management, and day-to-day operations of your business. Limited liability companies are much different — and much more flexible! — than all other entity types, so this document is *absolutely imperative* to have. You can adapt your corporate bylaws or your current partnership agreement for your operating agreement, but you need a document that's specifically tailored to your brand-new LLC, so you can't use these documents as they are. Go through the steps outlined throughout Part III of this book to create your custom operating agreement.

Getting around the contractual stuff

At this point in the process, you've managed to sort out the tax stuff and arrange your conversion so that you don't have to dish out too much dough. You do the conversion and . . . ouch! You get served with a lawsuit from one of your vendors stating that you voided your contractual obligation and owe them a lot of money. And unless you did a statutory conversion, they're probably right.

If you look at the fine print on the contracts that your company has signed over the years, some of them say that the contracts can't be assigned or that they'll be terminated upon the termination of the company that entered into the contract. This means that after you convert and terminate your old business structure, you may have problems with the people or companies to which you were contractually obligated.

The following common contracts may be affected:

- Lease agreements for office space
- Equipment lease agreements
- Bank loans
- Personal loans
- Contracts with vendors
- Employee agreements

In some cases, you may need to renegotiate the contract or buy your way out of the legal trouble, which can cost you a lot of money. Speak with an attorney before starting any negotiations. I've found that the money spent on attorneys in these cases is money well spent.

If you can't get out of a contract, you may want to consider leaving your old company active so that the contract doesn't have to be terminated. Whether you can do so depends on the contract, the type of business entity you are currently using, and your attorney's opinion on the matter.

Transferring your assets

After the LLC is set up, the next step is to transfer the assets. Again, in rare cases, transferring assets to your new LLC can be an expensive proposition — especially if you're transferring assets from a corporation, in which case you may have to pay some pretty hefty taxes on them when you take them into your possession. This entire process can be taxing (literally!). Before transferring assets to your new entity, be sure to read "Navigating the Tax Minefield" earlier in this chapter, where I go into some ways to alleviate the tax burden.

If the assets are currently held in your own hands, or if you are a sole proprietorship or general partnership, you can simply invest those assets in the new LLC in exchange for membership shares. LLCs make this process pretty easy because contributing assets to an LLC is, for the most part, a tax-free event. Just be sure that if you and/or your partners have personally guaranteed any debt for the business, nothing changes in that regard. Otherwise, as I discuss in the section "Converting from a sole proprietorship," earlier in this chapter, you can get hit with a *deemed cash distribution* on which you must pay tax.

While you're going through the process of transferring assets and moving operations from one entity to another, make sure to document everything properly. Transferring assets into your LLC can be a pretty formal procedure. If you're not familiar with how to do it, work closely with a qualified small-business attorney, or contact my office (info@docrun.com) for guidance.

Dissolving your old entity

After your new LLC is set up and all the assets and contracts have been transferred, you can begin winding up the affairs and dissolving your old business structure. Again, I am assuming that you are *not* currently operating as a sole proprietorship or general partnership and you have not executed a statutory conversion, which simply transforms your current entity into a limited liability company, eliminating the need to dissolve the old entity.

If your previous business structure was a sole proprietorship or general partnership, then you don't need to complete any special filings. You just need to make sure that you don't accidentally revert to old habits and put contracts, notes, correspondence, and debts in your own name. You also need to avoid combining personal funds with those of your business.

In some states, a partnership must publish a *notice of termination* in a local newspaper before it can be terminated. This public notice may even be required before the conversion can be effective. To find out whether this is the case in your state, call your secretary of state's office. I put a list of contact information for every state online at `www.docrun.com/dummies` (password is **onesmartdummy**).

If your old entity was a limited partnership or corporation, then you must file a *certificate of dissolution* (also called a *certificate of cancellation*) with the secretary of state's office. This certificate terminates your old entity in the eyes of the state and keeps old ghosts, such as company creditors, from haunting you. An officer, director, or member of the company must sign off on the certificate, and it can be filed only after all the company's owners approve. To make sure that the dissolution is legal and thorough, be sure to hold a meeting, document the meeting minutes, and have all owners sign the company resolution to dissolve. In Chapter 13, I tell you how to hold meetings and prepare meeting minutes properly.

If your entity is registered to transact business in states other than the one in which you initially formed, then you'll need to *withdraw* from those states before filing for a dissolution in your home state. This step is usually accomplished by filing a *notice of withdrawal* with the secretary of state of each state in which you're registered, along with the requisite filing fee.

Before you can file a dissolution with the state or withdrawal from a state in which you're foreign-filed, you must make sure that the company is in good standing with the secretary of state's office and that no fees are due. You must also make sure that the company has paid its taxes. If the entity isn't in good standing, the certificate of dissolution probably will be rejected.

Although the dissolution of an LLC has key differences from other entities, you may want to read Chapter 16 to get an overview before contacting your secretary of state to obtain more information on how to dissolve your particular entity type. An alternative to doing so yourself is to have a formation company handle the dissolution for you. Because all the assets and contracts are being transferred to the new entity, filing the paperwork with the state is the last step in completing the dissolution. A good formation company handles dissolutions all the time, so it can make sure that you have all your bases covered. You still have to pay the state filing fees, but the fee that formation companies charge for this service is usually pretty nominal. For instance, `MyLLC.com` charges $99 for dissolutions or withdrawals, regardless of the state.

Part III

Structuring Your LLC

Five Things to Remember When Looking for a Business Partner

- **Recruit based on knowledge and experience.** Reach out to anyone you think would be a good fit and set up those meetings! Keep your first contact with the person short and sweet; at this point, your goal is only to entice him to a meeting.
- **Tell others in your industry what you're looking for and plead their help in your recruiting efforts.** You'd be surprised how helpful others can be when asked.
- **Remember that the most likeable choice in a partner may not be the best one.** After you begin meeting with potential partners or co-founders, make sure to ask the questions that will give you insight into whether they're a good personality fit. You should be looking for someone who complements you, shares your vision for the company (a must!), and has strengths that align well with your weaknesses.
- **Be realistic and honest about a potential partner's workload and compensation.** If you don't have the funds to pay this person much (if anything at all), you have to be even more vigilant about getting her excited about the potential of the business and the freedoms she'll enjoy from its eventual success.
- **Don't use the term *co-founder* lightly.** It has quite a bit of value in the long run. Co-founders aren't just any old partners; they're generally considered to be the core drivers of the business.

Visit www.dummies.com/extras/limitedliabilitycompanies for an article on reasons why even a single-member LLC needs an operating agreement.

In this part . . .

- Finish structuring your LLC.
- Decide how you want to be taxed and tell the IRS.
- Get started on your operating agreement.
- Discover how to claim ownership of your company.
- Explore all things membership and voting rights.

Chapter 8

Tell Uncle Sam How It Is! Choosing How You Want to Be Taxed

In This Chapter

- Knowing which tax classification is right for you
- Watching out for tax traps
- Electing a tax designation with the IRS

In 1997, the United States Treasury established the current entity classification laws (which you may hear referred to as the *check-the-box regulations* because the corresponding IRS form is comprised of a series of check boxes). This profound move established LLCs as one of the few entity types whose owners can dictate to the IRS how they want their company to be treated for tax purposes. LLCs can be taxed in four main ways — partnership taxation, disregarded entity taxation (if you're a single-member LLC), corporation taxation, and S corporation taxation — and in this chapter I discuss them at length.

The chosen taxation has no bearing on the actual integrity and structure of the LLC; for instance, an LLC that elects to be taxed as a corporation is still considered an LLC by state law in every sense of the word. The key benefits of an LLC — dual liability protection, flexible management and ownership, and so on — are all still in full effect. The LLC simply pays taxes like a corporation does.

The default taxation for multiple-member LLCs is *partnership taxation*. If you file no **Form 8832, Entity Classification Election** with the IRS, you'll be subject to partnership taxation at the end of the year. This rule applies to all LLCs except those with only one member (commonly referred to as *single-member LLCs*). I go into all this information in this chapter.

Before you get too excited about how simple this arrangement can be, however, know that the IRS isn't as forgiving as it first seems. After you make a taxation election, you're stuck with it for about 60 months (5 years). This strict rule has a few work-arounds, but they aren't easy. So whatever decision you make, it better be a good one! Don't worry; by the end of this chapter, you should have enough information to make an informed decision about what type of taxation is right for your circumstances.

Getting to Know the Tax Types

The IRS recognizes only the following four tax types:

- Partnership
- Disregarded entity
- Corporation
- S corporation

As an LLC, you have the option of being taxed like any of these entities. The only exception: If you want to be taxed as a disregarded entity (think sole-proprietorship), then you must be a single-member LLC.

But with great power comes great responsibility; make sure you fully understand all your options and make an educated choice on which form of taxation to choose. The following sections detail each of these four taxation types.

Partnership taxation

All LLCs are created with a default tax status. It's like hair color; you're born with one color, but as you get older you can choose to change it if you want. If your LLC has at least two partners and the LLC doesn't make any tax classification election with the IRS, then your LLC is automatically assigned the default, which is *partnership taxation* — a favorable form of pass-through taxation. I actually really like partnership taxation. In most cases, this arrangement isn't such a bad deal.

All forms of taxation that I address in this chapter, with the exception of corporation taxation, are forms of *pass-through taxation.* The various forms have some differences, but the premise remains the same: The business itself doesn't pay federal income taxes; instead, the profits of the business pass through to the owners to be reported on their individual income tax returns. The individual owners then pay regular personal income tax. Similarly, any loss the LLC takes for the year flows through to the owners, and they can use these losses to offset other income they may have. See the section "Deducting LLC losses from your other income" later in this chapter for the details on this process.

Unfortunately, if you're a single-member LLC, you can't elect partnership taxation. Your default status is disregarded entity unless you elect corporation or S corporation taxation, all of which I describe later in this chapter.

Partnership and S corporation taxation differ dramatically from one another, and the regulations on structuring are different (for example, S corporations have more restrictions on who can and can't be an owner). Don't make the mistake of forming a corporation and electing pass-through S corporation tax status, thinking it's the same as the partnership taxation of an LLC. Corporations can elect to have a form of pass-through taxation (creating what is called an *S corporation*), but it's not the same as the default partnership taxation of an LLC. Check out the later section "S corporation taxation" for more detail.

Understanding allocations and distributions

To understand partnership taxation, you need to understand two concepts: allocations and distributions. At the end of the year, your company generates either a profit or a loss, which passes through to the owners on their personal tax returns. This number is referred to as the *allocation,* and each owner pays individual taxes on this amount. A *distribution,* on the other hand, is the actual cash you get from your LLC (or, sometimes, hard assets). It's usually what you're able to deposit into your personal bank account and spend as you please.

More often than not, the amount of profit you're allocated at the end of the year and pay taxes on isn't the amount of hard cash that drops into your pocket. Why not? Well, you'll most likely decide at some point that you want to retain some money in the company to pay for growth or to keep as a buffer. Or perhaps you or your partners will make a company expense or two that isn't deductible. When this situation happens, you have to pay taxes on these profits, yet you don't actually get to cash the check and go hit up Vegas for a nice little shopping spree.

Getting creative with flexible allocations and distributions

One of the coolest features of an LLC that has elected partnership taxation is that it has the ability to vary its allocations and distributions. This designation means that the company profits and/or losses don't have to be allocated or distributed according to the percentage of ownership.

An example of how you can use varied allocations and distributions to your advantage: Say you really need some last-minute capital to grow your business, and you're even willing to give up a 30 percent stake in your LLC in exchange. As an enticement for an investor to give you an infusion of capital, you offer to structure the deal so that she receives 100 percent of all company profits until she is paid back. After that point, the profits will be distributed according to ownership percentage, with the investor receiving 30 percent and you receiving the remaining 70 percent. This scenario is just one of thousands of ways you can use this flexibility to your advantage. Don't underestimate how powerful this concept is!

Unfortunately, this concept of varied allocations and distributions opens up the system to abuse by shady folks, and the IRS has gotten savvy. The IRS wants to know that you're using flexible allocations for legitimate business purposes and not simply for tax evasion. This crackdown throws a wrench into things a bit because in order for you to vary the allocations among you and your partners, you need to prove to the IRS that varied allocations result in what's referred to as *substantial economic effect,* described in IRS section 704(b). Long story short: If you're not trying to evade taxes, you'll likely be okay; just make sure you run the scenario by your CPA before making any promises.

Deducting LLC losses from your other income

If you have sources of income other than your LLC, you may be able to deduct your LLC's losses from that other income to pay less in taxes. The IRS recognizes three types of income:

- **Portfolio income:** Such as dividends from stocks held.
- **Active income:** Wages and 1099 compensation.
- **Passive income:** Income from a business or rental property in which you aren't an *active participant.* In other words, you don't make the day-to-day operational decisions for the business, and you don't work very many hours in the business.

Assuming your LLC has elected partnership taxation, you can use your share of the business's losses to offset any additional passive income that you may have received from other sources.

If you aren't an active participant in your LLC, you can't deduct your LLC's regular business losses from your personal portfolio or active income, such as the income from your day job. In other words, under the passive income rule, if you're not active in the business and your LLC passes on $50,000 in losses to you, you can't use it to offset the $50,000 you made when you made a good trade on Wall Street (portfolio income). So you can sound like a smarty-pants when talking to your accountant, this situation is called a *passive loss limitation.*

All forms of pass-through taxation — not just partnership taxation — are subject to the passive loss limitation. However, as a member of an LLC that has elected partnership taxation, you get a wicked bonus those other guys with S corporations and sole proprietorships don't get. Say you've shunned the slacker lifestyle and are regularly (and on a continuing basis) engaged in the day-to-day operations of the LLC, making you an *active participant* in the eyes of the IRS. Never underestimate the value (literally!) of hard work, because you now get to deduct your portion of the LLC's losses from all other income, including wages and stock dividends, without limitation. Starting a small business and not yet ready to quit your day job? This incredible tax deduction is reason alone to form an LLC and elect partnership taxation.

To help clarify the ins and outs of what partnership taxation allows you to do, check out Table 8-1.

Table 8-1 Offsets Allowed by Partnership Taxation

	Can Offset Portfolio Income with LLC Losses	*Can Offset Active Income with LLC Losses*	*Can Offset Passive Income with LLC Losses*
Active in LLC	Yes	Yes	Yes
Passive in LLC	No	No	Yes

If your LLC holds rental property, to be considered an active participant you have to be so actively engaged in the managing of the property that you qualify as an active real-estate professional. Otherwise, your involvement in the LLC holding is deemed passive, and any losses the LLC distributes to you are subject to the passive loss limitation rules. Personally, I can't think of a better incentive to learn how to fix toilets . . .

Avoiding self-employment taxes

If you elect partnership taxation, you're assessed a 15.3 percent self-employment tax in addition to the personal income taxes you're required to pay on the profit that's allocated to you. In addition, even if you're an active member of your LLC, you aren't allowed to hire yourself and use payroll taxes as a way to get around the hefty self-employment tax bill each year. This taxation is one of the only drawbacks of LLCs when compared to S corporations, which only assess self-employment taxes on the amount of salary you choose to pay yourself, assuming it's within the norm for your industry.

One caveat, however, lands this guideline in the LLC's favor. Although you may not be able to officially hire yourself (and thereby avoid self-employment tax), you can slack off a bit, to the point where you're no longer considered an active participant but rather a passive participant. In the case of an LLC electing partnership taxation, only active participants are required to pay self-employment tax, whereas inactive participants aren't. The income itself is considered passive, which, as far as income goes, is about as favorable as the IRS gets. However, depending on your industry and specific situation, the rules can be murky. I strongly suggest you let your CPA help guide you in this area.

Disregarded entity taxation

The *disregarded entity* tax status is the default for single-member LLCs. Essentially, it's the same tax status you'd pay as a sole-proprietorship (as if you haven't filed your LLC at all). It's the one form of tax status that LLCs with multiple members can't elect.

Similar to partnership taxation, disregarded entity tax status is a form of pass-through taxation, and in this case the sole member pays personal income taxes and self-employment taxes on the company's profits and/or losses on his personal tax return. The LLC is treated as a separate entity for the purpose of paying employment and excise taxes only.

Just because the IRS "disregards" your LLC for tax purposes doesn't mean that the same liability protection doesn't apply. It does. Assuming you have a solid operating agreement and practice good record keeping, you won't be held personally responsible for the liabilities of your business.

Single-member LLCs aren't allowed to elect partnership taxation; however, if you're a single-member LLC and don't want to be treated as a disregarded entity by the IRS, you may want to consider electing corporation or S corporation taxation, which I describe in the following sections.

Corporation taxation

Whether you're a single-member LLC or you have multiple members, you can always elect to be taxed like a corporation. Corporate taxation is completely different from partnership taxation. First and foremost, the IRS considers a corporation (or an LLC electing corporation tax status) to be an entity completely separate from its owners and treats it as if it were an individual. Instead of passing through profits and losses to the members, the corporation files its own tax returns. All a member must report on his personal tax return is the actual cash the company decides to distribute to him, whether in the form of dividends or salary. The member can't report the LLC's losses and therefore can't deduct them against other personal income. You don't have to worry about allocations, tax bases, phantom income (allocations that you have to pay taxes on, but don't actually get the cash to cover the tax bill), and deemed cash distributions because they aren't relevant to corporations.

Although corporations are taxed as completely separate entities and are treated as individuals in the eyes of the IRS, they do receive a few benefits individuals don't get. Individuals are required to pay federal income tax on all income. Granted, a good chunk can be deducted, but those deductions usually aren't so "adequate" at the end of the year because they rarely add up to the amount of money you're forced to fork over. Corporations, on the other hand, only pay federal tax on the profits that the company generated throughout the year. This point may not seem very significant, but as someone who's operated both entity types over the years, I can tell you my business always ends up paying less tax with the corporation tax structure.

When it comes to the corporation tax structure, many people worry about something called double taxation. It's understandable; who wouldn't balk at a term that implies paying double the amount of tax? *Double taxation* occurs when the owners of the corporation take the profit out of the company and the profits are taxed on the individual owner level. This scenario means that the same profits are taxed once at the corporate level and then again at your (the member's) level when they're paid out. As horrific as this situation sounds in theory, it's usually not so bad in practice. Check out the following section to find out why.

Knowing when to choose corporation taxation

To explain why corporation taxation may result in less tax than any of the forms of pass-through taxation (such as sole-proprietorship, partnership, and S corporation taxation), I'll use an example from my own life. As an entrepreneur, I often use loans from my established businesses to help cover the cost of establishing new businesses (instead of paying double taxation by taking the money as personal income before investing it into the new business). All of my companies are owned by me, so approval for this practice doesn't present much of a problem.

After the company is established, I may pay myself a salary (which is taxable to me, but deductible by the corporation); however, I rarely issue dividends. Instead of taking a lot of money from the business, I reinvest it and use it to help propel growth, which is the only way a business can achieve exponential growth. If you reinvest those profits into further building your company — a tax-free endeavor — instead of just buying yourself a fancy car, you're compounding your resources, and the results you can achieve are much greater.

By following this plan, you manage to grow your company while maintaining a nominal — almost nonexistent — tax burden. And when the company reaches its peak, you can sell it. I keep my stock for over one year, so any income from the sale of my ownership of the company is considered long-term capital gains, which are only subjected to a 20 percent long-term capital gains tax. The government is happy because creating new companies creates new jobs and helps stimulate the economy, and you're happy because now you can get the fancy car you've been wanting!

With an LLC, you don't have to make this tax election right away. If you're going to be putting a lot of money into the company and want to be able to deduct the losses of your initial, formative years, you can maintain default partnership taxation for a few years and then make the tax election to switch to corporation tax status. However, this change may have other tax implications that aren't obvious at first glance, so run any strategies like this one by a qualified accountant before committing.

Until you're profiting more than $75,000 per year, you may want to elect corporate tax status. Generally, until you start profiting above that level, the corporate tax rates are lower than the individual tax rates of the members who will be paying taxes on the LLC's income.

Seeing how corporation taxation can be a terrible idea

In a few instances, you should never elect corporation taxation for your LLC — namely, if your LLC holds real estate. In today's litigious America, the idea of putting your personal assets in another name to protect them is a generally accepted practice; using an LLC to hold real estate is a good move, but you're going to find yourself in a world of hurt at tax time if you elect corporate taxation in this scenario.

If you hold a piece of investment property in a corporation or an LLC electing corporation taxation, you're subject to double taxation on all the income that property receives, such as the rent it collects. Also, you're going to face a problem when you want to offload the property, because removing the property from the entity is a taxable event. Switching back to partnership tax status before selling the property won't do you much good, either. You may be forced to calculate the appreciation that occurred during the corporation tax election and pay a BIG tax on that amount. Literally! *BIG* is an acronym for *built-in gain,* and it's one well suited to the tax term, considering it's currently hovering around 35 percent! When you make the corporation tax election, you're stuck with it for five years, so this appreciation period can represent a pretty hefty chunk of change.

In addition, myriad other tax problems can pop up if you subject your rental property to corporation taxation. You can spend time and money getting a second opinion from a CPA, but I think you'll find it's a universally accepted rule: *Never* elect corporation tax status for an LLC that's being used to hold passive investments such as real estate. An LLC with partnership taxation is a better option. (Flip to the earlier section "Partnership taxation" for details on this election.)

S corporation taxation

S corporation taxation is the corporation's answer to a pass-through tax status. Just like a corporation can elect S corporation tax status, so can a limited liability company that has elected corporation taxation. You may think this move is a waste of time considering LLCs already have a pass-through tax status by default, but S corporation taxation differs from partnership taxation on some pretty big issues — namely, in what taxes you pay when you take money out of the company.

If you're a single-member LLC and therefore not allowed to choose partnership taxation, you're allowed to elect corporation taxation and then elect to be taxed as an S corporation. This method provides favorable pass-through taxation without the need to take on a partner. Just be aware that S corporation taxation differs substantially from partnership taxation and, should you take on a partner sometime in the future, you may be restricted in your ability to change back.

Reducing your taxes

S corporations get a pretty big advantage when it comes to taxation, though at first glance the situation looks comparable to partnership taxation status. If you're a member of an LLC electing partnership taxation, you're required to pay personal income tax on all company profits that are allocated to you. In addition to personal income tax, you're also required to pay a 15.3 percent self-employment tax, which is simply both the employer's and employee's shares of Social Security and Medicare taxes. But with an S corporation, you're allowed to pay yourself a salary, which is a deductible expense for the company, and any amount over that isn't subject to self-employment tax. You simply pay personal income tax on those profits and nothing more after they're allocated to you. This setup differs substantially from LLCs (which have elected partnership taxation) because all profits you derive from the company in that scenario are subject to the 15.3 percent self-employment tax.

In other words, if you're taxed as an S corporation, the amount of Medicare and Social Security you pay is limited to the amount you take as a salary. As long as your salary is comparable with others in your position and your industry, any profits the company takes above that amount aren't subject to extra taxes.

In a nutshell, this designation means you save 15.3 percent in taxes on all profits above an appropriate salary. So if you have a business from which you intend to remove a substantial amount of profits — more than the reasonable salary you're taking — you'll probably see some pretty hefty tax savings by electing S corporation taxation.

Dealing with the restrictions

Unfortunately, even if S corporation status is the best choice for you, you may not be able to elect it. When the IRS created the S corporation election, it wanted to make sure that the status was employed by genuinely small businesses and not exploited by large enterprises strictly as a tax-saving strategy. Therefore, you must meet quite a few restrictions in order to take advantage of S corporation taxation:

- Your corporation must not have more than 100 shareholders.
- Shareholders can only consist of natural persons, individual trusts (for estate-planning purposes), and tax-exempt nonprofit organizations. This list specifically excludes any other entity or business structure, such as limited liability companies or corporations.
- Shareholders must be citizens or alien residents of the United States.

- The corporation is only allowed to issue one class of stock and all owners are treated equally. You'll have to save the preferred shares for your IPO.
- Banks and insurance companies are barred from being shareholders.
- All shareholders must unanimously consent to the S corporation tax designation. In other words, a majority vote just won't do the trick.

In addition to these ownership restrictions, you may want to take into consideration a few other downsides before committing:

- **There's no step-up in basis on assets after you die.** When your heirs inherit your assets in an S corporation, they'll have to pay capital gains tax on the appreciation from the date you first purchased the asset, rather than just from the date that you passed it on to your heirs. I discuss this snag in more detail in Chapter 14.
- **You can't add debt to your tax basis.** Earlier in this chapter, I discuss that LLCs allow tax free distributions to the extent of your tax basis, including the amount of debt the company has that you can be held personally responsible for. With S corporation tax status, you receive no tax benefits for being personally responsible for the company's debt, unless it's a loan that you've made personally.

These rules (plus many more) make S corporations a bad choice for holding real estate. Even though S corporation status lets you get around the double-taxation nightmare that comes with a regular corporation, you're still limiting yourself by not being able to personally deduct the mortgage.

Check to see how your state taxes LLCs that elect S corporation taxation. Most states conform with the IRS on this matter, but about a half dozen states tax S corporations as corporations. Don't underestimate state taxes! If you're holding real estate or are in another form of business where double taxation can kill you, you may be in trouble. Make sure to speak with your local accountant or do some research on local state law before making this election.

Notifying the IRS of Your Election

Making a tax election for your LLC is as simple as filling out a single form: IRS **Form 8832,** one of the simplest tax forms you'll ever complete. They don't call them check-the-box regulations for nothing — all you have to do is check a box! In this section, I walk you through the process of making your tax election, starting with the necessary background work.

Applying for your tax identification number

All businesses must obtain an *employer identification number* (EIN for short, but also called a *tax identification number* or *tax ID*) from the Internal Revenue Service. The IRS uses this number to identify your LLC when the LLC pays its taxes. Over the years, the EIN has become an important number for the government, financial institutions, and other businesses to identify different entities. After all, an LLC in Georgia can have the same name as your LLC in California; how would Uncle Sam be able to tell them apart? Think of it as a Social Security number for your enterprise.

Obtaining credit, paying taxes, and even opening a company bank account are virtually impossible without a tax identification number, so don't delay! Some attorneys, accountants, and incorporating companies may charge you an arm and a leg to obtain this number for you, but you're smarter than that. With a few little tips, you can have your tax ID within an hour.

You can obtain a tax ID immediately online by going to `www.irs.gov` and doing a search for *EIN online application*. This should pull up the page that you need to get your application started. When you're asked for your Type of Entity, you'll notice that there is no LLC option. Here's what to select:

- If you're a single-member LLC electing the default disregarded entity tax status, check the box next to Sole Proprietorship.
- If you're a multi-member LLC electing partnership tax status, check the box next to Partnership.
- If you're electing corporation tax status for a single- or multi-member LLC, check the box next to Corporation, and in the following field, enter the form number **1120**.
- If you're a single- or multi-member LLC electing S corporation tax status, check the box next to Corporation, and in the following field, enter the form number **1120S**.

If you can, file your **Form SS-4** online; you'll likely receive your tax identification number instantly. Otherwise, you should be able to find the most recent IRS **Form SS-4** at `www.irs.gov/pub/irs-pdf/fss4.pdf`.

Your tax identification number stays with your company no matter whether you change owners, do a statutory conversion to another entity type (see Chapter 7), redomicile your LLC to another state (see Chapters 5 and 15), or change your tax status.

Making the tax election: Filing Form 8832

The best time to file **Form 8832, Entity Classification Election** is when you form your LLC; otherwise you're automatically assigned your default tax status (disregarded entity taxation if you're a single-member LLC or partnership taxation if your LLC has more than one member). After you file **Form 8832,** you don't need to continue to file it each year; the taxation election automatically lasts until you file another **Form 8832,** electing a different form of taxation.

Note that this entity classification is for income tax purposes only and has no bearing on how you're treated by the state, especially for liability purposes. For instance, if your LLC elects corporation taxation, you still have the protection of the dual-layer liability protection that's unique to LLCs.

Form 8832 itself is pretty straightforward. I provide a current one with instructions at `www.irs.gov/pub/irs-pdf/f8832.pdf`. The first section (lines 1 to 3) asks you a series of questions to determine your eligibility.

When you choose a tax classification, you're stuck with it for 60 months (5 years). The IRS does this to keep you honest. It figures a business process needs a few years to work the kinks out. It doesn't want shady tax avoiders to exploit the classifications for their personal benefit.

This rule has an exception: If you elect a taxation classification within the first 12 months of formation and, on the **Form 8832,** specify the "effective date" as your LLC's date of formation, then your LLC is allowed to switch to another form of taxation at any time. From that point forward, however, any additional switch will be subject to the 60-month rule.

Under line 6 of **Form 8832,** you're required to select your type of entity. If your LLC is formed within the continental U.S. (and I'm assuming it is), only the first three options apply to you. You notice that none of these options allows for S corporation taxation, and that's because you need another form, **Form 2553,** to make that election. Select Corporation taxation on **Form 8832;** then attach a completed **Form 2553** and file them both together.

In order to make a tax election for your limited liability company, all members must agree and sign. If for some reason you and your partners don't want to be listed on this form, you can stipulate otherwise in the articles of organization and your LLC's operating agreement by putting this decision-making power in the hands of the manager(s).

Your LLC's tax election should also be indicated in your LLC's operating agreement. Your *operating agreement* is an internal document and isn't publicly accessible, so by recognizing the tax classification in the operating agreement, you show that all members agree on it. You should also document any further tax classification changes by special resolution of the members of the LLC (I show you how to draft resolutions in Chapter 13).

Most states, but not all, comply with the federal tax election you make on **Form 8832.** Before making any assumptions, consult with a qualified accountant in your state.

Chapter 9

Make It Official! Getting Started on Your Operating Agreement

In This Chapter

- Knowing the ins and outs of the operating agreement
- Customizing the basics of your operating agreement

You're probably tired of hearing it, but I'm going to say it again — one of the most groundbreaking things about an LLC is its *flexibility.* Although corporations are subject to a strict legal structure, the options for LLCs are limitless. When you look up your state's laws surrounding LLCs, the rules are pretty clearly defined. However, one key phrase is usually repeated over and over again — "unless otherwise stated in the company's Operating Agreement." You see, with an LLC, you're allowed to make your own rules. That is where the ever-important *operating agreement* comes in.

In this chapter, I give you a basic understanding on what an operating agreement is and does and get you started on the bones and structure of the document. Then, throughout the remainder of this book — but especially in the next few chapters — as I help you make certain key decisions, I guide you on how to document those decisions in your operating agreement. By the end of this process, you should have a pretty built out and *customized* document that serves the majority of your business's needs.

What Is an Operating Agreement?

Your *operating agreement* is the blueprint for your business and is the first thing you should get started on after you file your articles of organization (see Chapter 6). It lays out everything relating to your business, including how the ownership is structured, the rules regarding transferring the ownership, how your business is managed, how important issues are decided . . . everything.

In a perfect world, very few operating agreements should look the same — the document should be perfectly customized to your business and your exact needs.

For the majority of important issues, LLCs are allowed to use their operating agreements to "replace" state LLC law. For the most part, if you place something in your operating agreement that contradicts your state's LLC statutes, your operating agreement will almost always win in the event of a lawsuit or disagreement among members. You'll want to check your state's laws before creating your operating agreement to verify which provisions cannot be overwritten by your operating agreement.

What the operating agreement governs

Operating agreements generally don't get into specific issues such as minor employment matters and day-to-day business operations (with the exception of major decisions and/or purchases). You don't look at your operating agreement to see what sort of commission structure you should impose on your new sales reps. Nor should you look to your operating agreement to tell you what credit terms or payment plans you can give to your customers.

Your operating agreement covers the bigger issues, such as large purchases, the decisions to take on debt, profit and loss distributions, selling membership shares, and assignment of duties . . . the things that can make or break your business. It paints the big picture as to how your entity is to operate. If you are a small business, creating an operating agreement may seem like overkill, but it's absolutely necessary — not to mention a legal requirement in most states.

As your business grows, you'll need guidance, and you should be able to turn to your operating agreement. If you and your partners negotiate and decide on everything in the beginning, then you're likely to experience less chaos and fewer disagreements when your company hangs in the balance.

Creating a clear-cut ownership structure

In my career as a corporate consultant and mentor to start-up accelerator companies, I can say that, without a doubt, the most common reason for a new venture to fail can be boiled down to discord among the partners. The thing is, starting a new venture is exciting . . . especially that initial idea phase, where you start painting a picture of the brilliant future that awaits you and your partners.

Usually it transpires somewhat like this: A few friends are together and one has a seed of an idea. He tells his buddies and then it steamrolls. Ideas are excitedly thrown into the mix, some are tossed, and others are kept — until a rough blueprint for a business model has been fleshed out. Sometimes this happens over a few hours, and sometimes the process takes months. Regardless, when a plan finally comes together, everyone is excited to jump on board the moving train. It's usually at this stage that most failed startups set up their eventual demise.

Here's the rub: Everyone is equally excited, and everyone took equal part in the business planning, so everyone should share equally in the ownership of the business, right? *Wrong.* Business ideas don't hold much value — they aren't even patentable — it's the execution of those ideas that matters. *That* is where the ownership needs to be distributed. You need to take an accurate count of what every owner will be contributing and then structure the ownership of your LLC to support those contributions. You need to have built-in safeguards for *accountability* — in other words, if a partner doesn't deliver what she promised, she doesn't get the membership shares.

In Chapter 10, I show you in detail how to structure your partnership in a way that keeps folks honest. But for now (if you have partners), you need to keep in mind that this is one of the core functions of your operating agreement.

LLCs can have different classes of membership, so all members don't have to be treated the same. Some members can get voting rights while others have to remain silent. Some members can also be managers and take charge of the company's day-to-day operations, while others can only watch from afar. Also, some members have certain powers that are inherent to owning the company, such as deciding who manages the LLC and whether to accept new members. I go over membership-related topics in detail in Chapter 10.

Assigning manager titles and duties

Regardless of whether your LLC is manager-managed or member-managed, the managers need boundaries and guidelines. Even if you are the only manager and you want unlimited decision-making power, you need to allow for this in your company's operating agreement. Some states require it by law, but regardless — it will keep you out of trouble when one of your non-managing partners contests that lease agreement you entered into or that building you purchased.

Forming your operating agreement is the perfect time for you and your partners to sit down and delineate all the specific roles and titles that each manager will take on. For instance, one manager may be great at numbers and will take on the role of chief financial officer, whereas another manager may have a solid vision of the company and is the person to lead the others on the path to success — this person can be named president or chief executive officer.

In certain situations, you may also want to consider adopting the "corporate" management structure for your LLC. This structure comes with the preset roles of President, Secretary, Treasurer, and Director. (Of course, since we're talking about an LLC here, you can adapt those roles to your needs however you want.) One example of where this may be helpful is if you have an investor who wants the immediate tax deduction that an LLC can offer (assuming the LLC doesn't bring in a profit its first year), but prefers the traditional management structure of a corporation. I show you how to elect a corporate management structure at `www.dummies.com/extras/limitedliabilitycompanies`.

Keep in mind that although managers are legally called *managers* by the state, they can have whatever titles they want. So, even if you don't elect the full corporate management structure, don't think you're missing out on the title of president or CEO if you're forming an LLC!

Why you need an operating agreement

Most folks get their filed articles back from the state and assume that they're in business. Or maybe their formation company sent them a form operating agreement and they assume that they can just fill in the blanks and be good to go. If this is you, not so fast, Tiger! You're not officially in business until your LLC has a complete operating agreement that, among many other things, issues ownership to the members.

A game where everyone plays by different rules

If you're still not convinced of the importance of an operating agreement, let me throw something else at you. Imagine a game (or a season, eek!) of NFL football in which each team played by its own rules. Chaos would ensue before the 2nd quarter . . . and probably some pretty gnarly fights. One team would call its failed red zone pass a touchdown, while the other would invent a "5th down," and the entire concept of pass interference would go out the window. And when the time came for the players to justify their behavior, they would all say the same thing: "There are no rules, so shut your trap" or "Whaddya gonna do about it?!" or . . . well, you get the picture.

When things start gaining traction and the stakes get higher, a business without a rule book is just asking for chaos and friction. So get with your partners and take the time to build out a comprehensive and *custom* operating agreement for your business so everyone knows upfront where their boundaries are. Then, when issues pop up, you have guidelines for dealing with the situation. You can rest assured that your business is safe from all kinds of internal disputes that could land you in court.

Aside from the clear necessities of an operating agreement, keep in mind that if you don't have one, you leave yourself open to being judged by your state's statutes — which you have no control over — and you probably won't like the outcome. You want your LLC to be governed by *your* rules, not those created by a state legislator who has no interest in your business or, most likely, business in general.

The easiest way for me to convince you of the necessity of an operating agreement is to describe what you may face without one. Here are a couple of scenarios of what could happen if you face problems in your business sans The Agreement:

- One of your members passes away, and his family wants to step in and take control of your business. Without an operating agreement with a provision protecting the surviving partners, you could end up losing everything that you have worked so hard for to a partner's relative who knows nothing about your industry.
- You and your partner, each owning half of the company, decide to give your partner's assistant 2 percent of the company for her loyalty and service. One day you come back from vacation to find that the company has been liquidated and dissolved in your absence. When you go to your attorney to see what can be done, you find out that because your LLC had no operating agreement stating that all members need to agree for dissolution to occur, state law prevailed. Unfortunately for you, your state's law says that a company can be dissolved with a majority of the members agreeing. Your partner and his assistant outvoted you while you were away.

Although oral agreements may technically be valid in most states, you should never rely on them in lieu of a written operating agreement. Oral agreements are just *asking* for a lawsuit. And not only are they subject to different interpretations by the members, but they are often taken with a grain of salt by the court system. In other words, if two members disagree, the judge deciding your fate can completely disregard the so-called agreement.

Establishing Your Framework

How you put your operating agreement together isn't nearly as important as what it contains. However, if you're going to take the time to create it in the first place, why not make sure that it's organized and easy to read? It isn't hard to make your document look like a million bucks — or at least like the thousands of bucks it probably would cost to have an attorney draft it from scratch.

Later, throughout the rest of Part III, I show you how to develop the *content* of your operating agreement, but first I want to explain how to build the structure and get the formatting down.

Achieving A+ form and structure

When it comes to style and formatting, the operating agreement is laid out similarly to the articles of organization (see Chapter 6) in that it has articles, sections, and subsections, all designated with letters, numbers, and/or Roman numerals. The layout may look something like this:

Article I

  (Section) A

    1.

    2.

    3.

  (Section) B

Or something like this:

Article 1:

  (Section) A

    (Subsection) I

    (Subsection) II

    (Subsection) III

  (Section) B

    (Subsection) I

    (Subsection) II

    (Subsection) III

Article 2:

  (Section) A

If you use a lot of legalese or industry terminology, you may want to consider making the first article a "Defined Terms" article with a list of definitions so that readers understand what certain words mean as they read through the document. After all, if they are binding themselves to the contract, they need to understand it fully.

Building your outline

Here's a sample outline of a basic operating agreement:

I. Organization

  A. Formation and Qualification

  B. Name

  C. Principal Office

  D. Governing Law

  E. Term

  F. Registered Agent and Office

  G. Purpose of the Company

II. Membership Interests

  A. Initial Members of the Company

  B. Percentage of Ownership

  C. Membership Classifications

  D. Management by Voting Members (if Member-Managed)

  E. New Members

  F. Capital Accounts

  G. Liability of Members

  H. Transfer and Assignment of Interests

III. Allocations and Profit Distributions

  A. Allocations of Profits and Losses

  B. Distributions

IV. Meetings and Voting

  A. Notice of Meetings

  B. Quorum

C. Meetings

D. Voting

E. Proxies

V. Management and Duties

A. Election

B. Delegation of Powers

C. Compensation

D. Indemnification of Members and Managers

VI. Miscellaneous

A. Books and Records

B. Financial Records and Reporting

C. Liability of Members

D. Indemnification

E. Dispute Resolution

F. Dissolution

Drafting Basic Provisions

You pretty much have all the freedom in the world when creating your LLC; you just have to state what you want in the operating agreement. Your operating agreement is composed of different pieces of text, which are called *provisions*. Each provision deals with a different topic relating to your company, such as how it is managed or how new members are admitted.

Unfortunately, people are often intimidated by all the legalese, so they don't create the agreement for fear of saying something wrong or using incorrect terminology. If you feel this way, just remember that something is better than nothing. The agreement doesn't have to be perfect — just do your best.

To make things easy for you, let's get started on some of the basic provisions that you can use when creating your operating agreement. For the most part, you can pick and choose which ones you want. First, in the preceding section, I give you a good outline for the operating agreement, and then, throughout the remainder of Part III of this book, I show you how to make the important decisions and then build out your operating agreement in a way that documents those decisions.

Laying out organizational matters

You may as well just copy and paste the text from your articles of organization (see Chapter 6) into the Organization section of your operating agreement because, for the most part, that's all it is. Unfortunately, as redundant as it may seem, state law often requires some of these statements to be drafted in the operating agreement as well, so it's better to be safe than sorry and make a quick reference to them.

The reason for this is clear: Your articles may have been signed and submitted by an organizer who, for the most part, has no actual involvement in your business. By placing this information in your operating agreement, you tell the world that all the members and managers of the LLC are in full agreement with the terms outlined in the articles of organization that were filed with the state.

In this section, I show you how to include provisions such as the ones under these subheadings:

- **Formation and Qualification:** The opening statement, showing the members intent on forming the LLC with the state
- **Name:** The name of your LLC
- **Principal Office:** Your LLC's main office address
- **Governing Law:** The state in which your LLC was formed and whose laws your LLC will abide by (can also be alluded to in the Formation and Qualification subheading)
- **Term:** How long your LLC is to remain in existence
- **Registered Agent and Office:** The name and address of your registered agent in all states in which your LLC transacts business (see Chapter 5)
- **Purpose of the Company:** The purposes for which your LLC was formed

Of course, all operating agreements are different, so feel free to arrange your information however you like — as long as it's there!

Formation and Qualification

This provision basically states that the members of the company all agreed to form the LLC under the laws of a particular state. If you have a formation date, you can include it here. If you haven't yet received your filed articles from the state, then feel free to omit the date.

Here's a sample provision that you may want to adapt to your needs:

On April 13, 2014, the members formed the LLC by filing articles of incorporation with the Secretary of State of Indiana in accordance with the Indiana Business Flexibility Act.

Name

Under the "Name" article of your operating agreement, you simply list the legal name of your LLC as it was formed with the state. Again, if you haven't received your filed articles, you can simply list the name as it appears on your articles of organization. In the event that the state rejects your name, you and your partners can amend your operating agreement to reflect the new name.

Here, you may want to list any DBAs that your company intends to operate under or have a blanket statement that allows the members and/or managers to operate the company under DBAs in the future. You may also want to specify any rules for changing the business name. For example, who has the authority to change the name — the members *and* the managers? Or just the members?

Here is a sample provision that you may want to adapt to your needs:

The Company may conduct its affairs under the name ABC Trucking, LLC. Upon written unanimous consent, the members may change the company name or adopt one or more fictitious firm names ("DBA"s) for the company, to the extent permitted by law.

Term

Back in the day, LLCs were required to have a limited life span. Long story short, the IRS wouldn't grant LLCs the benefits of partnership taxation unless they contained a few facets of traditional partnerships — namely, they can't live forever. But as LLCs have evolved to become the business structure of choice, this requirement has been phased out. Unfortunately, traces of it still exist in some states' laws.

For this reason, I strongly recommend that all LLCs have a basic statement stating that the company will exist perpetually until the members elect to dissolve it (the specifics of which are described in the Dissolution section of your operating agreement).

Here is a sample provision that you may want to adapt to your needs:

The Company will exist perpetually unless either a.) the Company is dissolved by the Act, or b.) the Company is dissolved under this Agreement.

Your company may *want* a limited life span. I go over this possibility in Chapter 6, where you would state such a desire in your articles of organization. If this is the case for your company, then you'll want to make sure to state your duration in this section of the operating agreement.

Purpose of the Company

When friends ask you why you formed your LLC, you're likely to give a somewhat specific answer, such as "I want to flip houses," or "I want to sell bacon cupcakes to pet owners." But when it comes to your operating agreement, you want to keep your purpose as broad as possible.

This provision should match the provision that you place in your company's articles of organization that you file with the state (see Chapter 6). It should state something such as this:

> *The purpose of the company shall be to carry on any and all activities as may be lawfully conducted by a limited liability company under the laws of the state of Indiana.*

Only under certain circumstances — which I go over in Chapter 5 — will you want to limit your company's purpose.

Giving specifics on company records and reporting

In most states, an operating agreement is legally required to specify who handles the company's records and reports and where they are stored. Sometimes these provisions appear in their own section of the operating agreement, and sometimes they are buried at the bottom of the operating agreement in the "Miscellaneous" section. Regardless of where they're located, these specifics are important because they tell the members where they can access the crucial information that pertains to their participation in the company.

Books and Records

Five years ago, this section would have made reference to the "company kit," which includes a transfer ledger that is legally accessible by all members of the LLC. Technology is changing everything, and this is a good thing for members. No longer are all the vital company records stored in a single leather-bound kit, usually accessible only to the member who has physical custody of it. (You'd be surprised how many of these kits get "lost" when disputes arise.) Now, things are migrating online, and these important records are stored digitally by third-party companies and accessible to all members.

Most states' laws are pretty firm on what information LLCs are required to share with their members. This rule often can't be overwritten by the LLC's operating agreement. In other words, you cannot elect to keep your members in the dark if they ask about certain key things. So before you decide to stray from the standard, you may want to check your state laws.

Here's a sample provision if you're using digital records:

> *The Members shall digitally maintain at* `www.docrun.com/ABC_Trucking` (replace link with whatever digital corporate kit you're using) *the following records of the business: a current list of the full name and last-known business or residence address of each Member, together with their capital contribution and membership interest; a copy of the Articles and all amendments thereto; copies of the Company's federal, state, and local income tax or information returns and reports, if any, for the six (6) most recent taxable years; and a copy of this Agreement and any amendments to it.*

If you're going with the traditional, leather-bound company kit, here's a variation of the first sentence that you may want to use:

> *The Members shall maintain at the Company's principal place of business the following books and records:*

Financial Records and Reporting

This section gives members the right to inspect all the business's financial records. It should tell them where the financial records are held and what sort of financial reporting they can expect as members. After all, as a member, wouldn't you want to know what's going on with your investment?

Following are a couple specific things you should include in this section:

- **Accounting and the Company's Fiscal Year:** This provision states what the company's year-end is and who the company bookkeeper or accountant is. Listing the name and contact information of your company's accountant is optional. It's not vital, but it may be nice to have, depending on your situation.
- **Financial Reporting:** It is common practice for the company manager to provide regular financial reports to the members. The types of financial reports to be provided (balance statements, profit and loss statements, and so on) and the frequency of distribution should be noted here.

It's common to want to state in this section that certain financial reports will be e-mailed quarterly (or whatever time frame you agree on); however, I don't recommend doing so. If something comes up and the company fails to live up to these promises, you could be opening the company up to liability with your investors or other partners. I recommend simply allowing these records to be inspected in person upon the request of an individual member.

Here's a sample provision for LLCs that have partnership taxation and that report to the IRS on a calendar-year basis. Feel free to customize it as necessary:

> *The complete and accurate accounting and financial records of the Company shall be held by the Managers at the Company's principal place of business. Such records shall be kept on such method of accounting as the Managers shall select. The Company's accounting period shall be the calendar year.*
>
> *The Managers shall close the accounting records at the close of each calendar year, and shall prepare and send to each Member a statement of such Member's distributive share of income and expense — in the form of a Schedule K-1 — for income tax reporting purposes.*

Who is responsible for maintaining the company's books and records? Will one person be in charge of this task? If you have a larger company, everyone will likely go about their daily business and not have a care in the world about dealing with the random record-keeping tasks that come up. You may want to assign one person to handle everything; that way, someone is responsible for the job and can be held accountable if it isn't completed.

Getting the boilerplate provisions out of the way

Boilerplate provisions are those that tend to appear in most agreements (if desired). They include such things as how disputes of the agreement are handled and who is legally (and personally) responsible for what.

Liability of Members

Although state law normally provides a default liability protection for the LLC's members, it's always good to throw in a provision that calls for it anyway. It doesn't have to be lengthy. Here's an example of a limited liability provision that you can use:

> *No Member shall be personally responsible for any debts, liabilities, or obligations of the Company solely by reason of being a Member. All debts, obligations, and liabilities of the Company, whether by contract or not, shall belong solely to the Company.*

Indemnification of Members and Managers

Although all managers and members are provided a basic level of *indemnification* (a fancy word for limited liability), it's always good to restate it in your operating agreement. Essentially, you're telling the world that all the LLC's managers, members, and employees are free from and not responsible for the obligations and debts of the company.

Now, this provision can be taken further. If you so choose, you can elect to have the company take complete financial responsibility for all the actions of any member or manager of the company made on behalf of the company — even criminal actions. This means that the company is responsible for paying not only any legal fees, but also any judgments that arise. This is often called *uncapped indemnity* in the legal world, meaning that there is no "cap" (or ceiling) on the amount the company is forced to pay in full defense of and in taking full responsibility for a member's actions.

Except in some cases, such as a single-member LLC, I generally don't recommend providing uncapped indemnity for *all* acts, including criminal ones. If anything, you may want to cap it (that is, cut off the funding) at a certain dollar amount or under certain conditions, such as "in the event of a misdemeanor." Doing so protects your company (and its solvency) should one of your members do something shady in the name of your LLC.

Here's a sample indemnity provision (excluding unlawful acts) that you can adapt as needed:

> *The Company shall indemnify any person, to the fullest extent permitted by law, who is a party defendant or is threatened to be made a party defendant, pending or completed action, suit, or proceeding, whether civil, criminal, administrative, or investigative (other than an action by or in the right of the Company) by reason of the fact that the person is or was a Member of the Company, Manager, employee, or agent of the Company, or is or was serving at the request of the Company, so long as the person did not behave in violation of law or this Agreement, for instant expenses (including attorney's fees), judgments, fines, and amounts paid in settlement actually and reasonably incurred in connection with such action, suit, or proceeding.*

Dispute resolution

Whenever a lot of people get together and work on a project for an extended period, disputes are bound to come up. Often, they come out of nowhere, blindsiding you at the worst times. Unless they are dealt with properly, they can seriously harm your business, and resolving them can take time and precious resources that your business needs to grow and prosper. To prevent these situations from happening, you and your partners should be forward-thinking enough to add guidelines on how to deal effectively with disputes when they come up.

First, you should specify the state in which disputes are to be dealt with. Handling lawsuits and disputes in states other than the one in which your company headquarters is located can be incredibly expensive. And even then, a court may not allow a lawsuit to be filed in a jurisdiction other than where the transgression took place. Therefore, a great policy is to require that all members take legal action only in the state in which your company is located.

Second, you'll likely want to keep your disputes out of the courtroom. Lawsuits can be costly and, at times, debilitating. You should provide your members with a means to handle their disputes in a friendlier, more laid-back way. Specifically, you'll want to bind them to *mediation and arbitration* (a diplomatic way to handle disputes in which a third party hears both sides of the disagreement and then makes a decision about the outcome).

Here's a sample provision that you can use:

> *The Members agree that in the event of any dispute or disagreement solely between or among any of them arising out of, relating to, or in connection with this Agreement or the Company or its organization, formation, business, or management, the Members shall use their best efforts to resolve any dispute arising out of or in connection with this Agreement by good-faith negotiation and mutual agreement. The Members shall meet at a mutually convenient time and place to attempt to resolve any such dispute.*
>
> *However, in the event that a member dispute cannot be resolved, such parties shall first attempt to settle such dispute through a nonbinding mediation proceeding. In the event that any party to such mediation proceeding is not satisfied with the results thereof, then any unresolved disputes shall be finally settled in accordance with an arbitration proceeding. In no event shall the results of any mediation proceeding be admissible in any arbitration or judicial proceeding.*

Addressing the other stuff

After filling in your operating agreement with the specifics I address in this chapter, you will still have quite a few holes! Don't sweat though because throughout the rest of the book (especially Chapters 10, 11, 12 and 16), I show you how to make the right decisions and document those in your operating agreement. So flip to whatever chapters interest you most and get started!

Chapter 10

Structuring Your Partnership

In This Chapter

- Boning up on LLC membership
- Choosing the right partners
- Issuing and vesting membership shares
- Organizing a single-member LLC
- Deciding on the rules for managers

In the eyes of the law, your LLC is a separate entity unto itself — almost like a separate person. But because it's not alive and can't think or act on its own, someone must do so on its behalf. In this case, the owners (that is to say, *you*) make sure the business stays alive. Until membership in your LLC has been issued — in other words, until the LLC is actually owned by someone — the business doesn't really exist.

The LLC's members are the company's major decision makers. For the most part, the business's success falls on their shoulders. Even if they don't manage the day-to-day affairs, they still control who does. Who owns the company and how that ownership is structured are the most important decisions you can make when starting a new venture.

In this chapter, I help you understand membership terminology, and I dive into finding the right partners to ensure the best chance of success for your new business. I outline all you need to know about membership of your LLC, showing you how to take ownership of your LLC by issuing membership interests to yourself and your partners. I also explain how you can structure your membership in a way that incentivizes all members to do their best and hold up their ends of the bargain.

Don't have partners? Don't fret. If you're flying solo, I show you how to structure your single-member LLC.

Understanding the Terminology: Members, Interests, and Certificates

As you probably know by now, the legal term for the owners of an LLC is *members*. The best way to understand the concept is to think of the ownership of the LLC as a big pie made up of *membership units* or *membership interest*. (Different states tend to use slightly different terms, but they all mean the same thing.)

For instance, if the company has a total of 100 membership units and you personally own 35 membership units, you own 35 percent of the company. In other words, you have a 35 percent membership interest in the LLC. An easy way to calculate your membership interest is to divide your membership units by total number of membership units the company has issued. When you issue membership interests, the entire pie must be consumed, so to speak.

Your LLC's membership is issued in its operating agreement. It's a strange thought: You can invest thousands into an enterprise, and all you get is a few pieces of paper signed by all members! But that agreement gives you the most important thing in business — control. Without evidence of your ownership, you have no say in how the LLC is run, how the money is spent, or how the company is structured. The business could be terminated tomorrow, and you'd get nothing.

Your LLC may elect to offer membership certificates to its members. A *membership certificate* is a piece of paper that helps prove a person's or company's membership in an LLC and includes the name of the member, the date that the membership was issued, the amount of membership interests, and the signature of one or two members and/or managers. As the world goes digital, physical membership certificates are being slowly phased out. However, some industries or jurisdictions (such as certain places in Eastern Europe) still may require you to serve one up as proof of your ownership.

Before putting anything in writing, do a quick review of your state's laws regarding LLC ownership to figure out what terminology the state uses. You can peruse various state laws applicable to LLC membership at `www.docrun.com/dummies/membership` (password is **onesmartdummy**).

Locating and Recruiting Key Partners

A business partnership is a lot like a marriage, so you should take as much care in choosing your partner(s) as you would in choosing a spouse. The choice may not seem like a big deal during the initial stages, but trust me; after things get rolling and the stakes get high, who you're with in the trenches is the key factor that can make or break your business.

Finding the yin to your yang

Finding the right partners or co-founders isn't just about skills, although that should be an important consideration; it's also about personality types. I've found that in the best relationships, opposites attract. For example, what happens when the stuff hits the fan? Is one founder more laid back while the other freaks out? In these moments, this mismatch in personalities tends to lead to the best outcomes. For example, if both partners are too laid back, they may not take the situation seriously enough, leading to trouble. If both partners are freaking out and losing their cool, chaos will likely ensue.

Another example: A very successful friend of mine, Scott, is in a partnership where he considers himself the idea guy who's good at being the face of the company, and his partner is more detail- and task-focused and likes being behind the scenes. Again, opposites attract. If Scott and his partner were both the visionaries, they'd have a lot of great ideas but very little execution. Not to mention that both would be competing over the limelight.

The lesson here is this: When coming together, all potential partners need to have an accurate view of themselves, knowing full well their strengths and weaknesses. If you know that you're more of a big-idea person who can excite and align others to your vision, then you should surround yourself with finishers — folks who know how to execute a project to completion. The reverse is also true.

Easy tiger! Don't let excitement cloud your judgment

When an idea has momentum, taking a moment to get real about who's going to be involved and what their contributions are going to be is hard. Having those honest, difficult conversations that may ultimately result in one or more potential partners being dropped from the project is even tougher. Those conversations stink; trust me, I know. But addressing those types of crucial conflicts early and head on — and knowing how to do it gently, honestly, and with tact — is what separates the great leaders from the weak.

Before deciding your membership structure, I recommend you read this chapter fully so you have a good idea of your options. Then sit down with your (potential) partners and begin an open and honest dialogue about what each of you is going to bring to the table in terms of skills and effort. Write this information down; it's going to be useful when you're drafting your operating agreement.

After your discussion, get honest about the partners' personality types. Lay it all out on the table. Don't stray away from the awkward and uncomfortable. If a potential partner doesn't see her own weaknesses (or thinks she doesn't have any of note), this unawareness tells you quite a bit about that person. In a perfect world, each person's weakness is another's strength. But very likely, you'll have some overlap and also some holes you need to fill. That's when you have an honest conversation about who should really be on the team.

If you have some holes you need to fill on your team — especially things like being detail-oriented and able to execute systematized processes (or even create the systems in the first place) — you may not have to find an additional partner. If you have a budget, you may be able to fill these holes with key hires. You can still incentivize these folks with ownership, but you can do it through a membership option plan or profit sharing plan that you create for employees. I discuss these different strategies in more detail later in this chapter.

If you have a partner who was a crucial part of building out the idea and could offer some value moving forward, but you don't feel he's a good, permanent match for the team, you can always keep him on in an advisory role and issue him some membership in exchange for his advice (when you ask for it) and continued support. That way, you still have him at arm's reach, and he gets to benefit (in a small way) from the future success of the company. This strategy usually involves creating an advisory board and allocating a portion of membership to advisors for their continued involvement.

Getting the good ones on board

Especially if you're flying solo and/or don't have the budget to fill the holes on your team with key hires, you have some recruiting to do! Recruiting can be an agonizing and time-intensive process, but it's worth it. At this stage, unless you have an extra $10,000 to $20,000 to spend, I don't recommend going to a recruiter. Instead, I suggest you roll up your sleeves, go on sites like LinkedIn and even Twitter, and start reaching out. Here are some things to keep in mind when looking for partners:

- **Recruit based on knowledge and experience.** Reach out to anyone you think would be a good fit and set up those meetings! Keep your first contact with the person short and sweet; at this point, your goal is only to entice him to a meeting.
- **Tell others in your industry what you're looking for and plead their help in your recruiting efforts.** You'd be surprised how helpful others can be when asked.

- **Remember that the most likeable choice in a partner may not be the best one.** After you begin meeting with potential partners or cofounders, make sure to ask the questions that will give you insight into whether they're a good personality fit. You should be looking for someone who complements you, shares your vision for the company (a must!), and has strengths that align well with your weaknesses. This candidate may or may not be the same person you'd like to have drinks with after work.

- **Be realistic and honest about a potential partner's workload and compensation.** If you don't have the funds to pay this person much (if anything at all), you have to be even more vigilant about getting her excited about the potential of the business and the freedoms she'll enjoy from its eventual success. Don't sugarcoat the amount of work she'll have to put in. It won't be a walk in the park, but hopefully it will be worth the risk in the end.

  Then, you'll have to be generous with the ownership. Just make sure that whatever ownership in the company you offer them is subject to vesting, which I describe in the later section "Making Folks Earn Their Share: Membership Vesting." That way, if the partnership doesn't work out, all parties can quickly part ways, and you still have a good chunk of that ownership to offer to the exiting partner's replacement.

- **Don't use the term *co-founder* lightly.** It has quite a bit of value in the long run. Co-founders aren't just any old partners; they're generally considered to be the core drivers of the business. The co-founder title is an important one for a new venture, especially if you're seeking funding. Be careful doling that out to someone who hasn't yet proven herself. Unless she is a rock star in your industry and you need to give her this title to get her on board, consider making her put in a certain amount of time or hit specific milestones before she can claim the title of co-founder.

Issuing the Membership

Your company's initial members are usually the ones who are investing their money or time in the business in the first place because they believe in the idea. In the early stages, excitement prevails and things are usually fine and dandy among partners. However, when a lot of people have a lot at stake, emotions are bound to get involved, and people tend to act irrationally. That's why you need to create some guidelines from the get-go that clearly delineate what each member's responsibilities are and what members can and can't do.

Also, many situations such as the following can be fatal to the business if they aren't dealt with properly:

- How can a member sell or transfer his membership shares?
- What happens when a member gets divorced, passes away, or goes bankrupt?

- What happens when a member wants to retire?
- How can the company take on more members if needed?
- How can the company expel members?
- What sorts of contributions are allowed?
- Does the company have different classifications of members?

The operating agreement also needs to address these topics so that you have a contingency plan that allows the business to not just stay afloat but also prosper.

The reality of membership shares

Although issuing membership is a vital part of setting up your new LLC, structuring the specifics of the membership and the members' individual rights can be even more important. Consider this example: Childhood friends Ed, Sal, and Greg have dreamed forever of opening their own motorcycle shop. Although they all work odd jobs, they soon realize that together they could finally make this vision a reality. Ed owns an excess of equipment for building custom bikes, including the paint and specialty tools. Sal has full access to, but doesn't own, an old vacant warehouse, and Greg has saved $50,000 in his successful entrepreneurship. Together, they possess all the pieces to build their own custom bike shop, ESG Motorbikes.

They form an LLC and divvy out their membership shares. Although Greg is fronting the capital to get the business afloat (providing the largest set of funds), Sal and Ed aren't letting Greg overlook the value of their contributions, so after some persuasion, Greg finally relents and agrees to spread the shares out evenly at one-third. The LLC protects the members from losses that can't exceed what they invest into the company, but it seems Greg has much more at risk and may deserve a bigger piece of the pie.

Unfortunately, after the excitement wears off and things get tough, Ed and Sal don't have the work ethic Greg thought they did. His investment ends up going toward hiring a manager — an okay guy, the best they could find at the time — who runs the day-to-day operations of the company.

A couple of years down the road, when the going isn't great, a private investor offers to purchase ESG Motorbikes for $100,000. Greg, having invested the most money, isn't too happy about this plan, but Sal and Ed outvote him and decide to sell. Sal and Ed make a quick profit; however, because Greg's membership certificate states that he owns one-third of the company and no special provision has been made for him in the operating agreement stating otherwise, Greg is only entitled to one-third of the proceeds from the sale of the business. Because Greg never took any profit from the company, he only gets roughly a $33,300 return on his $50,000 while his friends make out fat and happy. Greg's risk in the venture exceeded his reward, while his buddies gained probably more than they should've. Had Greg required that they structure the operating agreement differently, he could've at least gotten his investment back.

If not all members have to abide by the same rules and restrictions, you should create a *buy-sell agreement* for each member. That way you can have many different rules and provisions for many different members, such as who can transfer membership shares and how. Buy-sell agreements use a lot of these same provisions relating to membership interests and can range from 2 to 50 pages, depending on the size and scope of your LLC and the investment being made.

Naming the initial members and their contributions

Unlike corporations, which have a fixed meeting structure, LLCs have a more informal process for issuing ownership. Standard practice is to list the initial members of the company in the operating agreement. If your LLC has a lot of members, you may want to list them on a separate piece of paper and refer to it as *Addendum A.*

First and foremost, you generally have a provision in the operating agreement, under the Initial Members of the Company section in the document structure I provide in Chapter 9, that states who the members are. Here's an example of a provision you may want to use if your company has multiple members:

> *The name, address, and proportion of total ownership of the Company held by each Member (the "Percentage Interest") are stated in the attached Addendum A. Each Member's "Membership Interest" includes the Member's right to participate in the management and operation of the Company as specified in this Agreement, as well as the right to receive distributions when made and to share in all items of Company gain, loss, income, deduction, credit or similar items (the "Economic Interest").*

Here's the information you should include for each member on the addendum:

- Full name
- Home address
- Type of contribution made (cash, equipment, services, and so on) and its value
- Membership share or percentage of the company that was issued
- Class of membership shares issued to each member (if your operating agreement allows for multiple classes, as described in the "Establishing membership classes" section of this chapter)

As long as you don't intend on electing S-corporation taxation for your LLC (see Chapter 8), your company can have an unlimited number of members. These members don't have to be people, either; they can be corporations, trusts, or other partnerships, such as other LLCs.

Understanding some complexities of member contributions

Member contributions are pretty straightforward when it comes to drafting the operating agreement. Listing them in the addendum next to the contributing member's name is usually sufficient (see the preceding section for a sample provision). However, real life may not be so cut and dried.

If all members contribute cash and the membership interest that they receive in return is proportional to the percentage of cash they contribute, then the situation is pretty easygoing. It's when some members are contributing things such as services, real estate that they have a mortgage on, and so on that things tend to get hairy. The "value" of such contributions may be clear to you and your partners (such as the value of the hard work you agree to contribute) and executed perfectly in the operating agreement in accordance with state law; however, the IRS tends to see things differently.

For example, the IRS doesn't see services as having any inherent value; only cold, hard cash matters in its eyes (not surprising, right?). If all founding partners are only contributing services, all is well; as far as the tax man is concerned, the company has zero value at inception. You're all good! But if one or more founding partners are contributing cash, the non-cash contributing partner may have to do some work-arounds to keep from getting hit with an unexpected tax bill.

Especially if not all members are contributing only services or not all members are contributing only cash, you need a qualified small-business CPA to guide you on any tax implications that may arise when you're structuring your LLC. Involving an accountant may sound like a pain, but keep in mind that you'll need this person anyway when filing your taxes, so getting her on board early is a good practice, regardless. A CPA can help with sticky tax situations like the following:

- If some of the partners are contributing services and the others are contributing cash, you may want to consider having the non-cash contributing partners be issued membership first (when the company has no inherent value) and then take on the cash-contributing members at a later date.
- You'll likely want to make sure that partners who are contributing services actually do their services before getting their share of the pie. That's where *membership vesting* comes into play, and I highly recommend this strategy to keep everyone in line with his or her obligations. Just keep in mind that vesting has even more tax implications for all members. I go over membership vesting in the later section "Making Folks Earn Their Share: Membership Vesting."

- Another common partnership scenario that can cause some tax snags occurs when a partner is personally liable for debt that is contributed to the company, such as a mortgage on a piece of property. This concept may not seem like such a big deal to you and your partners — after all, anyone with good credit can cosign a loan — but it may affect all of you quite a bit when tax time rolls around. I go into more detail on this in Chapter 8.

Determining profit and loss distributions

Considering that all the LLC's founding members have contributed a portion of the upstart capital — whether in the form of cash, equipment, or services — everyone should be due a portion of the business's profits. Generally, this amount should be proportionate to each person's ownership percentage or capital account (explained in the following section). After all, the more time or money you invest into the company, the more you should profit, right?

One of the great benefits of operating as an LLC is that you don't necessarily have to distribute the company's profits and losses according to the members' percentage of ownership. You can vary the distributions however you like as long as you make sure you can give the IRS a good reason for doing so that doesn't include tax avoidance. (You didn't think the government would let you get away with that, now, did you?).

Allocations of profits and losses

An *allocation* is the amount of company profit and loss that is passed on to each member for him to report on his personal tax returns. An allocation doesn't necessarily reflect how much cash is actually distributed to a member, which in some cases means the IRS holds him responsible for income when cash was never distributed to him. (This scenario is called *phantom income,* and I discuss it further in the following section.)

Allocating profits and losses to members in accordance with how much they actually own is customary, but if you want to change it up, you can — provided that you follow the IRS's stringent rules. The IRS allows allocations to vary from member to member, regardless of their ownership percentage, as long as you can show a valid business reason, such as you invested a lion's share of the start-up capital or you took on more risk than the other partners.

For instance, some members may want to be allocated more losses than other members. Why? Well, they may have a lot of passive income from real estate properties and such that they want to offset. In this case, they can deduct the LLC's passive losses from their passive income in their real estate endeavors. The remaining amount is what they're taxed on.

Here's a standard provision that you can include in your operating agreement (under the section "Allocation of Profits and Losses") that allows you to vary the allocations whenever you and your partners choose:

> *The profits and losses of the Company shall be allocated to the Members in proportion with their individual ownership percentages. Should the Company wish to make special allocations, they must comply with Section 704 of the Internal Revenue Code and the corresponding regulations.*

Make sure you work with your accountant before varying allocations so she can help you avoid potential tax pitfalls. When I say that your reasoning for varying distributions needs to be logical for the business and not just to give one or more partners a tax benefit, I mean it. Read all of IRS Section 704 (`www.docrun.com/irs_section_704`). The IRS doesn't mess around.

Distributions

When the cash actually hits your pocket, it becomes a *distribution*. Although all company profits have to be allocated to the members (for them to pay taxes on), not all company profit has to be distributed; you can leave some in the business. And you can schedule your distributions whenever you want; they don't necessarily have to be once a year. You can make the payouts quarterly or even monthly if you like.

To avoid the phantom income situation I mention in the preceding section — a situation where you're essentially paying taxes on money that you never see — you can create a provision in your operating agreement that requires a *mandatory tax distribution*. This stipulation basically means that each year, the LLC will distribute whatever cash is necessary to cover each member's tax bill. Here's a sample provision that you can use to require this sort of mandatory tax distribution:

> *The Company will annually distribute cash to each Member in the amount of that Member's share of the Profits multiplied by the sum of the highest federal and state income tax rates based on the state in which the Member resides.*

You should also specify in your operating agreement the kind of distribution that can be made. For the most part, you'll be distributing only cash to the members. If the company doesn't have the money to pay a member, that member can't demand an asset in lieu of the cash. He'll just have to wait until the LLC has the money or the entity is dissolved. Here is a sample provision that you can use (under the section "Distributions"):

> *Subject to applicable law and limitations elsewhere in this Agreement, the members may elect to make a distribution of assets at any time that would not be prohibited by law or under this Agreement. The amount and timing of all distributions of cash, or other assets, shall be determined by a unanimous*

vote of the Voting Members. All such Distributions shall be made to those Members who, according to the books and records of the Company, were the holders of record of Membership Interests on the date of Distribution.

The Voting Members may base a determination that a distribution of cash may be made on a balance sheet, profit and loss statement, cash flow statement of the Company, or other relevant information. Neither the Company nor any Members shall be liable for the making of any Distributions in accordance with the provisions of this section.

No Member has the right to demand and receive any distribution from the Company in any form other than money. No Member may be compelled to accept from the Company a distribution of any asset in kind in lieu of a proportionate distribution of money being made to other Members except on the dissolution and winding up of the Company.

Make sure that your operating agreement contains a contingency plan for members who come and go in the middle of a fiscal year. Typically, the distribution those members receive is calculated according to the number of days that they held membership. You and your CPA can create whatever formula you think works best for your situation.

I often recommend that clients structure their LLCs in such a way that the managers are the ones to control the profit distributions. After all, a growing business will probably want to reinvest most, if not all, of the profits back into the company for at least the first couple of years. The managers are the ones in the trenches. If they're good at what they do, they'll be able to walk the delicate line of retaining that additional revenue in the company in order to fuel growth while still keeping the investors happy.

When special distributions make sense

Chris decides to partner with his best friends Brian and Aaron. They've been thinking about setting up a construction company since they were kids and have decided that now is the time to jump in. Brian and Aaron will be putting in the upstart capital ($30,000 each), and the three of them will be sharing equally in the work.

Chris, knowing that splitting the profits equally would be unfair, works out a deal with Brian and Aaron. Each partner will own one-third of the company, so they all have equal voting power and control over the company, but Brian and Aaron will receive 100 percent of all company distributions until they've been paid back their initial investment plus 20 percent. Brian and Aaron agree, and the three decide to form an LLC — the only entity that allows them to distribute the profits and any deductions from company losses not according to the percentage of ownership each member has.

If your LLC is manager-managed and you want to have the managers control the profit distributions, you can adapt this provision to your needs and place it in your operating agreement:

> *The Company may, but need not, distribute cash or other assets to the Members. Any distributions will be made in amounts and at times as determined upon the unanimous approval of the Managers.*

Note: If you require that only a majority of the managers approve a distribution, you can simply replace "unanimous" with "majority" in the sample provision.

Establishing membership classes

The LLC is the most flexible entity around, allowing you to tailor it completely to your needs, and it definitely lives up to its reputation when it comes to the ownership. You can choose to set up different classes of membership in your LLC. *Membership classes* designate certain rights and rules for different groups of members. Often, these different classes are marked with a letter (Class A membership, Class B membership, and so on).

After you have these different classes at your disposal, what can you do with 'em? Anything! The state laws are pretty lax on the whole thing — as long as the attributes of the classes are fair and are clearly listed in the company's operating agreement, you can go to town! With membership classes, you can give some of your partners more voting rights than others. Or the rules regarding the transfer of the membership shares can be different among members. You decide. Hey, no one said life is fair, and your LLC needn't be, either.

To establish membership classes, you create one set of rules and procedures for the Class A membership and another set for the Class B membership. For instance, you can create different classes of membership for the operating partners, the investors, and the employees. Their control in the company can be limited according to their respective positions. You can also use membership classes as an incentive for investors to contribute more money to the business. After all, it makes sense that the investors who contribute the most money should have more influence in the company than those who barely invested at all.

If your company has decided to issue membership certificates to its members, these certificates should list the membership class information. You usually do so by putting the class (such as *Class A, Class B,* and so on) on the front of the certificate. Then you put a *legend* — a paragraph stating the class restrictions — on the back of the certificate.

If you want to allow some but not all of your members to manage, you need to make sure your LLC is designated as manager-managed in your articles of organization. In most states, if you designate your LLC as member-managed, then all members are equal managers in the business, regardless of the classes set forth in your operating agreement.

If you want to create different membership classes, here's a sample provision that you can adapt to your operating agreement (under the section "Membership Classifications"):

> *The Company shall issue Class A Voting Membership Shares ("Voting Shares") to the members who vote (the "Voting Members"). The Voting Members shall have the right to vote on all company matters, as outlined in this Agreement.*
>
> *The Company shall also issue Class B Nonvoting Membership Shares ("Nonvoting Shares"). Nonvoting Shares hold no voting rights whatsoever, and members who own only Nonvoting Shares will have no right to vote on any matters. Members may hold both Voting Shares and Nonvoting Shares.*

If you intend to issue only one type of membership in the beginning but you want the option of issuing the other type of shares in the future, you can specify this intention by replacing the phrase "The Company *shall* issue . . . " with "The Company *may* issue . . . " in the second paragraph of this sample provision.

Deciding on how the members decide

Corporations are subject to more stringent rules regarding how decisions are made within the company, but LLCs have much more flexibility. When making company decisions, you must follow these three rules:

- Decisions must be made according to the terms you and your partners have laid out in the operating agreement.
- Decisions are documented properly in company *resolutions* (I show you how to do so in Chapter 13).
- The decision-making process can't conflict with any state law.

In other words, you and your partners specify in your operating agreement who decides on what. However, your state may have a few firm laws on how certain topics are decided on that you can't override in your operating agreement. For instance, you may not be able to state in your operating agreement that only a majority of the members can decide to dissolve the company because your state may require that *all* members agree to dissolve the company. Basically, these rules are in place to prevent the minority partners of any company from being disenfranchised.

Now, the good news is that your LLC isn't subject to the same strict meeting requirements that corporations are held to. You can opt to force all members to abide by a strict meeting schedule, where important decisions are made, but I don't recommend this setup. With any schedule that's too strict, occasional failure to meet requirements is inevitable. Setting yourself up for legal failure is always a bad idea; you're just giving someone a basis to sue you. So I suggest that you structure your operating agreement in such a way that allows you and your other partners to document your major company decisions in the form of *resolutions*.

I get into the ins and outs of company resolutions in Chapter 13, but for now you just need to know that resolutions are where you formally document the important decisions that you and your partners make that pertain to the company.

Voting requirements

The first thing that you need to determine is what percentage of members is required to approve a company decision or action in order for it to be valid. Common voting requirements that you can assign to certain important topics are *unanimous* (where all the voting members have to agree), a *simple majority* (where most of the members have to agree), or a set percent of the members with voting privileges. It's entirely up to you.

To prevent minority partners from being disenfranchised and not getting a say, most states have some firm, overriding laws in place about what percentage of members approving certain key decisions requires. In these cases, no matter what you put in your operating agreement, the state law will still win out. A common example of this approach is California, where all members must agree in writing that the company is going to be manager-managed, thereby taking the management control out of the hands of the members. Another example is the common requirement for all members to agree to liquidate and dissolve the company.

Make sure to check state laws before creating your operating agreement and, when in doubt, elect a requirement of unanimous consent. That's the better way to take care of the minority members anyway.

Voting

Not only do you have to determine what specific issues require a vote of the members, but you also have to determine how members get to vote (usually called their *voting interests*). You can structure voting interests two ways:

- **Allow each membership share to have one vote.** If your membership shares represent 55 percent of the company, you have 55 percent of the vote. This setup is the most common way to structure voting interests.
- **Give one vote per member.** If you have 55 percent of the company, you have one vote, which is equal to the member who owns only 1 percent of the company.

You also have to take into account that you may have different classes of membership shares: voting and nonvoting (see the earlier section "Establishing membership classes"). If you have both types, only the voting shares receive votes — no matter how you structure it.

If you're structuring your company voting so that each share gets one vote, here's a sample provision you can use (under the "Voting" section) in your operating agreement:

> *Except as expressly set forth elsewhere in this Agreement or otherwise required by law, all actions requiring the vote of the Members may be authorized upon the vote of those Members collectively holding a majority of the Membership Interests in the Company. The following actions require the unanimous vote of all Members, who are not the transferors of a Membership Interest:*
>
> *i. Making an Amendment to the Articles of Organization or this Agreement;*
>
> *ii. Absolving any Member from the obligation of making a capital contribution or returning money or property that was distributed to such Member in violation of law or this Agreement;*
>
> *iii. Approving the sale, transfer, assignment, or exchange of a Member's interest in the Company and the admission of the transferee as a Member with full rights therein;*
>
> *iv. Purchasing, by the Company or its nominee, the Membership Interest of a transferor Member.*

Note: Feel free to add any additional matters to this list that you feel need to be decided upon by a unanimous vote of the members.

You may want to calculate each member's voting interest from the get-go and place it in the operating agreement where you state their names, addresses, and initial capital contributions. This way, when a vote takes place, the voting interests are already calculated, and the members have already approved and signed off on their individual voting interests.

Making Folks Earn Their Share: Membership Vesting

One of the biggest causes of discord among partners is when one or more don't live up to their ends of the bargain. When a partner agrees to provide certain value to the company (namely, in the form of services) in exchange for a certain percentage of the membership, he's expected to make good on his promises. Unfortunately, even the best-laid plans fizzle out; people can be lazy, or life can simply get in the way. Having a partner that doesn't pull his weight usually dampens the enthusiasm of the other partners; after all, why should they work so hard when he's off having fun and still getting the same ownership percentage? Resentment builds, and thus begins the slow, painful disintegration of a perfectly good business.

Luckily, you can prevent this all-too-common scenario through *membership vesting.* In this section, I give you a quick overview of this (highly recommended) practice and guide you on how to implement it for those founding members who aren't contributing much more than future promises.

The best way to protect your company in the event that one of the partners becomes dead weight is to make sure that he simply earns his membership as time passes and/or as he meets certain milestones. If a member departs as an employee/manager of the company (whether he leaves on his own or is kicked out), he takes with him only the membership interests that he's already earned up to that point.

Deciding on a fair vesting schedule

The timeline in which members earn membership is called a *vesting schedule.* The most common arrangement for founding members of a new startup is a three-to-four-year vesting period, with membership vesting every quarter. For example, if a founder only contributing services is placed on a four-year vesting schedule, then on the three-month anniversary of his starting "employment" with the company, he receives one-sixteenth of his membership. Then, every three months, he receives an additional one-sixteenth of his membership until, on his four-year anniversary, he receives the final increment and owns all his membership in full.

Note: Vesting typically doesn't apply to membership earned in exchange for a contribution of cash or property, only services.

If you have only one other partner and you each own 50 percent of the total membership interests, you may have a difficult time kicking out your ineffective partner. In this case, I suggest having an advisory board in which you issue a small interest (such as 1 percent) to a trusted third-party advisor and then require a simple majority vote (see the "Voting requirements" section earlier in this chapter). This person can serve as your tie-breaker. An extra benefit to having an advisory board is that you can bring on additional advisors as needed. After all, it takes a village to raise a child. This applies to companies too!

Alternatively, have the membership vest based on specific milestones. That way, you may not be able to officially kick out your ineffective partner immediately, but at least he won't keep receiving more membership he isn't earning. When you've vested enough membership to have the majority of the interests, you can vote him out of there.

Understanding membership cliffs

You may have heard of the term *membership cliff* — when a company decides to make a partner wait an extra-long time upfront before her membership vests. For example, a one-year cliff on her vesting schedule means she doesn't get any of her membership until the one year anniversary of the date she started employment (although the membership accrues during that time). On that date (assuming a four-year vesting schedule), she receives the accrued one-quarter (four-sixteenths) of her membership and then continues vesting quarterly as normal.

Companies often use membership cliffs to incentivize a partner or employee to stay with the company for a certain amount of time (a year, for example). If the partner leaves early, she receives no ownership in the business. Personally, I'm not a big fan of membership cliffs lasting longer than six months. If a partner is only sticking around for the membership she was promised, do you really want her on board just biding her time? No way! I'd say *adieu* and find someone who is a better fit.

However, cliffs are sometimes useful. If membership vests monthly (rather than quarterly), you should heavily consider implementing a three-month cliff. This way, if the new partner/employee doesn't work out, you can quickly part ways without the hassle of having an extra member on board or, even worse, a bad hire who isn't invested in your business.

Using the Repurchase Option method

Because LLCs generally require that all their membership units be issued upfront, you can't always easily have each member be granted new membership every quarter. Therefore, an easy strategy is to reverse the situation and give all the membership to the partner upfront but give the company the full right to repurchase that interest from the partner. As the milestones are met, the company incrementally loses that right, and the partner's interest becomes more and more secure. This approach ultimately results in the same concept as regular vesting, but it's much easier to execute and is more tax friendly.

If you want to use the Repurchase Option strategy, you must allow for it in your operating agreement. It's relatively straightforward; however, you need to add many provisions that can be adapted in multiple ways. Adding entire pages of sample provisions here doesn't really fit with the scope of this book, so refer to your trusted small business attorney to execute this vesting method.

Avoiding common tax pitfalls

When you agree to earn your share of a business over time, it's generally because you believe that the company is going to increase in value. And if there's one thing everyone knows about the startup world, it's that when the big wins happen, they generally happen rapidly and gloriously, resulting in a huge increase in valuation.

If this jackpot happens to you, you're on cloud nine. You may not see any of the cash for a while, but, gee, does your personal balance sheet look great! You're living the dream, right? Well, yes — until you receive your tax bill. You see, the IRS will want to tax you on that new valuation even before you actually see any cash from the transaction. And unless you have enough cash lying around to pay taxes on the millions of dollars that you're now technically worth, you're going to be hurting.

Luckily, the IRS gave the tax-savvy an out, and it comes in the form of an *83(b) election.* When you make this election early on (generally right after you receive your membership grant), you lock in the valuation of the company at the time you joined. This setup means that even though your membership interest may potentially be worth millions in six months, you'll only pay taxes on the hundreds it's worth now (or nothing, if your CPA structures it in a certain way).

Making 83(b) elections is pretty straightforward and definitely something that you want to get a jump on as soon as your membership is issued. However, if you're going to implement vesting as a strategy, you really need to run everything by your qualified small-business CPA first. This tax issue isn't the only one that may affect you, and a good CPA can make sure that your butt is covered on all fronts. You may spend $100 now getting a consult, but that's peanuts compared to the tax bill you may face later if you proceed unaware.

Setting Up a Single-Member LLC

If you're planning on being the only member of your LLC, your LLC will be designated as a *single-member LLC* (SLLC).

Several states' courts have ruled that single-member LLCs don't offer the dual-layer of liability protection, called *charging order protection,* that regular LLCs offer. And unless you're completely diligent in your record keeping and dot every *i* and cross every *t*, SLLCs can also lack the basic liability protection that an LLC offers — protection that is one of the LLC's fundamental benefits.

Keeping your SLLC's liability protection

Although in some states single-member LLCs don't offer the same peace of mind as multiple-member LLCs, you can still take steps to ensure the basic liability protection that a multiple-member LLC or corporation offers — that which protects your personal assets if the company gets sued. This process can be somewhat tedious, though, because you must be rigorous in making sure you file everything correctly, and you have to go above and beyond to treat your entity as though it were truly separate from yourself.

To keep the liability protection in your SLLC, do the following:

- **Elect corporate tax treatment on IRS Form 8832, Entity Classification Election.** When you elect corporate tax treatment, you're automatically saved from being considered a proprietorship by the IRS. Head to Chapter 8 for details on electing a tax status.
- **Be diligent about keeping your business assets and cash flow *completely* separate from your personal assets and cash flow.** You must have documentation to this effect. In other words, no using that business credit card on that personal shoe splurge at the mall.

If, as a single-member LLC, you claim a home-office deduction (IRS **Form 8829, Expenses for Business Use of Your Home**), your home can theoretically be considered a business asset and be seized if you lose a lawsuit.

- **Sign all your filings as owner, on behalf of your LLC.** Never sign any business documents without this designation.
- **Add your federal EIN and your LLC's filing number (provided by the Secretary of State) to your Schedule C.** Adding your LLC's file number makes your LLC look much more legitimate and can deter those looking for a lawsuit.
- **Act like a corporation.** This approach involves complying with all corporate formalities, such as having meetings of the members and managers, keeping extensive minutes, and passing resolutions. Even if you're the only person involved in your LLC, don't think you can get out of these tasks. Having a meeting with yourself may seem silly, but doing so is necessary to document all decision making affecting the company.

Being a multiple-member LLC doesn't make you exempt from having to abide by these same formalities. These are simply good business practices that help you prevent the courts from classifying your company as an alter ego of yours and removing that barrier of liability protection. I just stress these points more for single-member LLCs because those entities — without any additional partners — are more at risk for having their companies disregarded by the courts.

Creating an operating agreement for an SLLC

Is your LLC a single-member LLC owned only by you? Although it may go against common logic that you need an operating agreement — after all, why would you need to create your own rules just for yourself? — having one is even more imperative for you, the single-member LLC owner. If you're ever taken to court, your operating agreement will help ensure that your personal veil of limited liability remains intact. (See Chapter 17 for more on the veil of limited liability.)

The operating agreement for a single-member LLC isn't much different from that of a regular LLC with multiple members. In most places, you simply change the verbiage, replacing "Members" with "Member" (singular). See Chapter 9 for the details on how to start your operating agreement.

Setting Up Rules for Managers

Some businesses have two kinds of partners: operating partners, who manage the day-to-day affairs, and silent partners, who keep their noses out of the daily goings-on. If this is how you've structured your LLC, with only one group of your members doing the managing, do you really want your silent, nonvoting members to be muddling in your daily operations? Not likely.

First, you need to make sure that your LLC is manager-managed (not member-managed, because not all members will have equal say in the management), and then set up two classes of shares. Remember, you can set this up however you want. For this example, I've used voting and nonvoting classes. Then you state that one class shall have full management rights and shall be managers, while the other class has no management rights at all. Here's an example of some provisions that you can draw from:

> *The Voting Members shall manage the Company. In their capacity as Managers, they shall have the right to make decisions and vote upon all matters as specified in this Agreement, in proportion to their respective Ownership Percentage of the Company. Voting Members need not identify whether or not they are acting as a Member or a Manager when they take action.*
>
> *Nonvoting Members have no right to participate in the management of the Company, nor vote on any matters of the Company. No Nonvoting Member shall take any action or enter into any contract or obligation on behalf of the Company without the prior written consent of all of the Voting Members. Likewise, no Nonvoting Member shall perform any act that is in any way pertaining to the Company or its assets.*

Outlining the Basics

This section is especially important for manager-managed LLCs. If your LLC is managed by the members, as opposed to a separate manager or two, then all members have equal say in the management of the company. On the contrary, if your LLC is manager-managed, then you have the option of bringing in an outside person (or group of people) who may not even be associated with the business. They don't even have to own a percentage of the company.

The *manager* is the person who runs the company. His actions determine whether the business succeeds or fails. He is a pertinent player in the game, and, for this reason, the members must choose wisely. The members must also retain control of the manager. If the manager screws up, the members need to have the power and authority to replace him on a dime. If you are a manager-managed LLC, this is probably the most critical part of the operating agreement.

Unless you plan on changing your managers out often, you'll probably want to place the names of the initial managers in the operating agreement. If there are more than a few, you can attach a separate piece of paper with the names and refer to it as *Addendum A or B.*

If you have multiple managers, you'll want to state in this section who is the Big Boss. You'll probably want to give the Big Boss a more official title like CEO, president, operating manager, Chief Yahoo, or whatever you want. If you have other positions that you can place managers in, feel free to list them here. You may want to list things such as chief financial officer, treasurer, vice president of yadda yadda yadda . . . . Make up whatever you want; just make sure to include what that position entails, such as the limits of responsibility and the day-to-day duties.

Electing the Managers

If you are in business for a while, you'll probably see a lot of people come and go. You see it happen with Fortune 500 companies all the time — they recycle leaders on what seems like a weekly basis. If you're like most people investing in a business, you'll want to make sure that if the people you put in charge aren't cutting it, you can kick them to the curb and find someone who can do the job better. Hey — it's your hard-earned money you're talking about. You wouldn't entrust it to some yackahoo, now would you?

I didn't think so. That's why you need to sit down with your partners at the beginning and decide how you're going to manage your managers. If you want to give your managers some job security, you may want to state in this section that the managers stay in power for a one-year term; then the members have to vote to reinstate them. At this point, the members can choose someone more qualified if they want to.

If you're a little more cutthroat, you may want to write the provision so that the manager can be replaced at any time by a vote of the majority of the members. At that point, the members will elect a new manager or select someone to serve in the interim.

Here's a sample provision you can use:

> *The Company shall be managed by one or more appointed Managers. The name and address of the Managers of the Company can be found in Exhibit B, attached. The Members, by a majority vote, shall elect and appoint as many Managers as the Members determine shall be in the best interest of the Company, though no less than one.*
>
> *One manager shall be elected to take the position of Chief Operating Manager. The Chief Operating Manager shall be held responsible for managing the operations of the Company and shall carry out the decisions of the Managers.*
>
> *Members shall serve until they resign or their successors are duly elected and appointed by the Members.*

Delegation of Powers

This question will come up: "What can and can't we do as managers?" Although managers must use common sense to avoid overstepping their boundaries and making important decisions without consulting the members, the operating agreement must have a section that gives them guidance. This section tells them what decisions they can make on their own and what decisions require a resolution of the members. Here's a sample provision you can use:

> *The Managers are authorized on the Company's behalf to bind the Company to contracts and obligations, and to do or cause all acts to be done deemed necessary or appropriate to carry out or further the business of the Company. All decisions and actions of the Managers shall be made by majority vote of the Managers as provided in this Agreement. The Managers have in their power to authorize or decide the following:*
>
> *i. The employment of persons or institutions for the operation and management of the company affairs.*
>
> *ii. The execution of all checks, drafts, and money orders for the payment of company funds.*
>
> *iii. The delivery and execution of promissory notes, loans, or security agreements.*
>
> *iv. The purchase or acquisition of company assets.*
>
> *v. The sale, lease, or other disposition of company assets.*
>
> *vi. The granting of security interests in the company assets in exchange for capital.*

vii. The prepayment or refinancing of any loan secured by the company assets.

viii. The execution and delivery of all contracts, franchise agreements, licensing agreements, assignments, leases, and subleases that affect the company assets.

For the most part, your managers can bind the LLC to contracts and other obligations. You can limit their powers in this section of the operating agreement. However, even if they act out of their authority, it doesn't necessarily void any contracts that they entered into. Ultimately, it's up to a judge to decide.

You may want to include a paragraph that states that any expenditure over a certain amount (say, $5,000) requires an additional authority. This can mean that a vote of the members is required. Or perhaps more than one manager or member has to sign off on the expense.

Compensation

The managers' compensation isn't something normally decided by the managers — for good reason. Generally, most LLCs are structured so that before any high compensation or bonuses can be doled out, the members must take a vote, and the majority must approve. This is a great provision which can really keep company costs from spiraling out of control. It maintains a checks-and-balances system and is a great way to keep payroll in check.

You can also throw in a sentence or two that states that the company is required to reimburse the manager for all expenses she incurred on behalf of the company. Here's a sample provision that addresses reimbursement of expenses:

> *Any Manager who renders services to the Company shall be entitled to compensation in direct proportion to the value of such services. Additionally, the Company shall reimburse all direct out-of-pocket expenses incurred by the Managers while managing the Company.*

Chapter 11

Using Your LLC to Attract Investors

In This Chapter

- Taking advantage of what makes LLCs attractive to investors
- Getting around securities laws (legally) with SEC registration exemptions
- Navigating tricky state laws

If you're an entrepreneur, one of your most fundamental tasks when starting a company is seeking out and acquiring capital to fund your startup. This process can be as simple as asking friends and family members to pull up their couch cushions and donate some extra change or as complex as raising millions in private equity or venture capital. Regardless of your methods or the amount you're raising, you have to contend with some hurdles. Namely, the Securities and Exchange Commission (SEC) — a government agency endowed with the task of keeping the little guys from being swindled out of their life savings.

Luckily, when you know the federal and state securities laws you're contending with and can navigate them with ease, raising financing should be a breeze. Well, aside from the talking people out of their money part; sometimes that's easier said than done! Thankfully, you were smart enough to form an LLC for your fundraising activities, and with the flexibility in membership rules, management, and profit distributions, you have the freedom to come up with some pretty creative incentives that make the prospect of investing with you much more attractive than, say, with a stiff, old corporation.

In the following sections, I explain why LLCs are one of the most alluring entities to investors. I go over federal and state laws regarding investments and show you ways that you can get around the detailed process of registering your offering with the federal and state securities commissions. These tactics are called *registration exemptions.* Remember that term, because these exemptions are your lifeline when navigating the securities law minefield.

Structuring Your LLC to Attract Investors

More often than not, upstart capital for budding enterprises comes from the founders and people willing to finance it for a piece of the action (otherwise known as *investors*), which is why raising capital is a vital aspect of any up-and-coming business. Unlike sole proprietorships or general partnerships, LLCs can actually sell portions of the ownership, the membership shares. Membership shares are normally given to investors in return for cash, property, or other assets. You can also give them to employees or contractors in exchange for their services. Issuing membership is a great tactic to use if you're just starting out and don't have a lot of money to pay employees.

In some states you can give *promissory notes* for future money, property, or services that someone intends to contribute. That way, you can issue the shares first, and then the person can make his contribution. You can always note in your operating agreement that if the individual doesn't live up to his promises, his shares are confiscated. Promissory notes can be a big incentive for investors to get on board, but be careful! Make sure the investor does in fact have the money to invest and is committed to living up to his end of the agreement.

One of the reasons LLCs are quickly becoming the entity of choice for raising money is because they provide unmatched limited-liability protection for everyone involved in the business. Not only are the members protected from

Maintaining an accurate record of members

When setting up your LLC and creating your operating agreement (a process I walk you through in Chapter 9), make sure to list all the members, their membership interest, and all the contributions received from them. Although keeping a current list of all membership information in the operating agreement isn't a legal requirement, I strongly recommend you do it anyway. When membership changes, having this setup forces you to update your operating agreement, and all new and existing members to have to reaffirm their agreement to the policies outlined in the operating agreement. If you have so many members that this strategy isn't practical, you can use what's called a *membership roll* to maintain an updated record of the company's members and their individual membership interests and ownership percentages.

Although you don't have to issue membership certificates, I always recommend them. They add legitimacy to the investment, and investors like to have them. If your operating agreement includes restrictions about transferring the membership, you should print a notice of these restrictions on the actual certificate. This notice is commonly called a *legend.*

the liabilities of the business, but LLCs also get the benefit of *charging order protection* — a second layer of liability protection that protects the business from the liabilities of the owners. (See Chapter 17 for more on limited-liability protection.)

Appeasing the SEC with an LLC

As I note in the preceding section, an LLC is the best entity to use when raising capital. Now the question is whether you legally can. After all the hard work of finding investors, you're nearing the finish line and just need to cut a deal, right? Unfortunately, you may not be able to just take people's money. Special *securities laws* protect the innocent from bad investments, and you must comply with these laws before legally raising financing. I know it seems like a pain in the neck — and it is — but trust me when I say that you do *not* want to mess with securities laws. The penalties for noncompliance are steep and include huge fines and jail time.

Most people think of securities laws and the SEC as only applying to large public corporations trading on exchanges such as NASDAQ and NYSE. Not so! If you sell shares of your small business or real estate property to the general public, then the securities laws apply to you.

The federal government considers anything to be a *security* if an individual or entity invests cash, property, services, or other assets into a business and isn't involved in the business's management decisions. This definition means that whenever you accept any form of contribution in exchange for your membership shares, you're dealing in securities. And you thought you had to be some big Fortune 500 company to do that!

Two major pieces of legislation control all U.S. securities: the United States Securities Act of 1933 and the Securities and Exchange Act of 1934. Both pieces of legislation have their own sets of rules and regulations and have been amended numerous times over the years. These acts were set up to protect investors, but complying with them is difficult for most small businesses. First of all, the process of registering your securities with the Securities and Exchange Commission not only is lengthy but also comes with some enormous expenses, including registration fees, CPA fees, attorney fees, underwriting fees . . . the list goes on and on.

So what's a small business to do if it can't afford the huge costs of raising just a little bit of money? Well, the feds got smart, and they now allow registration *exemptions* for businesses that want to raise a limited amount of money and don't mind playing by some pretty strict rules. I get into exemptions in more detail later in this chapter in "Exploring securities registration exemptions."

Securities laws protect you and the economy

Believe it or not, the securities laws in place help make the United States the economic superpower that it is today. Before the United States Securities Act of 1933, the stock market was a pretty rogue business. No regulations were in place, and anyone investing in the market was definitely doing so at their own risk (and risky it was!). Criminals could easily create fictitious companies with the sole purpose of taking the common man's life savings and heading for the border. Because of these dishonest practices, when many of these seemingly legitimate companies failed to report any earnings, the great stock market crash of 1929 rocked the nation. When the U.S. dove into the resulting Great Depression, lawmakers knew that something had to be done. With lessons learned, the Securities and Exchange Commission was born, and laws were drawn up that protect innocent people from fraudulent investments.

Seeing how the laws apply to you

One of the first ways to legally get around securities laws is to make sure that when you raise capital, the membership shares you offer aren't considered securities in the first place. The best way to determine whether securities laws apply to your organization is to take a good look at how the management will be structured after you raise the financing.

- If the investors have a full and equal say in the management of the company, then the securities laws don't apply.
- If the LLC is managed by separate managers or the investors have limited managerial powers, then the securities laws *do* apply.

I generalize the stipulations of the laws into a few loose rules to determine whether you're selling securities. If any one of these rules applies to your LLC, you're automatically required to comply with securities regulations:

- Your LLC is manager-managed.
- Your LLC is member-managed, but some or all of the investors are junior managers and don't have a full say in the business's day-to-day operations.
- Your LLC has hundreds of members. Even if they all have a say in the company's management, they can't all realistically manage the day-to-day operations.
- You're widely advertising the investment and looking for multiple investors.

These guidelines are loose and based on federal interpretations of the law. When it comes to states, the laws and the interpretations of what a security is differ greatly. For instance, New Mexico, Ohio, Vermont, and Alaska consider *all* membership shares to be securities, whether the LLC is manager-managed or not. I discuss state security registrations in "Flying through State Securities Laws (Blue Sky Laws)" later in the chapter.

If you're just looking to raise a little bit of money, I suggest that you find an investor or two who may have good input in the business operations. This way, you can avoid a lot of the securities laws, but your investor can also be an asset in terms of knowledge and experience.

When you want to create a member-managed LLC for bringing on investors, make sure that the articles of organization and the operating agreement both specify that each member is equally responsible for the operations and success of the LLC. Unlike corporations, your LLC should have no centralized management in which the shareholders elect directors who then elect the officers who manage the LLC. Avoid that structure and instead get used to managing as a team. To make sure the government doesn't classify your membership shares as securities, all members collectively must be in charge of the major decision making and have the power to select or remove key employees. (Head to Chapter 6 for info on how to form a member-managed LLC.)

If you transfer your membership shares to someone (such as a family member) as a gift, the securities laws don't apply. However, you can only make such a transfer once; you may not make multiple gifts of unrestricted membership shares.

Exploring securities registration exemptions

If you review the rules in the preceding section and find that securities laws apply to your situation, you may still want to sell membership shares as securities if you don't want your investors to have control over the operation of the business. If you just want them to sit back and be silent partners, that's okay. As a matter of fact, because the federal government knows how difficult, costly, and time consuming registering your securities with the SEC can be, it provides some exemptions that mostly apply to small businesses or small projects that are looking to raise a small amount of capital.

The exemptions that I discuss here apply only federally, so you still need to look at the laws for each and every state in which you intend to sell your securities and determine what applies to you and whether you can meet state criteria for an exemption from registration.

To help navigate the laws, I recommend working with a securities attorney who is familiar with conducting searches on securities laws in multiple states. You may be able to work out a money-saving agreement with the attorney in which you take on some of the workload yourself. Just make sure that, no matter what, the attorney specializes in securities laws. A regular business attorney typically won't cut it.

In the following sections I outline the federal exemptions available to small businesses. Rules 504, 505, and 506 are called *Regulation D exemptions,* and they all belong to Sections 3 and 4 of the Securities Act. If you're using a Rule 504, 505, or 506 offering exemption, you must read and follow some corresponding general rules, Rules 501, 502, 503, 507, and 508. You can find them at `www.docrun.com/dummies/regulation_d` (password is **onesmartdummy**).

Rule 504 exemption

If you're looking to raise less than $1 million, you're automatically exempt from having to register your securities with the SEC. This guideline is the *Rule 504 exemption,* one of the *Regulation D exemptions.* In general, you can't advertise the investment opportunity, and you aren't required to make any specific disclosures about the investment. However, the money must be raised within a 12-month period. After that time, you must register the securities with the SEC or find another exemption.

After you first sell some of your securities, you have to file a Form D with your state securities commission. This form includes some basic information about the company, such as the names and addresses of its owners and stock promoters. You can download a Form D at `www.sec.gov/about/forms/formd.pdf`.

You can only use this exemption if your LLC isn't selling any other securities that are registered with the SEC. For instance, if your LLC has another class of membership that's being offered for $50 million and is registered with the SEC, the same LLC can't use this exemption to raise less than $1 million.

The Rule 504 exemption is by far the most popular of all securities exemptions. Not only does it directly apply to most small businesses looking to legitimately raise financing, but it also means your LLC isn't required to bear the burden of state qualifications if your company is selling its securities with a Rule 504 offering. The LLC simply needs to abide by the exemption rules and make the requisite state securities filings for each state it's selling its securities in. I show you how to do this in "Flying through State Securities Laws (Blue Sky Laws)" later in the chapter.

Rule 505 exemption

If you plan to raise less than $5 million, you may be able to use the *Rule 505 exemption.* It has a few more limitations than the Rule 504 exemption in the preceding section (but that isn't surprising, considering you're raising more money):

- **You can't use *general advertising* (any advertising that's targeted to the public at large, such as newspaper ads, TV ads, and so on) to sell your securities.**
- **Like the Rule 504 exemption, you can't take longer than 12 months to raise your funds.**
- **Your LLC's financial statements must be certified by a CPA.** This step assures prospective investors that the profit/loss and assets/liabilities you state on your financial statement are factual.
- **You can only have a maximum of 35 regular-Joe investors (*nonaccredited investors*).**

When selling to the nonaccredited investors, you must adhere to the SEC rules regarding investment *disclosures.* These disclosures outline the risks inherent in the investment. This includes things such as competition or market barriers to entry — essentially, anything that could hinder your company's success and stability. You must be completely forthright and disclose everything that the SEC requires you to. Your attorney can help you write disclosure statements that comply with both federal and state laws.

Although you're limited in the number of nonaccredited investors allowed, you can have as many accredited investors as you like. What's an *accredited investor?* It's a person or institution that meets certain financial criteria. These investors are well-off enough to suffer the financial hit of a bad investment. They normally have a net worth of more than $1 million. They generally are more educated about investing and can make better decisions on where to place their money than the average person can.

Rule 506 exemption

Rule 506 is the golden rule that most companies use to raise funds over $5 million. When offering securities under the *Rule 506 exemption,* you're doing what's called a *private placement,* and you can generally raise as much money as you like. The guidelines for Rule 506 are very similar to those for Rule 505 in the preceding section:

- You're limited to 35 nonaccredited investors, but you can sell to an unlimited number of accredited investors.
- If you sell any securities to nonaccredited investors, you must make very specific and comprehensive disclosure statements regarding the investment to all investors.
- You can't do any general advertisement of the investment.
- Investors are limited in their ability to resell the securities.

To streamline the process of a Rule 506 offering, many companies issue what's called a *private placement memorandum* (or PPM, for short), which adheres to the SEC guidelines on what needs to be disclosed regarding the investment. If you ever come across investment opportunities that aren't listed on the stock exchange, you'll most likely see them in this format. Or you may see what's called an *executive summary,* which is just a summary of the PPM that teases your interest in the investment. After the company has your interest, it gives you the full PPM.

A PPM is normally a complete business plan, 30 to 50 pages long, put into a special format that includes certain disclosures, such as who is involved in the business and what risks are inherent to the investment. I encourage you to be completely forthright when drafting your PPM. Most smart investors look for these disclosures and, believe it or not, are a lot more confident in the investment when they see that the company is being very open and honest about the risks involved.

You can purchase a template for a private placement memorandum online. However, you may want to have your attorney draft a PPM for you instead, even though the cost may be in the thousands. Most templates comply with federal laws only, and your attorney will have to make sure that your PPM and your financing plan comply with the state securities laws as well. Not to mention the fact that your presentation will end up looking much more professional to prospective investors.

Intrastate exemption

The *intrastate exemption* requires that you find investors or members in only the one state where your LLC operates. This exemption sounds better than it is because it has the following problems:

- All the members of the LLC must be in the same state where the LLC has its business operations.
- The LLC can't advertise for investors in any state other than the one where it has its business operations.
- The LLC can operate only in this one state. This rule is the worst of all and the one where most LLCs get disqualified because it means that anything related to your business can't take place in any state other than your home state. You can't market to people out of state, and you can't have customers in or purchase supplies from other states.

The world is getting smaller and smaller every year, and raising money under the intrastate exemption is increasingly impossible for most companies. However, if you're a small mom-and-pop business that operates only locally, this exemption may work for you; just make sure that you don't do any business out of state. Also, keep in mind that you'll still be required to file an exemption with your state's securities commission. To do so, file the SEC

Form D (which you can find at `www.sec.gov/about/forms/formd.pdf`) with your state securities commission. Just make sure to clear everything with a qualified securities attorney first.

Regulation A exemption

If you plan to raise less than $5 million, you may want to consider offering your securities under the *Regulation A exemption* rather than some of the Regulation D exemptions I discuss in the preceding sections.

With a Regulation A offering, you aren't limited to the number of investors you bring on board. You still need to do a *private placement memorandum* (a long-winded form that's comprised of your basic business plan and some hefty disclosures about the investment); however, Regulation A allows you to advertise the investment in more ways than a Rule 505 or 506 exemption does. For instance, you can use radio or mass mailing to advertise your investment. Also, when registering under a Regulation A exemption, you can advertise your investment before having prepared a private placement memorandum, so long as you don't take in any money. This freedom allows you to test your response rate before incurring the cost of creating all your disclosure and financial statements.

So if Regulation A offers fewer restrictions and downsides than the Regulation D offerings, why is it so rarely used? As with many things, the Regulation A is great in theory but doesn't work so well in practice. Unlike with Regulation D offerings, companies taking advantage of the Regulation A exemption must file an offering statement with the SEC. An *offering statement* is a circular for investors regarding the company's business, financial, and other pertinent details; the risk factors of the investment; and the management of the company. Not only does this statement result in public disclosure of your company's private details, but these offering statements can also be expensive to produce. In addition, Regulation A offerings are more difficult than Regulation D offerings to coordinate with state securities laws, which I discuss in the next section

As part of the disclosure, you must show financial statements; however, they can be unaudited if no audited statements are available.

Flying through State Securities Laws (Blue Sky Laws)

Think the federal security laws are a hassle? Well, the ride ain't over! Not only do you have to comply with federal laws, which are regulated by the SEC, but you also have to register your LLC and follow state laws — often called *blue sky laws* — in every state where you're prospectively looking for money. Just hope the investor you're targeting doesn't live in a backward, complicated state with expensive filing fees!

The term *blue sky laws* originated from a judge who said that a certain stock being advertised had "about the same value as an area of blue sky."

Because the laws differ from state to state, registering your securities in multiple states can be very time consuming and very expensive — especially if you have a securities attorney doing all the research and filing. You can get around the arduous and costly process of registering your offering with every applicable state securities commission, but it still takes some good old-fashioned research on your part. You can use the registration exemption offered by certain states after you find out which states offer it.

Registration exemptions started when the federal government decided to cut small businesses a break and let them raise money without too much red tape. However, even when companies could navigate the federal securities laws, they were still getting hung up by state securities commissions. So to help out the small businesses and real estate transactions that don't raise a large amount of financing (between $1 million and $5 million), the Uniform Commission of State Laws, with the blessing of the SEC, tried not only to put all the states on the same page but also to offer registration exemptions that matched those of the federal government.

The result was a set of provisions titled the *Uniform Limited Offering Exemption* (or ULOE), which basically took the federal registration exemptions 505 and 506, made a few simple variations, and then handed them over to the states, ready for the taking. The federal government offered the ULOE to the states on a silver platter, begging them to copy and paste that set of securities laws into their own state statutes. The idea was that if a company complied with the federal registration exemptions, then it'd be in compliance with the state securities laws. Some states agreed, but others copied only part of the code. Therefore, you and your attorney must go through each state's code to see whether that registration exemption is available in your desired state, and if so, what the specific rules are. If you want to file under the ULOE, you can get the SEC Form D document at `www.sec.gov/about/forms/formd.pdf`. Just remember: Run things by a qualified securities attorney before filing!

Most states offer some variation of the Rule 505 and 506 exemptions. Check the laws yourself or contact a securities attorney who can check for you. Unless you can find an exemption in the individual state's laws, you're required to register in that state if you advertise your investment there or take investment from it.

Chapter 12

Doing the Membership Shuffle

In This Chapter

- Understanding the basics of transferring membership
- Setting up your operating agreement to manage transfers
- Creating individual buy-sell agreements
- Finalizing and amending your operating agreement

In Chapter 9, I explain the basics of an operating agreement and help you start creating your own. In Chapter 10, I go over how to choose your partners (carefully!) and structure your partnership. In Chapter 11, I show you how to bring on investors. After reading these chapters and putting your plan in place, unfortunately sometimes things just don't progress as intended. In this chapter I show you what to do when your plans go awry and a partner needs to go. I also show you how to finish your operating agreement and how to amend it when needed. Think of this chapter as your insurance plan: You structure your company and your operating agreement now in a way that allows you to get out of future problem situations with your partners pain-free.

I know this is a touchy subject to bring up with your partners — especially when you're just getting started and things seem to be working flawlessly — but when else are you going to do it? When the you-know-what hits the fan? Not a good plan! The best way to broach it with your partners is to remind them that a change in ownership doesn't necessarily have to be the result of some argument or other fall-out. A change in ownership can occur for myriad reasons, good and bad.

Investigating Intricacies of LLC Membership Interests

Before getting into the details of how to handle specific exit scenarios with your partners, I first want to help you determine the value of membership interest and give you a basic understanding of how membership interests are transferred.

Determining the value of the membership interest

Generally, the value of a member's interest equals her interest's portion of the current fair market value of the company. In other words, if the company is deemed to be worth $150,000 and the departing member has 25 percent of the membership, the fair market value of that membership interest is $37,500. You and the partners can decide to go to a business valuation expert — who will usually charge between $3,000 and $5,000 — to determine the fair market value of your company. Or, if your company is relatively small, you may want to determine the value of your company on your own.

Regardless of how you determine the value of the membership interest, you need to specify in your operating agreement that the fair market value is the price to pay for membership interest. Here is a sample provision that you can amend as needed:

> *If a Member resigns with the Company's approval, the Company shall purchase the resigning Member's Membership Interest within 90 calendar days after the effective date of resignation. The purchase price will be an amount equal to the fair market value of the resigning Member's Membership Interest, to be calculated in good faith by the Company as of the effective date of resignation. If the resigning Member disputes the valuation reached by the Company, the value of the resigning Member's Membership Interest shall be determined by an independent third party appraiser to be appointed by the Company and approved by the resigning Member. The resignation of a Member will not cause the termination or dissolution of the Company.*

Don't want to worry about figuring out the fair market value? Instead of using the above provision, you and your partners can all agree that, should one of you leave, the value of the membership interest shall be equal to the capital account balance. When the time comes, have your accountant figure out the specific member's capital account balance. Here's a sample provision you can use:

> *If a Member resigns with the Company's approval, the Company shall purchase the resigning Member's Membership Interest within 90 calendar days after the effective date of resignation. The purchase price will be an amount equal to that Member's Capital Account balance, calculated as of the effective date of resignation. The resignation of a Member will not cause the termination or dissolution of the Company.*

After you figure out the member's interest or capital account balance and the member has relinquished her shares to the LLC, the other members can reconfigure their ownership percentages. For instance, if three members each own 33 percent of the company and one member decides to sell her shares back to the LLC, the remaining two members will each own 50 percent of the company.

You may want to consider adding a *right of first refusal* provision to your operating agreement. This means that before the departing member can sell his interest to the public, he must first offer some or all of it to the other members. If the company or its members do not elect to buy back the membership interest, the member can sell his membership to the general public.

All the rules regarding adding and withdrawing members can be laid out in your operating agreement or, if the requirements tend to be different for each member, individual *buy-sell* agreements. I show you how to draft a buy-sell agreement later in the "Creating individual buy-sell agreements" section of this chapter.

Transferring membership

By default, the membership in LLCs isn't freely transferrable. Unless you explicitly allow for it in your operating agreement, you can't just sell your ownership like you would a share of stock. Instead, your membership is broken into different rights, namely *voting rights* and *economic rights*. The reason for this dates back to the beginning of LLCs and the IRS requirements for allowing them to enjoy partnership taxation, but that's not important. The key takeaway is this: Typically, when you transfer your membership to someone, that person doesn't automatically receive all of the rights that you possess.

The default rule in most states is that when you transfer your membership interest, you transfer only the economic rights to that interest — entitling the new owner to the same profit and loss distributions as you were to receive as owner — but no voting rights. This law is to protect you and your partners from the uncomfortable event of waking up in the morning to find that you're now partners with someone completely different than who you started the company with. In most LLC structures, the full rights (both economic and voting) of the membership interest cannot be given to the new member without unanimous approval of the other members, which is taken during a member vote. The vote should be documented in a formal, written *resolution* that all voting members must sign.

For example, say you want to gift your LLC membership to your brother. That seems fair, right? After all, it's your membership and you can do what you want with it. Well, not so according to most states' laws. Your brother will have your economic rights and profit and loss distributions, but no voting rights, essentially making him a silent partner. He can enjoy the financial benefit of the membership interests (if there is any); however, he cannot be involved in any decision-making for the company.

This arrangement definitely creates some hassles, but it's not necessarily a bad thing: These laws can form the basis of *charging order* protection, one of the most powerful forms of liability protection out there. I discuss this in more detail in the next section.

Using transfer restrictions to your advantage

As I describe in Chapter 17, this "nuisance" of not being able to freely transfer membership forms the basis for a pretty hefty *charging order protection* strategy. In this strategy, say you're the owner of ABC Realty, LLC. One day you're at the grocery store, and a woman jumps in front of your car. You barely hit her, but lo and behold you have a lawsuit on your hands. Your membership in ABC Realty, LLC is considered a personal asset of yours, so when she goes after everything you own, she throws your ownership of the company into the mix as well. So, what do you do? You stop worrying and let her take it.

As long as your LLC is structured the way that I outline in this chapter, this unfair and angry creditor is about to get much angrier. You see, according to the rules, the creditor cannot foreclose on your *full* membership interest — only the economic interest. Then, after the creditor seizes this economic interest of the membership shares, you and the rest of the additional members can vote to withhold distributions of profit. The creditor is still required to pay taxes on her membership, even though she's not able to pocket any of the company's profits. Drag this on for a few years and I guarantee you'll have a creditor anxious to get out of the situation and settle at a more reasonable sum. I go over this strategy in more detail in Chapter 17, but the main thing you need to know is that this limitation to transferring ownership has an upside.

When drafting your operating agreement, add a provision under the Transfer and Assignment of Interests section that reinforces your charging order protection. Here's a sample provision that you can use:

> *If a creditor obtains a lien or a charging order against any Member's membership interest, or in the event of a Member's bankruptcy or other involuntary transfer of interest, this act shall constitute a material breach of this Agreement by such Member. The creditor or claimant shall only be considered an Assignee and will be limited to the rights of such. The creditor or claimant shall have no right to become a Member or have rights to management participation nor have the right to participate as a Member or Manager in any regard to the affairs of the Company. Said creditor or claimant shall only be entitled to receive the share of profit and losses, or the return of capital, to which the Member would otherwise have been entitled.*

You may want to take this a step further and state that the partners have the option of purchasing the assigned membership shares at a discount:

> *The Members may unanimously elect to purchase all or any part of the membership shares that is subject to the charging order, bankruptcy, lien, or other involuntary transfer at a discounted price. The price shall be equal to one-half of the fair market value of such shares. Written notice of such purchase shall be provided to the creditor or claimant.*

Preparing Now For an Easy Transition Later

When you're drafting your operating agreement, one of the most important topics to discuss with your partners is how to deal with one of the partners moving on from the company. You don't want to put off this discussion. Otherwise, you could find yourself in a bad situation with no means of fixing it, not to mention going through the hassle and expense of letting a courtroom decide.

Although a partner may move on from the company for many reasons, the three main situations you need to account for in your operating agreement are when a partner

- Peacefully moves on
- Gets ousted by the other partners
- Involuntarily loses his membership interest by an event such as a bankruptcy, divorce, or death

In the Transfer and Assignment of Interests section of your operating agreement, you have a lot of pertinent issues to sort out before you proceed with business. Some important subjects that you want to address in this portion of your operating agreement are

- When and how can a member resign?
- If someone resigns, does she get her contribution or capital back?
- What happens when a member retires or passes away?
- What happens if a member goes bankrupt?
- Can a member be expelled?
- How are membership shares transferred?

In this section, I show you how to draft your operating agreement in a way that accounts for all of these questions. Then, I show you how to create individual *buy-sell agreements,* allowing each member to have different terms for transferring his membership.

Parting on peaceful terms

Usually a member knows when a situation isn't right for her. Although you may still need to have a painful conversation, this is ultimately the best situation for everyone. After all, you don't want someone to be involved in your company against her will. Or maybe the member just needs cash and wants to sell her membership. Whatever the reason, a peaceful exit is usually just that — peaceful. However, it's good to specify in advance in your operating agreement the terms for such an exit.

When a member leaves on his own accord, the company has two options: it can either buy back that member's interest or force the parting member to try to find a buyer for it. If the company's operating agreement prohibits the member from resigning, then their interest can convert to a pure economic interest. In that case, hopefully the buyer is okay being a silent partner because he wouldn't get any voting rights!

In most cases, you want to leave the option open to the other partners. In other words, if the company has money, then the members can vote to buy back the membership interest of the departing member. If the company is cash-poor at the time, then the remaining members can opt to leave the burden on the departing member. Here's a sample provision you can use that allows for this option:

> *Any Member may resign from the Company at any time. However, the Company will not be obligated to purchase the resigning Member's Membership Interest without the unanimous approval of the other Members.*

Removing a member

You know that saying: *A chain is only as strong as its weakest link.* In business, it's no different. Sometimes you have to make the hard decision to eliminate a member. Sometimes, this is as easy as simply firing them, removing them as manager (if they were one), and letting them remain a silent owner.

If you and your partners decide that letting the member retain silent ownership is the best course, you can simply place this provision under the Expulsion section of your operating agreement:

> *No Member may be expelled from the Company.*

However, if you want to take a more hard-lined approach, you want to specify the terms under which a member can be expelled. First, decide if a member can be expelled *without cause,* meaning you don't have to give a specific reason. All other members can simply vote the reject off the island at their whim.

Because there are quite a few reasons why a member may become a liability for the company (aside from simply disliking a person), a more common approach is to list specific *causes* for the other members to expel a specific member. Here are some provisions that you can amend (simply add or remove causes) as you see fit:

> *The Company may only expel a Member for cause, upon the approval of a majority of the Members.*
>
> *Any of the following will constitute "cause" for expulsion of a Member:*
>
> *a) It is or becomes unlawful for the Company to carry on its business with the Member;*
>
> *b) The Member files a voluntary petition in bankruptcy or is adjudicated bankrupt or insolvent;*
>
> *c) The Member has engaged in misconduct that has caused or is likely to cause a materially adverse impact on the reputation of the Company or on its business or internal affairs;*
>
> *d) Commencement by the Member of a legal proceeding against the Company;*
>
> *e) The divorce or separation of a Member results in a transfer or assignment of membership interest to the Member's spouse, ex-spouse or dependents;*
>
> *f) The Member's conviction of a felony or misdemeanor (excluding routine moving violations or tickets);*
>
> *g) The Member's material breach of this Agreement.*

You and your partners can decide to state in the operating agreement that, when a member is expelled for cause, the value of the membership interest is lower. In other words, the company can be allowed to buy back the membership of the expelled member at, say, 50 percent of the fair market value of the membership interest. This would be drafted as a separate provision under the Expulsion section of the operating agreement.

When it comes to hiring, firing, and retiring members who are also *managers,* state law is usually silent on the issue. So you need to have provisions in your operating agreement that discuss how managers will be retained and replaced. If the LLC is manager-managed, the operating agreement should state that the members get to vote every year on whether to replace the current manager.

The members should also be able to take a special vote to expel the manager at any time, if need be. Managers should also be admitted in much the same way — with a vote of the members.

As for the manager withdrawing, you have to choose whether to allow it, and if you do not allow it, what penalties will be assessed for the damages incurred by his withdrawal. This should also be placed in the operating agreement. If your LLC is manager managed, feel free to amend some of the above provisions according to what you and the other members agree and place them in the Management section of your operating agreement.

Dealing with the death of a member

Sad as it is, death is the great equalizer in life. Young or old, rich or poor — it will happen to all of us.

Although you can decide on your own how your LLC behaves upon a member's death, the law always protects the remaining members' interests, especially from the passing member's heirs. Because membership shares of LLCs are considered personal property, those shares will go through estate and probate much the same as the other assets of the deceased. The membership shares will be distributed according to her will or estate plan. Therefore, you can easily end up with a new partner.

The plus side is that, if your operating agreement is worded correctly, the beneficiary of the LLC membership interests has no real power in the company, only an economic interest. So the beneficiary can receive only the portion of profits and losses that her membership shares entitle her to. When it comes to voting, she has no say. When it comes to managing, she must remain silent. She can only become a full partner if the other partners take a vote and agree.

Here's a sample provision you can use:

> *Upon the death of a Member, the deceased Member's legal representative, successors or heirs (collectively "Member's Estate") will retain the Member's Economic Interest subject to the terms of this Agreement, but will not be entitled to participate in the management of the Company. The Member's death will not release the Member's Estate from any obligations or liabilities incurred before death. The death of a Member will not cause the termination or dissolution of the Company.*

Don't like the idea of having a member's heirs as partners? You can also add a provision to your operating agreement that states that the LLC has the right to buy back the shares within a certain time frame. Here's a sample provision that you can edit accordingly:

> *The Company will have the option to purchase the deceased Member's Membership Interest by delivering written notice to the Member's estate within 60 calendar days after the death of the Member. The Company will then have 90 days from the date of the notice to pay the Member's estate an amount equal to the fair market value of the deceased Member's interest, to be calculated in good faith by the Company as of the deceased Member's death. If the deceased Member's estate disputes the valuation reached by the Company, the fair market value will be determined by a neutral third party appraiser selected by the Company and approved by the deceased Member's estate. The death of a Member will not cause the termination or dissolution of the Company.*

Make sure that all actions on behalf of the members of the company, especially those concerning adding and withdrawing members, are clearly documented in the company minutes. Recording these changes shows a history of the company procedures and will be invaluable if any actions are contested or if the company is taken to court.

Creating individual buy-sell agreements

In many cases, the members of a company aren't necessarily equal. They contribute different things and have varying levels of ownership. One member may run the day-to-day affairs of the business while others just sit back and reap the rewards. Considering this, you may want to have different membership transfer policies for different members. In this case, you generally don't place these provisions in the operating agreement. Instead, you give each member his own *buy-sell agreement*.

A *buy-sell agreement* simply outlines the rules that govern how a member may voluntarily or involuntarily transfer her membership. It also explains what the company and that member (or her estate) should do if she were to retire, go bankrupt, become incapacitated, or pass way.

If your buy-sell agreement covers all members in the company, then you just include these provisions in your operating agreement instead. But with LLCs, you don't have to hold everyone to the same standard. If you want, you can have individual buy-sell agreements for each of your members, each containing different rules and restrictions.

A buy-sell agreement must cover

- How much money a member's shares are worth
- Who controls the member's shares if she leaves the LLC for any reason
- The reasons why someone may be admitted as a member and issued membership shares
- What happens to a member's shares when the member departs or withdraws, for example:
  - The LLC or the other members can purchase the shares
  - The shares can be sold to the general public
- The process of transferring membership shares
- What happens if a member declares bankruptcy or gets a divorce

If you are using buy-sell agreements (rather than outlining general rules in your operating agreement), when the company issues membership shares to a new member, you must create a buy-sell agreement at the same time. Otherwise, a buy-sell agreement that you create after issuing membership shares may not be retroactive. If you've already issued your membership shares and now want to create a buy-sell agreement, make sure that

- The buy-sell agreement is in writing and in accordance with state laws
- All members vote on the agreement and sign the written resolution
- The agreement specifically states that it covers all *current* LLC members

Using your buy-sell agreement to say buh bye!

Say you gave membership to an employee, and six months later, you catch him stealing from the till. You and your partners are furious, so you decide that the only option is to fire him. Unfortunately, he still has the membership that was given to him. Considering that you and your members want to cut ties with the thief, you consult your buy-sell agreement.

Luckily, you were smart and included a provision that allows for the expulsion of a member. You and your members take a vote and send a letter to the excommunicated employee letting him know that he is being expelled as a member of the LLC and will receive the value of his shares in a structured payment plan that suits the company. This is all in accordance with the buy-sell agreement that he signed and received a copy of when he was issued his shares.

When drafting a buy-sell agreement, you can use the same provisions that cover membership transfers and would normally be found in the operating agreement. You simply adapt each provision to the specific circumstances you want outlined in the buy-sell agreement.

If you're using individual buy-sell agreements and don't have these important provisions drafted in the operating agreement, then you MUST make sure that each member has a signed buy-sell agreement on file.

Like operating agreements, buy-sell agreements can vary substantially, and what's in them is very particular to your state's individual laws on what's allowed and what's not. With that in mind, patching together an agreement from various fill-in-the-blank forms you find on the Internet (I know you've done it!) can be a dangerous proposition in this case.

Executing the Transition

Hopefully you've already outlined the terms in your operating agreement so that when the time comes for a transition in membership, all you've got left is the easy part.

Depending on how you structured your LLC in your operating agreement, you may have to decide whether the company should buy back the membership interest of the departing member. If the LLC has enough profits to repurchase the membership, this is usually the best move. Before committing though, you should make sure to go over your company's financials with your accountant. She can tell you whether or not a buy-back of the membership is a viable option for the company.

After the member has relinquished his shares to the LLC, the ownership percentages are reconfigured. For instance, if three members each owned 33 percent of the company and the company purchases back the shares from one member, then the remaining two members will each own 50 percent of the company. After reconfiguring the ownership percentages, you should amend your LLC's operating agreement with the new membership configuration. You must also outline the purchase amount and specifics of the sale in your amended operating agreement or a written resolution.

Making room for new members

When the LLC or its members do not buy back the shares, then you should make room for one or more new members on the team. The good news is that, unless you've structured your LLC to specifically allow the membership interests (including their voting rights) to be freely transferable, then you and your partners should have a say in how much power the incoming members are entitled to.

When the membership shares are sold, the incoming member(s) won't have full rights in the LLC; she has only *economic rights,* which means she gets the profit and loss distributions, but has no right to vote or manage the LLC. However, the other members can vote to allow the incoming member the rights that were previously denied her. At that point, she becomes a full member. When you take this vote, make sure to document it clearly in a written *resolution*, signed by all of the members.

Also make sure to amend your operating agreement with the new ownership percentages. The new member must also sign this amended operating agreement, agreeing to be bound by the same terms as you and your partners.

Giving old and new members their fair share

In a perfect world, membership would be transferred only on January 1 (or at the beginning of your fiscal year). Unfortunately, this is rarely the case, which presents a complication when it's time to dole out the previous year's allocations and distributions of profit (or loss, if you didn't have such a great year).

When a new member joins your LLC, you should prorate that year's distributions based on how long she has been a member during that current fiscal year. For instance, say a new member, owning 10 percent of the LLC, is admitted to the LLC on July 1. Should she get her full 10 percent of the profits at the end of that year? Of course not!

In this case, if the total profits distributed are $100,000, the new member should receive only 50 percent (for the half of the year she was a member) of the 10 percent (her ownership share) for a grand total of $5,000. After that distribution has been made, the remaining $95,000 can be distributed according to the other members' percentages. Your accountant can assist you in your exact calculations; this example is just a quick and easy (yet oversimplified) overview. When figuring out the exact amounts, you need to take other things into consideration, such as each member's individual capital account balance. More on capital account balances in Chapter 14.

Whether you bring on a new member or the company buys back the membership interest, the reverse is true for the departing member. If she relinquishes her interest on July 1, there is no reason for you to give her a full distribution at the end of the year. It can be prorated for the time she was a member with the company.

It would be smart to define these terms of prorated distributions in your operating agreement (or buy-sell agreements) now rather than later, especially because economic interests are usually the "freely transferable" part. Can you imagine the outcome if a member were to buy in on December 20, take a huge chunk of the distributions for that year, then sell out on January 2? Trust me, it's happened, and the only way to prevent that situation is to make sure your operating agreement or buy-sell agreement clearly states that distributions are calculated according to the number of days of the year that the member has been admitted to the LLC.

Wrapping Up the Operating Agreement

In Chapter 9, I give you an outline for a comprehensive operating agreement, the backbone of your business. Hopefully by now you've made some key decisions with your partners, checked some state laws, and have filled out the sections. If everything looks complete, you're very likely ready to go! In this section, I help you add the finishing touches to your operating agreement.

You should run your completed operating agreement by a lawyer-review service to check for anything you might be missing. Don't get suckered into paying an expensive retainer or high fee for a revised version. Unless your LLC's structure or requirements are unusually complex, an inexpensive, quick and easy lawyer review should be all that's required.

Signing and Ratifying

With an LLC, all your managers and members should sign the operating agreement. Some of the worst client problems I have seen arose because not every member had signed the operating agreement, resulting in thousands of dollars of legal fees and lost time from disputes.

To protect against this, not only should each member (and manager, if manager-managed) sign off on the operating agreement, but they should also sign off on their capital contributions, membership interests, and distributive shares that are listed in the agreement. If the company has a lot of members, you can include a separate signature page.

You should also make sure that you hold a meeting of the members (and managers, if you like) and take a vote to approve the completed operating agreement. You should draft minutes of this meeting to further document that all of the members got together and approved the document. This way, if the document is ever contested in court, you can prove that the contesting member was there when the document was up for a vote and could have disputed the document at the time. This is why it's a good idea to have *all* the members approve the operating agreement as opposed to a simple majority. (For more information on how to document company decisions and draft resolutions, flip to Chapter 13.)

Sharing the copies and storing the original

You should give a full copy of the operating agreement (including all signatures) to each of the members and managers who signed it. This ensures that everyone is on the same page and each person is familiar with company policies that they've agreed to abide by. Keep the original safely tucked away in your company kit (see Chapter 13).

Amending the operating agreement

As companies grow and change, so should their infrastructure. If you are in this for the long term, you'll probably reach a point when the operating agreement needs to be amended. How you amend your operating agreement should be specified in the most recent version of your LLC's operating agreement, otherwise, it's largely determined by the laws of the state that your company is domiciled in. If your current operating agreement states that it must be amended by unanimous consent, then all members will have to approve the amendment. If it states that a unanimous vote by the managers can amend the operating agreement, then all managers need to sign, approving the amendment.

This provision should be placed in the Amendments section of your operating agreement, which I showed you how to do in Chapter 9.

When amending your operating agreement, hold a meeting of the members (see Chapter 13), present the amendment for a vote, and draft a resolution stating that all (or a majority) of the members agree to amend the operating agreement. Again, you want to abide by whatever is stated in your current version of the operating agreement.

Having this proof that all members agreed on changing the operating agreement is vital because if a member ever takes you to court over something in the operating agreement, you can prove that he voted and signed off on the amendment. After the vote, make sure that all members have copies of the signed amendment and all resolutions.

Unlike when you amend your articles of organization, you don't need to file the amendments to your operating agreement with the state or local jurisdictions because your operating agreement isn't a public record. Your operating agreement is a private contract between the members (and managers) of the LLC. This means that your amendment is valid as soon as it has been voted on.

Part IV

Running Your Brand-New LLC

Five Steps to Impeccable Record Keeping

- Draft comprehensive resolutions that document important decisions as they are made.
- Store your records at a secure record-keeping storage site or in a physical company kit.
- Make sure that all members have constant access to the company records.
- Maintain an updated membership roll.
- Keep all tax and financial records organized.

Visit `www.dummies.com/extras/limitedliabilitycompanies` for an article to help you understand LLC tax distributions.

In this part . . .

- Learn the ropes of how to operate your LLC.
- Keep up your company records so your LLC stays in good standing with your members, the government, and your customers.
- Dive into all things taxes and get an overview of what tax filings to expect, no matter what form of taxation you've chosen for your LLC.
- Uncover the major tax traps so you can avoid them.
- Discover how to grow and expand your business.
- Know when to call it quits and dissolve your LLC.

Chapter 13

Maintaining Your Records (And Your Sanity)

In This Chapter

- Filing your initial report
- Acquiring the necessary business licenses
- Keeping your company's records properly

I'm sure you're hankering to jump right into building your business, but not so fast! You didn't think that you could simply file some articles of organization and the government would let you go scot-free, did you? Nope. You still need to take care of removing some red tape.

Although the amount of red tape varies depending on the industry you're in, it usually isn't too much of a hassle if you know how to stay under the radar. First and foremost, most states require you to file an *annual report* with your local secretary of state or franchise tax board. Each state refers to this report by a different name, and the requirements also differ substantially depending on where your company is domiciled. I show you how to file your report in the first section of this chapter. Then I discuss the necessary business licenses you need to obtain and the regular record keeping you need to do in order to protect your business's limited liability. With these details arranged, your LLC will be legit and protected, and you'll be free to begin transacting business.

Filing Your Initial Report

When creating your LLC, you create and file your articles of organization (as discussed in Chapter 6) and are well on your way to completing a customized operating agreement for your business (see Part III). At this point, you should have made certain decisions about how the company is to be managed and who the managers are, among other things. Well, if you remember correctly, one of the major benefits of an LLC is *privacy.* A lot of the decisions you make regarding your company remain in your operating agreement, which isn't public record. In a perfect world, you would be able to leave it at that. In *this* world, however, a few of those decisions you made must be revealed to the government and, subsequently, to the public eye.

The amount of disclosure required varies substantially from state to state. As I talk about in Chapter 5, these disclosure requirements can be a big incentive (or disincentive) to form your LLC in a particular state. The first and most important document that you may be forced to disclose is your company's *initial report,* which is usually filed within the first couple months of forming your company and, in most states, reveals the managers and/or members of your LLC.

Getting to know your state requirements

Each state requires different information to be listed on public record. For the most part, the initial report lists information such as:

- The names and addresses of your managers
- The name of your registered agent and your registered office address
- Often, if the LLC is not manager-managed, the members who own the LLC

The name and the filing processes also vary substantially from state to state. Some states refer to this initial report as an *initial list of managers or members* or an *information statement.* In some states, this same report is required to be filed annually or biannually (with updated information, of course). In those instances, this report is often referred to as an *annual* report.

The fee for the initial report can be hefty — sometimes as much as the fee for filing the articles of organization — and depending on the state, can be due either annually or biannually. Also, unlike the articles of organization, which can be submitted by a separate *organizer* (a person who files your articles but otherwise has nothing to do with your company), a manager or member of the LLC needs to sign the initial report.

Keeping your company current

Although this may seem like a trivial detail, if you don't file your initial report (or, subsequently, your annual reports) and pay your state taxes in a timely manner, you'll not only face some pretty hefty penalties and fees, but your LLC may go into a *default* or *revoked* status relatively quickly. After all, when it comes to the life of your LLC, the state giveth and the state sure can taketh away!

Filing public announcements in Arizona and New York

Two states — Arizona and New York — require you to file a public announcement of your articles of organization in a newspaper or other daily or weekly publication.

If you're setting up an LLC in Arizona, follow these steps to file the public announcement:

1. **Within 60 days of filing your articles of organization with the Arizona Corporation Commission, publish the entire text of your articles in the newspaper of your choice (as long as it is published at least weekly and has at least 5,000 subscribers) in three consecutive issues.**
2. **File your *affidavit of publication,* given to you by the newspaper, with the commission within 60 days of filing your articles of organization.**

   The affidavit of publication tells the state that you submitted your articles for print. Your LLC goes into effect only after the affidavit of publication has been filed.

If you're setting up an LLC in New York, follow these steps for the public announcement:

1. **After filing your articles of organization with the New York Department of State, publish your articles in two separate newspapers once a week for six consecutive weeks.**

   Your county clerk's office chooses the newspapers in which your articles will be published.
2. **File the affidavit of publication, given to you by the newspaper, with the department of state within 120 days of the LLC's filing date. Until this affidavit of publication has been filed, your LLC is not in full legal compliance with the state of New York.**

Often in these cases, the state doesn't even tell you that your status has been revoked; you may not find out until you've been sued and realize that you don't have the LLC protection you thought you had. When your LLC is in revoked status, it's considered an *administrative dissolution,* and you may very well lose all liability protection, which was a key component of why you created an LLC in the first place. Find out more about administrative dissolution and the other ways in which your LLC can dissolve (or reorganize) in Chapter 16.

Luckily, you're usually not required to go to the expense of filing an updated report every time your information changes. In most states, you're required to file the report only on its due date (typically on the anniversary of the LLC's filing date). Not only does this save you fees, but — in case you haven't caught on already — it may also be a good way get yourself and your LLC a little bit of privacy: If you have to list the names of the members of the LLC *only when you file the report,* you have an entire 11 to 23 months (depending on how often an updated report is due) to allow whoever you darn well please to own or manage the company.

Paying to Play: Business Licenses

After you file your initial report with the secretary of state, you'll likely need to get yourself a business license (or two or three!). Unless you're in the business of mass weaponry, drug development, or peddling junk bonds, the federal government usually keeps its distance and leaves business licensing to state and local governments. It's sort of like "pay to play," and the last thing you should ever do is open up shop without first forking over some cash for official government approval. Avoiding this step is the fastest way to get shut down. (Yes, the United States *does* have a free market, but you didn't think that means it's *actually free,* did you?)

Acquiring state, city, and possibly county business licenses

Most states require that all businesses apply for a standard *business license.* This is the "letter of approval," so to speak, that you need to legally conduct business within the state. The state tax board uses the licenses to keep track of all enterprises that are responsible for paying state and sales or use taxes.

In addition to the state license, you may be required to file for a city and/or county license, depending on where you live. If your business is located within city limits, you need to obtain a license from the city; if it falls outside city limits, you must obtain your license from the county. Contact your county clerk's office or the city's business license department and ask which local licenses and permits you need to obtain. Keep in mind that you'll likely be required to pay an annual fee and/or local taxes for each license.

Each state requires different details from businesses applying for licenses. Typically, you can expect a business license application to request the following information:

- Business name, physical location, and mailing address
- Type of business and formation date
- Prospective business activities and expected income
- Federal tax identification number (see Chapter 8)
- Names and addresses of managers/members and possibly percentages of ownership

To find out where to obtain a business license application and where your application must be filed, check the secretary of state's website for the state in which you filed.

If the ownership of your business changes, most states require that the new owners apply for a new business license under their names, even if the business name stays the same. Moving your business to a new address may also require a new business license application, especially if you are moving to a new city or county. Essentially, you just refile the form with the updated information. If a change doesn't significantly alter the structure of the business (such as adding or dropping a member who owns only a small percentage of the LLC), you normally don't have to file a new application. However, some states require you to submit a letter to the business license department describing the change. The department then uses the information to update your business license.

Applying for a sales and use tax permit

If you're selling tangible goods, then you're required to collect sales tax from your customers and pay the government. What is a *tangible good?* Although the definition may vary slightly between states, you can pretty much classify a tangible good as being any item that can be seen, weighed, measured, felt, or touched or is in any other manner perceptible to the senses. Real estate is excluded.

To collect sales tax on the products you sell to your customers, you need a *sales and use tax permit.* What's the difference between sales tax and use tax? I'll explain:

- **Sales tax** is imposed on all retailers (anyone who sells tangible goods — not services — in the state). Retailers are required to pay and report sales taxes to the state board of equalization, and they have the option to collect sales tax reimbursement from their customers at the time of the sale.

- **Use tax** is imposed on you when you purchase something from an out-of-state vendor and use, consume, or store the item in your state. Use tax also applies if you lease an item. And you thought you were avoiding tax when you bought that fancy TV off eBay!

You are typically imposed a statewide sales tax and a local sales tax that differs from city to city. If your business isn't located in an incorporated city, then you're required to pay the county at its local sales tax rate. By combining state and local tax rates, you come up with the amount of sales tax to charge your customers.

What if you aren't selling tangible goods? What if you run a dry-cleaning service or a dog-grooming facility? Aren't you in the clear? Well, in some states you are. Unfortunately, in other states, you are still required to go through the application process. State governments prefer that individuals aren't the ones deciding whether they are liable for paying sales and use taxes. The government prefers that a seasoned tax collector make that determination.

Although it may seem like a hassle, you *want* to go through this application process. The alternative is the harrowing experience of having a state tax auditor set up shop in your office for two (or more!) weeks and proceed to pore over each and every income and expenditure record, tallying up use tax on sticky notes you bought online and sales tax on small thank-you items you shipped to your clients. Not only will the auditor pull every single penny of unpaid taxes out of the woodwork, but the state will impose hefty fines on top of it all. Needless to say, not fun.

Most states call the department that collects the state taxes the *board of equalization.* (I have no idea what that means or why they decided to use such a dumb name — I suspect they decided that "board of tax collectors" didn't sound so friendly.) A lot of businesses pay this department a hefty chunk of dough every quarter.

Following special licensing requirements

If you are one of the lucky ones who decide to set up shop in a heavily regulated industry, such as healthcare, gambling, auto repair, or liquor, then you're probably going to be required to obtain special licensing. If you own your own building, you have to comply with building codes and obtain special permits. If you deal with any sort of food product, then health-code regulations come into play. Now that I think about it, if you're in business at all, you should read this section. I'm sure you'll find one thing or another that applies to you!

In this section, I go over some common special licenses that you may have to obtain. All states are different, though, and I can't possibly list every single license requirement in every single state. To make sure that you have everything covered, give your state's licensing bureau a call before starting business operations.

In most states, because you file so many documents with so many different state and local agencies, you are assigned a nine-digit *UBI* (Universal Business Identifier) *number* upon filing your state business license. You use this number on all your state and local filings so that state and local agencies can easily identify you. A UBI number is sometimes called a *tax registration number, business registration number,* or *business license number.*

State-issued licenses

In addition to the basic licenses required for most businesses, you may be required to file for other licenses, depending on your state. Here are a few that you may be required to apply for:

- **Licenses based on type of product sold:** Most states require you to obtain a license if you sell certain products, such as liquor, tobacco, lottery tickets, gasoline, and firearms. These licenses can be hard to obtain and are often heavily regulated.
- **Professional/occupational licenses:** If you (and/or your employees) will offer services in a specialized area that requires certain skills or training, then you, personally, and each of your employees performing that service are required to obtain a specific license before opening up shop. Some occupations that often require licensing are
  - Medical care — doctors, dentists, and so on
  - Auto repair
  - Real estate sales
  - Contractors
  - Cosmetology
  - Tax services
  - Legal representation/attorneys
- **Licenses for other regulated businesses:** Every state has industries it likes to control. They vary widely from state to state, which is one reason to do your research. Industries that may require additional licensing include jewelry manufacturing and sales, furniture sales, carnival operators, tree trimming, motorcycle sales, auto towing, dating services, swimming pool services, janitorial services, taxi services, movie and television productions, dance clubs, and adult entertainment–related businesses.

Locally issued permits

Some licenses aren't regulated by the state but instead are issued by local government, such as your city or your county. Here are a few licenses to be on the lookout for:

- **Fire department permits:** For those businesses that attract a large number of customers, such as nightclubs, bars, and restaurants, the fire department must conclude that the location is clear of fire and safety hazards.
- **Health department permits:** These permits are most often required for businesses that prepare and/or sell food but can apply to any business where the health of the general public is a primary concern.
- **Property use permits:** If you start a business that involves manufacturing or decide to operate a retail-type business out of your home, depending on your location, you may need to obtain a *land-use permit* from your city or county's zoning department that says you can use the land for something other than residential purposes.
- **Building permits:** If you're constructing a new building or expanding or renovating an existing building, you need to obtain a *building permit* from the city or county. Getting a building permit can take years, and you probably will have to submit a detailed set of plans to the department and work with your builder to gain approval.
- **Zoning permit:** Some cities require that all new businesses get a *zoning compliance permit* before they open. This permit proves that you aren't operating a business out of a location that is zoned for residential use only. Some locales are even more complicated. For instance, you may be able to operate a retail store only out of a property that is zoned specifically for retail.
- **Home occupation permit:** If your business is home-based, you may be required to obtain this permit when you file for your business license. It allows the state to keep track of which employees are working in what type of environment and whether your family members are involved in the business.
- **Use and occupancy permit:** In most states, when you apply for your business license, you must also apply for a *use and occupancy permit* from the building department (or its equivalent in your state). This application normally results in a building inspector (and possibly a fire inspector) visiting your business location to get an idea of what sort of conditions employees will be working under. The inspector looks out for the interests of the people working at the location and checks for fire hazards, life safety issues, code compliance, building permits, zoning issues, and so on.

Federally issued licenses

If you are in a heavily regulated industry, then a federal license in your area of expertise may be required. This license lets the public know not only that you know your stuff, but also that you are a reputable company operating under the watchful eye of the government. Here are some industries that are required to operate under special federal-issued licenses:

- **Selling securities or providing investment advice:** You are required to be licensed by the U.S. Securities and Exchange Commission (`www.sec.gov`). If you are only selling *securities* (membership shares in exchange for capital investment) and are looking for a small number of investors, you may be exempt. See Chapter 11 for more information on registration exemptions.
- **Interstate trucking or any other form of interstate transportation:** You are required to be licensed by the U.S. Department of Transportation (`www.dot.gov`).
- **Preparing meat products or other foodstuffs:** You are required to be licensed by the U.S. Food and Drug Administration (`www.fda.gov`).
- **Manufacturing tobacco, alcohol, or firearms or selling firearms:** You are required to be licensed by the U.S. Bureau of Alcohol, Tobacco, and Firearms (`www.atf.gov`).
- **Radio or television broadcasting:** You are required to be licensed by the Federal Communications Commission (`www.fcc.gov`).
- **Manufacturing, testing, and/or selling drugs:** You are required to be licensed by the U.S. Food and Drug Administration (`www.fda.gov`).

If you are required to secure a federal license before opening your business, consider having your attorney guide you through the application process. The applications can be lengthy, and you want to make sure you do everything correctly. Whether you are approved or not can make or break your business.

Meeting Other Pertinent Requirements

You thought you were finished? You're dealing with the government here, remember? Between the federal, state, city, and county requirements, the paperwork is never-ending. Regardless, all businesses *must* handle two more things. The first is your federal tax identification number — you won't get far without it! The second is workers' compensation insurance — don't even *think* about hiring employees until this is taken care of.

Federal tax identification number

In Chapter 8, I go into detail on how to obtain your LLC's tax identification number (*tax ID* for short; also called an *employer identification number* or *EIN*). If you haven't done so yet, flip back to that section and *do it now.*

If you're reading this sentence sans tax ID number, then you're asking for trouble! Not with me, but with everyone else you intend to do business with. As a matter of fact, I don't think you can even make any of the filings I address in this chapter without having that annoying number. You can't apply for business or professional licenses, hire employees, or even open a bank account without one. I'd be surprised if you don't know your company's tax ID number by heart by the time you finish this book.

Workers' compensation insurance

All businesses that have employees are required to carry workers' compensation insurance to protect employees in the event that they get injured on the job and can't work or have medical expenses that need to be paid. This insurance is provided by private insurance companies but is required by law for each employee who works for you.

If you have a payroll company, you should also ask them about unemployment insurance. They may be able to get you a good deal and also tie it directly to your payroll. That way you won't have to update them whenever you lose or bring on employees!

(Record) Keeping Your Liability Protection

As you may have read in Chapter 2, limited liability companies offer two forms of liability protection:

- That which protects your personal assets from the liabilities of the business
- That which protects the business from your personal lawsuits and creditors

This second form of liability protection is, for the most part, unique to LLCs and is commonly referred to as *charging order protection.*

The best way to understand basic liability is to think of it as a piece of fabric — a *veil* — that protects you and your personal assets from your business's litigious predators. The term *corporate veil* specifically refers to the protection that the LLC provides to your personal assets if a lawsuit is filed against the business.

When a creditor of the LLC breaches this veil of protection and seizes your personal assets, it is called *piercing the veil.* In short, the limited liability, perhaps the most important attribute of an LLC, has been lost.

The one and only way to keep your veil of limited liability intact is to keep perfect records. Therefore, you must keep a close eye on your company's record-keeping practices. Not only is properly keeping records a practical solution for keeping all partners on the same page, but it shows the courts that you are a serious business and motivates them to treat you like one.

To pierce your veil, the creditor has to add you, as an individual, to the lawsuit against your company. In the complaint, the creditor will seek to impose personal liability on you, the owner, for the business's debts or wrongdoing (in other words, the creditor pleads the court to pierce the veil of limited liability). Then the creditor has to prove to the court that the veil of limited liability should be pierced. If the creditor proves that the veil should be pierced, the court will make you personally responsible for the judgment. This means that the creditor can seize and liquidate your personal assets to settle the claim.

In Chapter 20, I list ten important steps you must take to keep your liability intact. Here I address the most important one: record keeping. In this context, record keeping entails the following:

- Drafting comprehensive resolutions that document important decisions as they are made
- Storing your records at a secure record-keeping storage site or in a physical company kit (see the section "Creating a company kit" later in this chapter)
- Making sure that all members have constant access to those records
- Maintaining an updated membership roll
- Keeping all tax and financial records organized

Piercing the veil of limited liability is one of the most frequently litigated issues involving small businesses. If a creditor is persistent enough to sue your LLC, you can be confident that it will attempt to pierce your veil. After all, adding you to the lawsuit costs the creditor nothing. So you must make sure that all your ducks are in a row *before* you ever hit the courtroom.

Documenting your decisions with resolutions

Luckily, the government is pretty lax when it comes to LLCs (as opposed to corporations); therefore, strict and formal meetings of the members and/or managers of the company aren't required. What *is* pertinent, however, is that you document each important decision made by the members and/or managers. The documenting is often done in the form of a *resolution.*

When you create your operating agreement, you specify what percentage of approval is required to make major company decisions, as well as what constitutes a major decision in the first place — it could range from things like taking on a new building lease to taking on an investor. If you and your partners specify in the operating agreement that a simple majority of membership interests is all that's needed to approve a decision, and you are a majority stakeholder, then you are the only member who needs to agree to and sign the resolution.

Because drafting a resolution is such an easy process, you should use this method to document as many company decisions as possible. Common decisions you may want to make by way of a resolution include:

- Allowing the treasurer to open and use LLC bank accounts along with a designation of authorized signers
- Adopting a fictitious firm name (a *DBA,* for "doing business as")
- Approving a contract
- Leasing of property by the LLC
- Acquiring an independent audit of the LLC's tax and financial records
- Changing the LLC's fiscal tax year
- Approving salaries and bonuses of key employees

Creating a company kit

All limited liability companies need to have a *company kit.* Your company kit keeps all your important documents organized for you and covers your butt if you ever end up in court.

In the old days, the standard for a company kit was a single leather-bound binder. However, technology has taken over, and more and more people are opting for a digital company kit. Not only does this kit protect against loss and misunderstandings, but it allows *all* parties to have continuous access to important corporate documents . . . not just the person who is in possession of the physical kit.

When you form an LLC with a formation company, you may be enticed to pay extra for a physical company kit. If you go this route rather than the digital route, beware of the fill-in-the-blank forms that come with it. Because LLCs are so customizable, a one-size-fits-all approach doesn't work. Besides, most of these forms aren't even tailored to your state's specific laws governing LLCs.

When you receive your kit, collect the following documents to upload to it (or place in it):

- Your state-filed articles of organization and company charter
- Your operating agreement (if you already have it)
- Any company meeting minutes and resolutions
- A list of your members, their contact information, and their membership percentages
- Any cancelled membership certificates
- Your federal tax ID number and filing
- Your business licenses and state filings
- Any foreign filings that you have made in other states
- Your company's registered agent information for each state

If your attorney is forming your entity, he may provide you with a physical company kit, where you keep all of your important company records. But beware — many attorneys insist on keeping your corporate kit at their offices. This isn't because they want to save you real estate on your bookshelf. It's because they know that if you want to make any changes or obtain your records to defend a lawsuit, you'll have to contact them first . . . and very likely end up paying for their services each time.

Creating and maintaining a membership roll

Creating a membership roll is very simple. You just go online and enter in each member's name, address, and the amount of membership interest she has. If you have a physical company kit, you should have gotten a blank form to use for this purpose. Make sure to update this information every time your LLC's membership changes. Some states even require that you supply your registered agent with an updated copy of your membership roll. Most online company kit solutions offer this functionality.

Tracking tax filings and financial information

Your tax returns and financial reports show the backbone of your business. These records undeniably prove that your LLC is an operational business. Because they are backed up by bank statements and receipts, the courts take them very seriously as testimony to the intricacies of your business.

You need to hang on to your pertinent tax records and financial statements for seven years. These tax records show the courts that your company is, financially, a separate entity than the owners — in other words, you and your LLC don't share a bank account. Your financial information proves that you have been actively engaging in business and not using the entity as an extension of yourself (also called an *alter ego*).

Your operating agreement (see Chapters 9 through 12) should designate what sorts of financial reports the members have access to and how they can go about viewing the records. Tax returns, balance sheets, and profit-and-loss statements should be kept at your corporate office in case one of the partners wants to view this information. Also, in the event of a lawsuit, you will likely be required to hand over copies of this information to the plaintiff.

Chapter 14

Making Cents of Taxes

In This Chapter

- Understanding how your LLC is taxed
- Finding out what to file based on tax status
- Saving on taxes with your LLC

Just the thought of taxes probably makes you want to throw this book across the room, but don't do it. This chapter isn't the most entertaining one you're going to read, but it's quick and painless, I promise. Although taxes can be a pain in the butt, by educating yourself about them you gain the upper hand and can end up paying less. Just think, after reading this chapter, you'll be able to stride into your accountant's office with your head held high, with no problem discussing the tax basis of assets, tax reporting requirements for LLCs, and how you can avoid sending a chunk of change to the IRS.

LLCs can be taxed a multitude of ways, but most LLCs just stick with the default partnership taxation. And why not? It's a great way to be taxed! In Chapter 8, I go through all the various forms of taxation you can choose. At this point, I assume you've already elected your company's tax structure and are now ready to deal with the ins and outs of managing it — maintaining books, filing your federal returns, and so on — and avoiding any potential hiccups you may encounter along the way.

Although I touch on all types of taxation in this chapter, I spend the most time discussing partnership taxation because it's the most common to LLCs and, in my opinion, the least understood form of taxation.

If you're like most people, you get confused by tax information at times. Don't get discouraged. You don't need to know everything — just enough for planning purposes and to have an informed conversation with your business accountant. After all, an accountant spends his days poring over tax law and dealing with the IRS, so take advantage of his experience. Although having a basic understanding of the tax information I cover in this book is helpful, use an experienced accountant for the important stuff, such as distributing money to the members and filing the end-of-year tax forms.

Reviewing the Tax Types

Because LLCs are allowed to elect pretty much any tax status that suits them, the federal returns, information statements, and/or notices they're required to file each year vary accordingly. To review, an LLC can choose disregarded entity, partnership, corporation, or S corporation taxation. Check out Chapter 8 for help on which form of taxation to choose.

Disregarded entity taxation

Disregarded entity isn't so much an election as a default tax status for single-member LLCs. Single-member LLCs don't qualify for partnership taxation because no partners exist, so they're automatically subject to disregarded entity status unless they elect corporation or S corporation tax status.

Disregarded entity taxation can actually be beneficial for some real estate and investment transactions. When considered a disregarded entity by the IRS, your company is treated as if it doesn't exist, and you're taxed simply as an individual (or as a sole proprietorship, to be exact). This setup can be beneficial when executing tax credits, deductions, and strategies that only apply to individuals (see Chapter 18).

Partnership taxation

Partnership taxation is the default tax status for limited liability companies with more than one member. It's a form of *pass-through taxation* (where the profits of the business pass through to the owners to be reported on their individual income tax returns). The primary benefit of partnership taxation over other forms of pass-through taxation is that you can vary the profit and loss allocations to the partners.

Corporation taxation

The corporate tax status differs dramatically from all others. It's the only non-pass-through form of taxation an LLC can elect. The revenues and expenses, and thus the profits and losses, of the company don't pass through to the members but instead are retained in the company and taxed at the applicable corporate income tax rate. Because the corporation tax rate is generally lower than what an individual pays, this status can often be beneficial.

Additionally, when a member sells his interests in the company, the profit from that sale is subject to a very favorable long-term capital gains rate, which can result in substantial tax savings. The major drawback of corporate taxation, though, occurs when ordinary profits (called *dividends*) are removed by the members, causing a *double-taxation* scenario where the amount is taxed both as corporation profit and then owner income.

S corporation taxation

The corporation's answer to pass-through taxation, S corporation tax status, came about when small, closely held businesses (such as independent contractors) needed the ability to operate under the liability protection of a corporation but without the heavy tax and regulatory burden that comes with the standard corporation. Note that *S corporation* isn't an entity type, but instead simply a tax election that can be made by either a corporation or an LLC.

The S corporation's claim to fame is the members' ability to hire themselves and pay themselves a salary. Although the resulting tax burden is ultimately equal to the income tax and self-employment tax they'd pay with partnership taxation, the members pay income tax on only amounts over the salaries they pay themselves (as opposed to members subject to partnership taxation, who have to pay income tax and self-employment tax on all profits over their salaries). Obviously, you can't just pay yourself $1 and be done with it. The IRS stipulates that your salary must be consistent with others in your industry and your position.

Filing Your Federal Returns

Although you'll most likely delegate the filing of your federal tax returns to a competent accountant, I still recommend that you have a good, basic knowledge of what your LLC needs to do at tax time. You'll have much more-educated conversations with your accountant and also be able to review his work. After all, you sign those filings; don't you want to know exactly what you're signing?

Up-to-date versions of all the forms I mention here can be found on the online resource center at `www.docrun.com/dummies` (passcode is **onesmartdummy**).

Sucking it up with sole-proprietorship status

If you have a single-member LLC, the IRS classifies it as a disregarded entity by default and taxes it as a sole proprietorship. This designation means that the company doesn't have to file an information statement with the IRS like an LLC does, and you don't have to issue yourself a **K-1.** You simply report your company's income and expenses on a **Schedule C, Profit or Loss from a Business,** and attach it to your personal income tax return (your **Form 1040**) like you do for any other side income you have. If you have rental property, the profit and loss information is instead listed on a **Schedule E, Supplemental Income and Loss**.

Keep in mind that as a sole proprietor, you can't pay yourself a salary. Therefore, all your income is subject to self-employment tax, which you report on a **Schedule SE, Self-Employment Tax,** that you attach to your **Form 1040.** You can, however, deduct other employees' salaries as an allowable business expense.

If you have less than $5,000 in expenses for the year, you should be allowed to file the short form of the **Schedule C,** the **Schedule C-EZ.** Double-check with your accountant to make sure that this is the case.

Ponying up with partnership taxation

With partnership taxation, you don't file an actual tax return for your LLC. Instead, you file only an information statement — IRS **Form 1065, U.S. Return of Partnership Income.** On this statement, you report the company's income, deductions, gains, losses, and the allocations that are being made to the partners. After this statement has been filed, the company then issues a **Schedule K-1** to each member that shows what income and deductions have been allocated to her. The member then reports the allocations made to her (individually) on Part II of a **Schedule E,** which she attaches to her personal tax return.

Before you can file your IRS **Form 1065,** or any return for that matter, you need to obtain a tax identification number for your LLC. You can do that by submitting a **Form SS-4, Application for Employer Identification Number,** to the Internal Revenue Service or applying online at `www.irs.gov` (enter the phrase *SS4 apply online* in the search box). I recommend that you apply online so that you can get your number immediately (and I explain how to do so in Chapter 8).

Preparing Form 1065

All partnerships, including LLCs, are required to file a **Form 1065** by April 15 of each year. The **1065** isn't a tax return; it's a summary and information statement that lets the IRS know who is responsible for paying which percentage of the company's tax burden for the year. It's four pages long and contains six different schedules. (About ten other schedules can be filed with the **1065** if your accountant deems them necessary.)

The company also must make some tax decisions called *elections*. Elections can include decisions concerning the research credit, for example, and also depreciation of assets. These decisions can affect all the members and can have huge tax consequences. Therefore, whoever is preparing and filing the **Form 1065** must look to the operating agreement for guidance on how tax elections are to be decided. If the operating agreement doesn't address them, then all members should come together for a vote.

After **Form 1065** is completed, only one member needs to review and sign it; however, that member must answer to all the other members if they have a question or problem with the filing.

If you're operating as a single-member LLC, you don't need to file **Form 1065** because the IRS treats you as a disregarded entity and you're taxed as a sole proprietorship. I go over what filings are required for single-member LLCs in the earlier "Sucking it up with sole-proprietorship status" section.

Taking your accounting system into account

On **Form 1065**, you indicate the accounting method that your company uses. If you have a bookkeeping service or an accountant, you can just ask that person. If not, you have to choose one yourself.

Cash-based accounting is the simplest method of accounting and is generally used by smaller companies that do their bookkeeping themselves. With cash-based accounting, you classify income only when you actually receive it, and you classify expenses only when the checks you wrote have posted to your bank account. If your register matches your bank statement, with no other debits or credits showing, you're likely on a cash-based accounting system. If your income is over $1 million, however, I recommend that you ditch this accounting method and go with accrual-based accounting instead.

Accrual-based accounting is a little bit more difficult to track, but it offers the most tax benefits. It's a standard for most professional bookkeepers because it provides a more accurate picture of how the business is actually doing. Essentially, with accrual-based accounting, you record income when the sale occurs, not when you actually receive the money. You also record expenses when the invoice is received, not when your check is cashed by the vendor. With this type of accounting, spending more money than you have is virtually impossible. Also, at the end of the year, you'll show less profit that you'll need to allocate and pay taxes on.

Form 1065 asks for the tax year of the LLC, which is customarily a calendar year. LLCs are required to have the same tax reporting period as their majority members, and majority members are normally U.S. citizens who pay taxes on a calendar-year schedule.

Distributing K-1s to the members

After she fills in the **Form 1065** for your LLC, your accountant creates a **Schedule K-1** for each member of the LLC. The **K-1** contains the allocation information for each partner, including how much and what type of company income the member has been allocated and what sort of deductions he can write off. It also provides an updated analysis of each partner's tax basis. See Chapter 8 for more about tax bases.

The operating agreement tells you what percentage of profits and losses each member is allocated, but unfortunately, filling out the **K-1** isn't always as simple as just writing in the portion of each member's profits and losses. The schedule calls for different types of income to be reported separately, such as short-term capital gains, long-term capital gains, charitable contributions, royalties, interest income, and rental real estate income, among others. Having to calculate percentages of different types of income for a multitude of members can be a huge headache, so I recommend you leave it to the professionals.

Remember that one of the benefits of an LLC is that the company profits and losses don't have to be allocated to the members according to their ownership percentages. LLCs allow for *special allocations,* which means you can own 10 percent of the company and feasibly receive 100 percent of the profits and losses for a specific year. Granted, you can't make these decisions without having a good reason (specifically, one that doesn't involve tax evasion); however, if your accountant determines that your situation is sufficient, special allocations are easy to do.

When your accountant creates the **Schedule K-1s,** she files the originals, along with **Form 1065,** with the IRS. You'll get a photocopy of your **Schedule K-1** that you can use when filing your individual tax return.

The amount of profit that's reported on your **K-1** isn't necessarily the money that was distributed to you. In other words, you may have to pay taxes at the end of the year on the company's profits when you haven't even seen a penny of a cash distribution. That's because there's a difference between what the LLC allocates to you and what it distributes to you. *Allocations* are the profits and losses that you have to report on your personal tax return and pay taxes on. *Distributions* are your cash portion of the profit that you actually receive. I go over allocations and distributions in detail in Chapter 8.

Paying the actual taxes

If you're a United States citizen, you pay your personal taxes on IRS **Form 1040.** But your **1040** tax return doesn't include a line that specifies LLC income. If you take a look at **Form 1040,** you see that line 17 mentions business income. So here, you list the total income stated on your **Schedule E, Supplemental Income and Loss,** which you submit with your **Form 1040.**

You use a **Schedule E** to report all income and losses from business activities that don't constitute your primary source of income. If you're managing the day-to-day business of the LLC, you should be on the company payroll, and your regular paycheck is what's considered your primary source of income. The allocations the company makes on a yearly basis are considered secondary income. In other words, if all you do is sit at home and collect profits from businesses that you don't actually operate, and you don't have any "job" per se, that income is still reflected on a **Schedule E.**

If you're a single-member LLC and you're also a manager of the LLC, this information doesn't apply to you, and you don't list your business income and deductions on a **Schedule E.**

When filling out your **Schedule E,** you report all the business income and deductions in Part II.

Because the **Schedule E** isn't as simple as copying and pasting the information from your **K-1** (a few other schedules are involved), I recommend leaving the preparation of this form to your accountant. I include the basic how-to here only so you can familiarize yourself with it. Armed with this information, you can check your accountant's accuracy and have intelligent discussions with your accountant about the documents that she prepares.

If you're actively engaging in the business, you're required to pay self-employment tax on your percentage of the company profit. You must calculate your self-employment tax on the **Schedule SE, Self-Employment Tax,** which you file with your **Form 1040.**

Coughing up cash with corporation tax status

When you decide to be taxed as a corporation, you're subject to the same type of taxation that corporations are — with no exceptions. If you aren't used to corporate taxation, just think of your company in terms of being an official person that's separate from yourself. You don't pay taxes on behalf of your company. All taxes are paid by the corporation on the profits that are left in the business at the end of the year.

Licensed professionals get a bad deal

If you're a Professional LLC, you may be subject to a special form of taxation unique to Professional LLCs and Professional Corporations. The IRS governs this form of taxation by special rules, and it can change your tax outlook drastically. If you're a licensed professional, finding an accountant who has experience with this sort of taxation and can guide you through the process of operating your company under these strict limitations is imperative.

You report all of your business's income and deductions on IRS **Form 1120, U.S. Corporation Income Tax Return** — a separate tax return. (You send a signed copy of **Form 8832, Entity Classification Election,** to the IRS with your corporate tax return.) Your profits are subject to the federal corporate tax rate, which averages around 15 percent (for profits under $50,000). Then, if you distribute them to the members, those same profits will be taxed again as dividend income to the members. This situation is called double taxation.

Shelling it out with S corporation tax status

If you elect to be taxed as an S corporation, you file an IRS **Form 1120S, U.S. Income Tax Return for an S Corporation,** rather than the traditional partnership returns. The **1120S** is more of an information statement than anything else, because S corporations don't really pay taxes; they just pass the profits on to the owners for them to handle the burden.

When filing a **Form 1120S,** you prepare a **Schedule K-1** for each member (referred to as *shareholders* on this form) and give a copy of the **K-1** to each member so he can use the information when preparing his personal tax returns. You then submit one copy to the IRS with your **Form 1120S.**

With the **K-1,** you must also send to each member a copy of the **Form 1065** tax classification election and **Form 2553, S-Corporation Tax Election.** Not only is this step an IRS requirement, but it also explains to your fellow members why their LLC is filing taxes as an S corporation. For someone who isn't hip on all the tax flexibility inherent in LLCs, getting a **K-1** for an S corporation can be pretty confusing without an explanation attached.

If you're taxed as an S-Corporation, you're required to file **Form 1120S** by March 15 of the following year; if you're on a fiscal year that isn't the calendar year, the deadline is the 15th day of the third month after the close of the fiscal year. Depending on your state, you may also have to send a copy of

Form 1120S and the corresponding **K-1s** to your state tax board. Or, they may have a similar form that you need to file. Your accountant can assist you in pulling together all of the required filings for your LLC.

Avoiding LLC Tax Traps

Business is business, and the unwary can easily fall into quagmires. Every entity has its tax traps, and LLCs are no different. As long as you plan around them, you'll be fine.

Transferring assets into your LLC

For the most part, when your LLC elects partnership taxation, transferring assets into your company in exchange for membership is a *nontaxable event.* This term means that, for income tax purposes, the IRS recognizes no gain or loss. Problems arise only when debt or liability is involved.

LLCs have a tax pitfall known as a *deemed cash distribution.* It occurs only when one of the members reduces the amount of his liability. The IRS considers the reduction in liability to be a cash distribution, and like a cash distribution, the member must pay taxes on any of this amount that goes over his tax basis. (I describe tax basis in greater detail in Chapter 8.)

A good example of a deemed cash distribution is a member who transfers a piece of property into the LLC. Say that the property has a mortgage on it for $80,000. When the property is transferred into the LLC, the two members decide to refinance the property to include the other member as a personal guarantor. Unfortunately, the partner who transferred the property didn't realize that by refinancing it he was reducing his debt by $40,000 and that the IRS would consider that $40,000 a cash distribution. So at the end of the year, the contributing member has to pay taxes on $40,000 that he never actually received.

Had the members talked to a professional early in the game and chosen to obligate the member in some other way than refinancing the property, the contributing member could've avoided a big tax surprise.

Dealing with phantom income

When a partner is allocated a sizeable company profit that she has to pay tax on but she isn't actually distributed any profits, that allocation is called *phantom income.* Phantom income can be dangerous because a partner in the LLC can end up with a pretty hefty tax bill but no cash to pay it with.

Triggering gains on securities LLCs

Although a *securities LLC* — an LLC created for the sole purpose of holding securities — can be a great way to diversify and protect your investments at the same time, it can also be subject to a pretty serious tax trap. A securities LLC may be exposed to the investment company rules stating that the transfer of appreciated securities into the LLC triggers capital gains. This guideline means that after you transfer your securities into your LLC, you have to pay taxes on the capital gains that you realized from the date you purchased the securities to the date you transferred them to the LLC.

These rules apply only if

- You're classified as an *investment company* (which means that more than 80 percent of your LLC's assets are in the form of publicly traded securities).
- The securities you've transferred aren't already in diversified portfolios, and the transfer results in the diversification of your securities.

If both of these stipulations are the case, then the tax basis is *reset,* which means all your appreciation thus far is subject to capital gains taxes.

Members often experience some phantom income — especially in your LLC's beginning stages, when you need to keep the profits in the business to help it grow. However, you can feel pinched in the pocket if the business doesn't even distribute enough cash to the members to help cover the tax burden. You'll have to scrounge up the dough on your own. Garage sale, anyone?

Phantom income has a good and a bad side. The bad side is that it can happen to you. The good side is that you can force it on a creditor who obtains a *charging order* on a member's interest. A charging order is all that a creditor can go after if a member is liable personally, and it gives a creditor access to only the allocations and distributions that a membership interest can receive. If you allocate only profits to the members (who include the creditor with a charging order) and don't give any cash distributions to pay the taxes on those profits, how happy do you think the creditor will be? Needless to say, he'll be running for the hills and eager to settle the lawsuit in the member's favor. (Chapter 17 covers this strategy in more depth.)

You can add a provision in your operating agreement that can force the company to distribute enough cash for the members to be able to pay the taxes on their allocations. You can figure out a percentage that works for all members and also includes a percentage for state taxes. However, by doing so, you completely undermine the strategy that gets rid of creditors who have obtained charging orders.

Minimizing self-employment taxes

Even though LLCs aren't imposed the same double layer of taxation on profits like corporations are, you can still end up paying more in taxes if you aren't careful. And aren't you're supposed to be saving on taxes, not paying more?

The IRS hits LLCs and sole-proprietorships the hardest with self-employment taxes. Self-employment (SE) taxes are Social Security and Medicare taxes, and they're imposed in addition to the federal income taxes that you have to pay. These taxes amount to about 15.3 percent of the total income allocated to you. About 12.4 percent goes to Social Security, which will be paid out to you when you reach retirement (I hope), and 2.9 percent goes to Medicare, which is a form of hospital insurance. You use **Schedule SE, Self-Employment Taxes,** to determine the self-employment tax that's owed, and file it with your personal **Form 1040** tax return.

You have to pay self-employment taxes if

- Your LLC offers licensed services to the public, including accounting, actuarial science, architecture, consulting, engineering, health, and law.
- Your LLC is actively engaged in business. If your LLC engages in only passive activities, such as holding rental properties with the rent the only profit distributed to the members, then it's passive income and not subject to self-employment taxes.
- You work more than 501 hours during the LLC's tax year. That is, on average, about ten hours per week.
- You have the authority to execute contracts on behalf of your LLC.

If you're an investor or partner in the business, you aren't required to pay self-employment tax on the money you earn.

Luckily, a cap limits the amount of earnings subject to self-employment taxes per year. Unluckily, that amount is $117,000, which is way over the national average — and that only applies to Social Security. Anything over that amount is still subject to the 2.9 percent Medicare tax. This increases to 3.8 percent if you are married (filing jointly) and make in excess of $250,000, or if you are single and make $200,000 or more.

Currently, you can only deduct half of what you paid in self-employment tax when calculating your *adjusted gross income* — the amount you have to pay income tax on.

Becoming a silent partner

Not everyone is required to pay self-employment tax. SE tax is for wage earners, not necessarily big fish. So if you're a silent partner who doesn't deal with the day-to-day matters of the business, you may be able to find a way around the mandatory self-employment tax.

First, make sure your LLC is manager-managed. If it's member-managed, it's hard to attest that you, as a member, aren't doing any managing of the day-to-day affairs! Then find someone trustworthy who can act as manager and will be able to enter into contracts with your and the company's best interests in mind. Finally, make sure that you work no more than 500 hours per year for that particular company.

Obviously, this work-around isn't possible if you're one of the operating partners. But if you're simply an investor, you may be able to eliminate the required self-employment taxes and keep a hefty chunk of change in return.

Choosing to be taxed as an S corporation

Unlike partnerships, the owners of S corporations can hire themselves. In fact, they're expected to hire themselves; an S corporation without any owners on the payroll is a sure path to an audit. The main benefit of hiring yourself is that you're paid as a regular employee, as you'd be if you had any regular job. This setup means that the income you receive isn't subject to self-employment taxes. You still have to pay regular payroll taxes, but this amount is often much less.

Of course, you must hire yourself for a wage that's standard in your industry. If your company hits a windfall, you can't necessarily take all the cash out as a bonus because you're limited to having a salary that's believable for an executive of your rank, in a company your size, in your industry. For instance, if everyone else in similar positions is pulling around $100,000 per year, you can't take home $10,000 and not expect to raise some red flags with the IRS.

Keep in mind that if you're an owner who is active in the business's day-to-day operations, the IRS considers you to be an employee. Therefore, you need to include yourself on the company payroll and pay payroll taxes on that income. Make sure to take enough of a salary that it's in line with the standard for your position in your industry. After that, the remaining income you take is classified as company profit, which you don't have to pay self-employment taxes on. You're only subject to personal income tax on this profit. That's a 15.3 percent savings!

Chapter 15

Expanding Your Empire: Going National!

In This Chapter

- Foreign-filing your LLC
- Handling business licenses in multiple states
- Managing a multi-state company

With technology advancing at a blinding pace, the world is getting smaller by the hour. Throw up a website, and all of a sudden you're transacting business with customers all over the globe! The world is yours for the taking. Just keep in mind that when you're wheeling and dealing all over the map, the various states and countries in which you touch down are going to want a piece of the action.

Although the implications of having physical operations in multiple countries can get very complicated and are beyond the scope of this book, there is a very good chance that eventually your LLC will go *national.* And that in itself can be a quagmire if you don't have a road map to guide you.

If you're simply selling to customers in a particular state, then you aren't beholden to that state in any way. However, things change when you get into hiring employees and owning or leasing property. You need to know whether, according to the laws of the state in question, you are considered to be *transacting business* there. The definition is usually left vague and open-ended . . . and most often ends up in the state's favor.

If you think that you may be transacting business in a particular state, you need to know how to formally take your company to the national level. With proper planning and the right help, the process of going national can be as exciting as it gets. So have fun with it, big shot!

Registering Your LLC in Multiple States

Say you have a restaurant in Florida, your home state, but want to expand into Georgia and North Carolina. When you open locations in those states, you are *doing business* there. By law, if you're doing business in states other than the one in which your LLC was formed, you must register in those states. This is called *foreign-filing*. The foreign-filing process is similar to the formation process, but it's always in addition to the initial formation. Your *domicile* (the state in which your LLC was formed) doesn't change; foreign-filing just makes it legal for you to transact business in the other states in which you've registered.

Not foreign-filed anywhere? Doing business only in the state in which your LLC was formed? Then you're simply called a *domestic LLC*.

Defining "doing business"

The term *doing business* is important in LLC law because it creates the guidelines under which you may or may not be required to foreign-file. Of course, you'll want to foreign-file in as few states as necessary. With each additional state comes additional laws to learn and red tape to follow, as well as some pretty hefty fees. Unfortunately, as you find out in the next section, foreign-filing is sometimes necessary.

Determining whether you're actually "doing business" in another state can be difficult. What if you tend to ship your products to customers across the country, yet your office and all your employees are housed in your LLC's home state? Which state's laws must you follow? Remember, each state's laws are different. However, if you think that you might be required to foreign-file in a particular state, here are a few questions to guide you:

- Does your LLC operate out of a physical office or retail store in the state?
- Are you often physically in the state, meeting with customers and vendors and transacting business (instead of just speaking with them over the phone or by e-mail)?
- Does a large portion of your LLC's revenue come from that state?
- Do any of your employees physically work in the state? (In other words, do you pay state payroll taxes?)

Knowing that you are *not* doing business in a state

The Revised Model Business Corporation Act (RMBCA) gives criteria for when an entity is *not* transacting business in a state. Although it was written for corporations, the act also applies to LLCs.

Not sure if you are technically doing business in a particular state? If your LLC is doing only one or two of the following things, chances are you aren't required to foreign file in that state. Regardless, you should double-check with a corporate consultant in that state, a local registered agent, or an attorney.

- Maintaining, defending, or settling any proceeding (that is, being involved in a lawsuit)
- Holding meetings of the board of directors or shareholders or carrying on other activities concerning internal corporate affairs
- Maintaining bank accounts
- Maintaining offices or agencies for the transfer, exchange, and registration of the corporation's own securities or maintaining trustees or depositaries with respect to those securities
- Selling through independent contractors
- Soliciting or obtaining orders, whether by mail or through employees or agents or otherwise, if the orders require acceptance outside this state before they become contracts
- Creating or acquiring debts, mortgages, and security interests in real or personal property
- Securing or collecting debts or enforcing mortgages and security interests in property securing the debts
- Owning real estate or other forms of property
- Conducting an isolated transaction that is completed within 30 days and that is not done in the course of repeated transactions of a like nature
- Transacting business in interstate commerce

You can view the laws regarding transacting business for each state at `www.docrun.com/dummies/transacting_business` (password is **onesmartdummy**).

If you answered yes to any of these questions, then there's a good chance that you are doing business in the state and are required to foreign-file your LLC there.

If you're an online retailer or service provider, don't freak out. Making money from customers in a particular state doesn't necessarily mean that you're transacting business there, as far as the law is concerned.

Foreign-filing to do business in multiple states

Yes, it's a necessary evil, but with the help of your registered agent and perhaps a good advisor, foreign-filing can be a breeze. Just be aware that if you're planning on doing business in numerous states, the filing fees can get pretty hefty, especially considering that a lot of states charge more for filing foreign LLCs than they do for domestic ones. Unfortunately, you can't get out of the fees, but at least you can try to incorporate these costs into your budget.

Registering (also called *qualifying*) your business in another state is remarkably similar to the formation process. This stuff should almost be second nature to you after creating your original LLC. (I cover those steps in Chapter 6.) Registering is relatively easy, and foreign entities generally have less paperwork to deal with in terms of certain licenses and permits after the registration is completed. Whew . . . something to look forward to!

When you register, you submit an application. In many states, this application is referred to as a *certificate of authority.* You can download the basic form off the secretary of state's website for the state in which you are attempting to register, or you can have a formation company create the application for you.

Tsk, tsk, tsk . . . Haven't foreign-filed?

So you've been doing business in a state and haven't registered there . . . what do you do? First, call your attorney. Second, drive to the police station and turn yourself in. Don't worry — just kidding!

The reality is that nothing major will happen to you. If your LLC is sued, you should be able to defend it in the local courts. You may simply have to get legit and foreign-file first. However, if you decide that you want to sue someone in that state, you definitely need to register there first.

As for penalties, some states are more harsh than others. You may have to pay the fees and taxes that should have been paid, plus fines and interest. However, if your tax burden wasn't huge, most states are happy to have the business and will waive the fines and fees just to get you in compliance. In other words, it's not such a big deal. Just make sure to register ASAP!

When filling out the application, you'll likely have to provide the following:

- **The name of your LLC:** List the name as it appears on the articles of organization in your home state.
- **The name of your LLC in the state in which you are registering:** If your LLC name isn't available in the state in which you're registering, you may have to select an alternative name under which to do business in that state.
- **Entity domicile:** This means the date and state in which the LLC was formed.
- **Registered agent name and address:** Give the name and address of your LLC's registered agent in the state in which you are registering to do business.
- **Your principal office address:** It's common to put your resident agent's address here as your principal office in the state. However, you can also list your corporate office address if you have an office in that state.
- **Name and address of each manager and/or member:** The information that is required here varies from state to state. Check the state form you are using or contact your formation company if you have any questions.
- **Signature of a manager or member:** One manager or member's signature is required to file the registration.
- **Signature of resident agent:** Your resident agent is required to sign the application stating that he has agreed to be your resident agent.

In most states, you must show a proof of good standing from your LLC's home state before you can file your application. This proof is often called a *certificate of good standing* or *certificate of existence.* The certificate shows the state with which you are foreign-filing that your LLC is in good standing in the state in which it was formed. To make it even *more* difficult, some states require that you provide a certified copy of your articles of organization. You can contact the secretary of state's office in your home state to obtain these documents, or you can have your formation company do it for you. After you've obtained your certificate of good standing (and your certified copy of your articles, if required), send it in with your application.

Before your application can be approved by the secretary of state, it must be signed by your resident agent in that state. If you're registering to transact business in multiple states, you may have a hard time keeping everything in order and staying on top of your filing dates. Running a company is hard enough without all the tedious paperwork involved in maintaining your LLC's compliance in a zillion jurisdictions. For a nominal fee, you can have a multi-state resident agent company serve as your resident agent in all the states in which you're doing business. The company can assist you with the filings, stay on top of your paperwork, and even let you know when your filings are due!

After your foreign-filing package is ready to be sent to the state, you mail it to the Secretary of State (called the Department of State in some jurisdictions), along with a check covering the cost of the filing. At `www.docrun.com/dummies` (password is **onesmartdummy**), you can find an up-to-date list of all Secretary of State offices and their respective addresses. Then, you just wait for it to be sent back with an "approved" stamp on it!

Maintaining Your Multi-State LLC

Although it may sound sexy to say that you're a nationwide company, every state in which you register to transact business brings a pile of paperwork and loads of fees. Your annual or biannual filings may include

- Annual report of members and managers
- Annual publication in a local newspaper
- Franchise tax reports
- Income tax reports
- Business licenses

Depending on the state, many other filings may also be required.

When you're operating in multiple states, you'll probably be required to go through a similar filing process for each and every state in which you are doing business. If you don't have a physical location in a particular state, some filings (such as building permits) may not be required; however, others, such as initial reports and business licenses, are still necessary. If you aren't sure about these basic filing requirements, contact the secretary of state's office (I provide contact information at `www.docrun.com/dummies` — password is **onesmartdummy**) or your registered agent in that particular state.

Working with a formation company to track your filings

Because of the multitude of filings that are required for every state in which you are transacting business, you may want to consider hiring a formation company to handle everything for you. That way, you can maintain compliance and spend your time running your business rather than struggling with strange filings for states you aren't familiar with and, worse, trying to remember when all those filings are due.

The Big Four registered agent companies offer services tailored to each state. The Big Four include

- Corporation Service Company or CSC (`www.cscglobal.com`)
- CT Corporation (`ct.wolterskluwer.com`)
- InCorp (`www.incorp.com`)
- National Registered Agents, Inc. or NRAI (`www.nrai.com`)

For instance, for $99 per state, InCorp offers a Company Compliance & Resident Agent Service that tracks your filings, filing dates, mail forwarding, and so on. It also has an online system where you can view all your filing dates, your filings, your corporate documents, a compliance calendar that lists the due dates of all your filings, and so on. These compliance tools — common among the Big Four — are a huge help because filing dates vary from state to state, and the tools can keep you from paying hefty late fees for missed filings. Most smaller registered agents don't have the technological proficiencies that bigger agencies can afford.

Submitting initial reports

In every state in which you foreign-file, you need to file an initial report. This report is usually identical to the initial report that you file when forming a new LLC, which I show you how to do in Chapter 13. You need to make sure that the information you submit in one state is the same as the information you submit in another state. When you're doing many filings in other states, sometimes it is hard to remember that your LLC is still only *one* entity with one set of members and one federal tax identification number.

Obtaining business licenses

If you are foreign-filed in multiple states, you need to apply for state and local business licenses, just as you would if you were forming your LLC in that state in the first place. Use your corporate office address in that state to determine your local jurisdiction (the city or county). If you're using your registered agent's address as your corporate office address, then use that zip code to find which local agencies you need to register with. Your registered agent should have this information.

In addition to general state and local business licenses, your LLC may need to obtain other special permits, depending on the type of business you're engaged in. For example, if you're operating a physical office in that state, then you may have to obtain a use and occupancy permit. If you're engaged in a heavily regulated industry such as alcohol, then you may need to obtain special alcohol permits. In Chapter 13, I show you how to file for and obtain the requisite business licenses for your LLC. This information is applicable to foreign-filed entities as well — the only difference is that you'll be doing it in multiple states rather than just the one in which your LLC is domiciled.

Paying taxes

If you determine that you are, in fact, doing business in multiple states, the tax man in each state will want a piece of the action. How much will you owe? Well, that depends. Each state handles taxation differently. In general, each state requires you to allocate a percentage of your sales according to an *apportionment formula,* because sales figures alone don't give a complete picture of how much business you are doing in that state. For example, you may have your headquarters and manufacturing operations based in Rhode Island but make most of your sales in other states. The formula entitles Rhode Island to a larger share of your income.

Fortunately, most states use a common formula involving three factors of your business:

- **The property factor** is the average value of your *in-state property* (furniture, equipment, buildings, inventory, and so on that's stored or used in that state) divided by your *total property* (the furniture, equipment, and so on that you own everywhere).
- **The payroll factor** divides your *in-state payroll* by *total payroll.*
- **The sales factor** equals your *in-state sales* divided by *total sales.* ***Note:*** Some states give sales a double weight because it's the most important factor.

The states average these three factors to determine how much business you are doing in each state. Because a particular state may use a different formula than the rest, you could end up paying taxes on more or less than 100 percent of your actual income. The LLC may even have to withhold taxes on non-US resident members. Be sure to consult with a CPA in each state to confirm the formulas and each member's tax obligations.

If you're selling tangible goods and will be paying sales tax in another state, you definitely need to open up a separate bank account for that state. Keep your sales receipts for each state separate so you know which states to pay sales tax to.

Withdrawing from a state

What happens when you're no longer doing business in a particular state and don't want to keep up with the paperwork of being registered there? Withdrawing (or *canceling*) your LLC is very simple — you just file a *certificate of cancellation* with the secretary of state's office in the state from which you want to withdraw.

The certificate of cancellation is a pretty standard form and contains some basic information, such as

- The name of the LLC as stated in the articles of organization
- The name of the LLC as it is doing business in that state, if different
- The effective date of the cancellation, if different from the filing date
- Any other information that the manager or member filing the certificate of cancellation feels is relevant

You can normally download this form off the secretary of state's website and mail it in with the filing fee. You don't really need an attorney to file the certificate of cancellation. However, you should seek legal advice if the entity you are withdrawing has assets or physical locations in that state.

Changing your home state

Sometimes, you don't want to expand your empire as much as you simply want to *move* your empire. This process is often referred to as *domestication* or *redomiciling,* and it means moving your LLC from one state to another.

If the state you're moving to allows it, you can keep your existing LLC and transfer it to the new state and then dissolve the record in the old state by filing a regular old dissolution. (I discuss dissolution filings in Chapter 16.)

If your state does not allow for this sort of easy transfer, then you need to form a new LLC in the new state, transfer over all of your assets, and then dissolve the old LLC. This isn't necessarily a simple process; however, if your LLC has elected partnership taxation, there is a good chance it can be a tax-free one. Make sure to speak with a qualified CPA before going this route.

Find out if your state allows a simple redomicile procedure (or if you need to create a completely new replacement LLC in your new state) on `www.docrun.com/dummies/redomicile` — password is **onesmartdummy**.

Sometimes the best solution is to start over

When Bart opened Bart's Bikes, he was a different man. He lived on Venice Beach and was a California boy at heart. But soon, the company grew and before he knew it, he was doing business in Oregon. Little did he know that Oregon was a bike lover's paradise and within months, Bart's Bikes took off there. Bart, getting older and wanting to trade in his surfboard for some hiking boots, decided that a move to Oregon was in order.

Within a year, all of Bart's business was in Oregon, and he decided to close up shop in Venice Beach, leaving that life behind for good. Now Bart faced a predicament. Bart's Bikes, LLC, was formed in California and foreign-filed in Oregon, but he wanted to change his company's domicile to Oregon. After all, why should anyone put up with California's high taxes and exorbitant fees if he doesn't have to?

Bart heard about a process called *domestication,* where he could file some forms with Oregon's secretary of state's office and make Oregon the LLC's new domicile. Unfortunately, Bart discovered that Oregon is one of the states that does not provide for domestication. In this case, he had his attorney assist him in withdrawing and dissolving his California-based LLC and transferring the assets to a new, Oregon-based LLC.

Chapter 16

Dissolutions: Every Beginning Has an End

In This Chapter

- Understanding what a dissolution means
- Examining reasons your LLC may dissolve
- Deciding whether a dissolution is right for you
- Knowing how the dissolution process works

"Nothing gold can stay." — Robert Frost

All things eventually come to an end to make room for new beginnings, and your LLC is no different. Sometimes, business simply doesn't go as planned and you're left with no option but to close up shop. Other times, legal or tax technicalities get in the way and force the demise of your business.

Whatever the reason, you need to make sure you do things by the book. If you don't cover all your bases before and after the dissolution, you may be asking for a fiasco later on. So before dissolving your LLC, I urge you to thoroughly review this chapter, get together with your fellow members, and create a detailed plan for dissolution.

After you create the dissolution plan, make sure your accountant reviews it thoroughly and clears you of any gnarly tax traps you may be inadvertently walking into.

Getting Clear on the Context

Listen up, 'cause this is important: Just because your LLC dissolves doesn't mean that it's gone for good. The term *dissolution* is used in so many varying contexts and so often changes meaning from state to state that it'll make your head spin. So to keep you from developing a migraine, I lay out the basic terminology for you in this section.

It's important to know the difference between a *dissolution* and a *termination.* When your LLC faces what's often referred to as a *dissolution* (an event that forces your LLC to re-organize), your LLC doesn't necessarily need to wind up its affairs and terminate all business activities. In many cases, you and your partners have the option of continuing business, just under slightly different circumstances. If your LLC faces a *termination,* though, your whole operation is at the oh-so-irreversible end.

The one exception to the difference between a dissolution and termination is a *tax termination* or *technical termination*. Just when you were getting pretty clear on the terminology, leave it to the IRS to come in and muddy things up, right? Here's the skinny: A tax termination is not fatal and generally doesn't affect your LLC (unless you want it to) and only results in the termination of your tax status. I go into this topic in the later section "Tax terminations: 'Cause the IRS says so".

It's Melting! Examining the Reasons Your LLC May Dissolve

Following is a list of common reasons your LLC may dissolve:

- **Voluntary dissolution:** When your business isn't working out — management is deadlocked over an issue, the company isn't profitable, or it was simply a planned event — and you and your fellow members unanimously decide to terminate the business, a voluntary dissolution takes place.
- **Administrative dissolution:** The secretary of state may revoke your company charter and terminate your LLC, causing an administrative dissolution. This usually occurs when you fail to file your state reports or don't pay your state fees for an extended period of time.

- **Judicial dissolution:** Upon the request of a creditor, the attorney general, the IRS, or a disenfranchised member, a court may order a judicial dissolution. If a judge orders you to dissolve your LLC, it's usually due to things such as bankruptcy, failure to pay federal taxes, a voting deadlock among members, or being caught red-handed engaging in criminal acts.
- **Tax termination:** Normally not fatal to your LLC, a tax termination takes place when 50 percent or more of your LLC's membership is transferred. When this happens, the IRS considers your old LLC to have been terminated and all your company's assets and capital to have been transferred to a new entity (which is really the same LLC that existed before).
- **Fictional dissolution:** The state's version of the tax termination, a fictional dissolution occurs when a member, intentionally or unintentionally, creates a *dissolution event (a legally defined occurrence that forces a restructuring of the partnership)*. The specific events that cause a dissolution event varies from state to state, but it generally occurs when a member (owning 50 percent or more of the company) exits the LLC for reasons such as bankruptcy, death, or retirement, or is simply kicked out by the rest of the members.
- **"Inept professional" dissolution:** Okay, so that's not the technical term, but it's the term I use for when the underlying licensed professional of a professional LLC — a doctor, lawyer, and so on — loses his license to practice and therefore has to dissolve his company. After all, what use is there for an LLC that's no longer allowed to transact business? I discuss Professional LLCs in detail in Chapter 2.

Don't worry if you don't understand the distinction among all these dissolutions just yet. This list is just a primer; in the following sections, I explain everything in much more detail.

Voluntary dissolutions: Even the mighty fall

Business is hard. Really hard. If you're tired of struggling and have decided to move onto greener pastures, don't beat yourself up about it. You aren't alone: One in ten businesses don't make it past their first year. All great entrepreneurs have had to call it quits on something at one point or another, and because you had the foresight to set up your businesses as an LLC, closing up shop is relatively painless. Well, aside from the unending slew of questions from your non-business-owner friends and relatives, of course.

Voluntary dissolutions aren't always cause for mourning. If an LLC is used for a short-term project, such as film financing or a real-estate deal, the members understand that the LLC will be dissolved when the project has run its course, thus allowing the members to dissolve the operation and split the cash, simple as pie.

A voluntary dissolution is relatively simple to perform. If all the members are onboard and no legal proceedings are looming, terminating the LLC is pretty straightforward: You wind up the affairs of the company and file articles of dissolution with the secretary of state. I cover the process in the "Undergoing the Dissolution Process" section later in this chapter.

Most states require that all members of the company agree to the dissolution before it can take place. This is to protect minority members from investing in companies and then having no say when the other members want to close up shop, take the money, and run.

If your LLC isn't up-to-date with state filings or has outstanding tax liabilities, your articles of dissolution may very well be rejected, and you won't be allowed to formally dissolve until you handle those burdens and pay up. Ironically, if you neglect these responsibilities long enough, the state dissolves your LLC for you, which I discuss in the next section.

Administrative dissolution: The state giveth and the state taketh away

When I was little and would disobey, my mother always used to threaten (jokingly, of course), "Jennifer Lee Reuting, I brought you into this world and I can take you out." Well, the secretary of state shares that credo, except in this case, there's no kidding around. If your LLC "misbehaves" — doesn't file its required disclosure statements or doesn't pay its state taxes — the secretary of state automatically dissolves your LLC, often referred to as an *administrative dissolution.*

Luckily, should you be faced with an administrative dissolution, most states have an option for *reinstatement* (also called a *revival*). In order for this to happen, you'll likely have to file an updated disclosure statement and pay all back taxes and fees, along with pretty hefty penalties. Upon reinstatement, the default is fully remedied, and it is as if no dissolution had ever occurred. Even the state forgives you fully. At the end of the day, they're just happy they got the extra money out of you!

Reinstatements must be completed within a set period from the date of dissolution; often two years, depending on state law. So don't dawdle!

Only the state in which your LLC is domiciled has the authority to dissolve your LLC, even if it's registered to transact business in multiple states.

Judicial dissolutions: When the gavel strikes

In rare cases, the court of law has the authority to dissolve and/or terminate the existence of your LLC with what is called a *judicial dissolution*. It may also be referred to as an *involuntary dissolution,* because, well, if it happens to your LLC, you can probably bet that the majority of your members weren't rooting for it to happen (to say the least).

Generally, judicial dissolutions are only done at the request of the state attorney general, one or more members of the LLC, or an unsatisfied creditor. Because of the irrevocable nature of this sort of dissolution, judges often consider it a method of last resort.

Courts are only granted the authority to perform a judicial dissolution if your state's laws have a specific statute allowing it. To understand how your LLC may be at risk, review your state's laws in regards to this. A list of state laws on dissolutions can be found here: `www.docrun.com/dummies/dissolution` (password is **onesmartdummy**).

Action by the attorney general

If you or any of your members are in the habit of performing criminal acts in the name of your LLC, you'll definitely want to plan for a sudden dissolution by mandate of the state attorney general.

What are "criminal acts," you ask? The term is pretty loose, but it generally refers to forming your LLC under fraudulent circumstances and/or engaging in illegal conduct, gross negligence, or fraud. Let's just say, if your business involves running a sweatshop or swindling elderly folks out of their pensions, you can pretty much assume you qualify.

Luckily for the consumers of the world, LLCs that have been dissolved by mandate of the courts often cannot be reinstated. Of all dissolutions, a judicial dissolution directed by the attorney general for criminal acts has the greatest chance of resulting in a permanent termination of the business.

Action by one or more members

Judges love operating agreements. Why? Because if every LLC had a well-planned and executed operating agreement in place, the judge could actually make his afternoon tee time instead of suffering through *another* case involving member disputes.

Most member-dispute cases arise from situations that could have been avoided from the get-go with a well-written operating agreement, such as a voting deadlock among members, or a disenfranchised minority member that feels her investment is being wasted. If, upon formation of the LLC, all rules and expectations were laid out in the operating agreement, then there would be a guiding framework in place to mediate any disputes or misunderstandings as they arise. Instead, the judge has the right to mediate by imposing a judicial dissolution that may fully terminate an operating company, all because of a simple disagreement.

If you happen to be the minority member with the bone to pick, a judicial dissolution can work in your favor. The law allows for LLCs to be dissolved at the request of a member for acts of misconduct or negligence by the other member(s) or for breach of the operating agreement. When this happens, your LLC is forced to terminate and liquidate.

If the judicial dissolution wasn't ordered for reasons of criminal acts or negligence, there's a good chance your state statutes provide for the ability of the remaining members to continue on with the business should they choose to do so. In some states, even a *minority* of the members has the option to continue! It simply needs to be allowed for in the operating agreement of the LLC. In this case, a formal dissolution would take place, thereby distributing the share of the company's assets to the disgruntled member, then the remaining members can decide to not take their share of the distributed assets and instead continue the existence of the company on their own.

The courts have more important jobs to do than referee disagreements among members, not to mention that the legal fees of using the court system make it incredibly cost prohibitive. The best thing you can do is sit down with your partners as soon as possible (*before* any disagreements arise) and devise an operating agreement containing a detailed procedure for dealing with disputes. I show you how to do so in Chapter 9.

Action by an unsatisfied creditor

If a creditor obtains a judgment for a claim against your LLC, or your company has acknowledged in writing that a claim is owed, he can drag your LLC into court and request a judicial dissolution. This step is usually taken on the grounds that the LLC is insolvent and will not have the ability to pay the debt at any point in the near future. Creditors must be paid first from the sale of assets in the event of a dissolution and liquidation, so forcing that sale may be the only way they can recoup their losses. In some states, if you've provided for it in your operating agreement, then you and your members may choose to patch the company back together after the creditor has been paid, and continue on with business.

In the case of a judicial dissolution and subsequent liquidation, the court will appoint a *receiver* (or *liquidator*) to receive the LLC's assets and distribute them to the creditors and then to the members.

Tax terminations: 'Cause the IRS says so

First, this section applies only to LLCs that are taxed as the default partnership taxation. If this doesn't apply to you (for example, your LLC has elected corporation or S corporation taxation or is a single-member LLC), you can skip this section.

Even though you're an LLC — the newest and most advanced of all business structures — as far as the IRS is concerned, you're no different than two wiseguys off the street who wrote a partnership agreement on a napkin and didn't remember to file a DBA (Doing Business As, also referred to as a *fictitious firm name*). And, as with partnerships, if one of you wiseguys leaves, the partnership is null, kaput, deader than a donut. Terminated. As in tax terminated. (Get it?)

If your LLC transfers 50 percent or more of its membership within a 12-month period, the IRS considers your partnership to be terminated and, assuming the remaining partners want to continue the business, a new one to be formed. This dissolution can happen easier than you realize — for instance, if an equal or majority partner retires or passes away, or if you decide to take on a sizeable investor. It also doesn't have to happen in one transaction — it can be caused by multiple transactions, added together, resulting in more than a 50 percent change of ownership.

Now, before you freak out, with the exception of this event possibly causing a fictional dissolution (which I address in the following section), your LLC inherently remains unchanged. You don't need to make any filings with the secretary of state. You don't need to notify your vendors, creditors, or employees. You don't even need to obtain a new tax identification number! It doesn't sound like much of a termination at all, does it?

Well, I *am* talking about the IRS here, so there's a downside. Here are two things to remember about tax terminations:

- You must make new tax elections. Any existing tax elections that your LLC made (see Chapter 8 for more info on tax elections) are terminated, and you must make new ones.
- Watch out for tax traps. Although tax terminations are generally nontaxable events, they can force the existing members to recognize a gain or a loss on their personal tax returns, so you definitely want to plan for any possible tax traps before transferring membership.

If you think you may have cause for a tax termination at any point in the near future, flip to Chapter 14 where I go over the whole muddle in more gritty detail.

Fictional dissolution: A bureaucratic hassle

To help you understand the quirks of the present, I need to first arm you with a brief history lesson. When LLCs first came around, the IRS had a bit of a fit. A few rogue states created this new entity — a sort of hybrid between a partnership and a corporation — and the IRS had no idea how to tax it. They finally decided that LLCs were subject to partnership taxation, but in order to qualify, the LLCs must be substantially differentiated from corporations.

Long story short, the IRS mandated that LLCs were forbidden from taking on two of the four main corporate characteristics: They couldn't have a *perpetual duration* (an unlimited lifespan) and they couldn't have free transferability

Does your LLC have a limited life span?

Way back in the day, in order for the IRS to allow LLCs to be taxed like partnerships, LLCs had to *act* like partnerships. One of the major suppositions of a partnership (unlike a corporation, for instance) is that it has a limited lifespan. After all, partners can't live forever right? Therefore, LLCs were restricted to a duration of 50, or sometimes 30, years, depending on the state. This meant that after 30 or so years, the members of the LLC would have to get together to specifically elect to continue and file a revised version of their articles of organization with the secretary of state, containing a new duration or dissolution date. If they didn't do this, then their entity would automatically be terminated by the state they are domiciled in.

Thankfully, the IRS and subsequently the states have decided that LLCs are no longer constrained to a set lifetime; however, if your LLC was formed prior to the "age of enlightenment," you need to check your articles of organization to make sure you don't have a set duration.

If you find that your LLC is limited to a certain length of time, you need to file an amendment to your articles of organization before that time elapses. Otherwise you're just looking at another reason the secretary of state could do an administrative dissolution on your LLC!

of ownership. To comply with the first restriction, the states ruled that a maximum duration (often 50 years) needed to be specified in the articles of organization upon forming the LLC.

As for the second restriction (no free transferability of ownership), well it's a bit more complicated. The states created their own version of the *tax termination* (see previous section), mandating that any transference of 50 percent or more of the membership results in a *dissolution event*. This means that unless the remaining members get together (often within 90 days of the dissolution event) in a formal and documented fashion and unanimously decide to continue the partnership, then the LLC is dissolved. Because a dissolution event is so easily remedied by a vote of the members, a dissolution of this sort is often referred to as a *fictional dissolution*.

Luckily, in the years since LLCs came on the scene, the IRS has seen the light (albeit slowly) and now no longer imposes these rudimentary partnership restrictions on LLCs. The limited-duration rule was the first to go, and most, if not all, states now consider LLCs to be entities with unlimited life spans, as long as you request it in your articles of organization (see Chapter 6). As for the free transferability of ownership, the states have been much slower to adapt to accommodate the new freedom allowed by the IRS. For the most part, the IRS allows free transferability of ownership interests, as long as the portion of membership being transferred doesn't exceed 50 percent. In this case, a *tax termination* may occur, which I discuss in the "Tax terminations: 'Cause the IRS says so" section.

If you look at all the state laws on the issue, you see that they're varied. The more progressive states now automatically allow free transferability of ownership — in other words, no more silly *dissolution event* business — unless the members specify otherwise in the operating agreement. Other states reverse that policy, keeping the fictional dissolution limitation as the default law while allowing the members the power to do away with it in their operating agreement. And some states haven't updated their laws at all.

The moral of the story is that depending on the laws of your state, the fictional dissolution may be a very real problem for your LLC. To make your life as easy as possible, I organized a list of all the state statutes that address the fictional dissolution so you can easily check to see what does or doesn't apply to you. You can view it at `www.docrun.com/dummies/dissolution` (password **onesmart dummy**).

Considering the Future Before Calling It Quits

Sometimes a dissolution isn't simply a dissolution, as in the case of administrative dissolutions, tax terminations, and the other types in which your business can continue to operate. If you and your partners are voluntarily dissolving the company, then that decision will undoubtedly lead to the termination and liquidation of your LLC. Winding up the affairs of a business can be super-simple or complex and troublesome depending on the circumstances. However, all terminations share one characteristic: They're pretty darn *final.*

In other words, you usually can't take it back. So you owe it to yourselves and the business you've created to do some preliminary work before closing that chapter for good. Read on to find out what steps you should take before termination.

Keeping your LLC on life support

First, you and your partners need to determine whether or not dissolution is even the right move for your business. I know that when the going gets tough, you may have trouble seeing any alternatives. And you're all probably looking forward to when you can completely resign the failed business to the past and move forward with a clean slate. I, like any entrepreneur, have been there before.

However, if there is any possible way you can avoid formally liquidating and terminating your LLC, do it. And the reason is this: The LLC actually has to be *in existence* in order to offer its impenetrable stronghold of liability protection. A dissolution substantially weakens your LLC's liability protection. In California, for instance, creditors of the LLC can go after the members *personally* for the debts of the company within four years after the date of dissolution or until the *statute of limitations* (the length of time after an act occurs that the law will allow you to be held responsible for it) has expired on the cause for action, whichever is sooner (see California Corporations Code Section 17355). Dissolving your LLC may give a greedy plaintiff complete access to your personal assets.

If your LLC has substantial debt, your best bet is to wind up the affairs as much as possible without formally dissolving the LLC with the secretary of state. In other words, keep your LLC on life support (for example, keep paying your state filing fees and tax returns) as long as you can. Or, at least, until the statute of limitations runs out.

Keeping your LLC on life support does have drawbacks. You'll have to continue paying state fees and maybe even franchise taxes. In high-tax states such as California, which has a minimum $800 annual franchise tax, the best move financially may be to take the liability risk and wind up your company.

An LLC with substantial losses that has elected to be taxed as an S corporation has an added consideration. Because you usually aren't able to deduct those losses against your personal income until the company has been formally dissolved, keeping your LLC on life support can become a costly endeavor. In this case, run the numbers, carefully taking into account any unforeseen liabilities your LLC may face, and take whatever path is more financially viable for the members.

All in favor? Taking the vote

If you've made it to this point, you're probably aware that LLCs are ridiculously flexible entities. You can generally structure your LLC however you want by placing certain restrictions and allowances in your operating agreement. A common restriction is forcing certain members into a sort of silent partnership by issuing them *nonvoting* membership interests. However, in the event of a termination of the company, most states are quick to override this restriction. Even if the operating agreement specifies that a certain class of membership isn't allowed *any* voting privileges whatsoever, most states still give those members a say in whether or not the LLC can be dissolved.

Unless you and your partners have already unanimously agreed to terminate the company, you need to check your state's laws and see where you stand when it comes to the voting rights. Some states require a unanimous vote, other states require a majority, and other states allow each LLC's members to decide for themselves by placing a special provision in the articles of organization. To make the arduous task of terminating your company a wee bit easier for you, I aggregate all state laws regarding this topic at `www.docrun.com/dummies/dissolution` (password is **onesmartdummy**).

When you're finally ready to take the vote for dissolution, make sure to hold a proper meeting, keep meeting minutes, and create a formal, written resolution that all members sign. I go into detail on how to document important decisions like these in Chapter 13. This way, the other members have no recourse if they change their minds afterward, and they can't claim that you did it without their permission.

If your LLC is managed by separate managers, your state laws likely require that the dissolution of the company be approved by a majority of the managers (in addition to approval of the members).

Planning for the future

Unfortunately, after you get all the members to agree to a dissolution, the negotiation process begins. I've found that, in the event of a termination of a business, the chances for amicable negotiations among the members is highly correlated to how extensive the operating agreement is. Hopefully, when starting the business, you and your partners had enough foresight to lay out terms and procedures for the possibility of your business not succeeding as you'd planned. Sadly, this isn't often the case.

When you decide that the end is imminent, you and your partners need to sit down and work out a few things. Going into this meeting, all members should have a pretty good idea of what they want to do with their lives after this chapter has been closed. Your future plans often play a big role in the negotiations, and things can get pretty sticky when two or more of the members are interested in continuing on in the same industry, whether they intend on starting new companies or going to work for competitors.

When creating — and often, negotiating — a plan for the future, you and your members may want to address the following questions:

- Are any of the partners going to remain in the same industry? If so, are any of those partners restricted from contacting the defunct company's customers, suppliers, and/or previous staff members?
- Do any members have the right to use the business's intellectual property? If so, under what conditions? You may have spent a small fortune building your brand, and you may want to protect it.
- Who will handle the dissolution process? The members need to agree on which of them will spearhead the process of dissolving, as described in the next section.
- Who is responsible for maintaining the company records so that they can be accessed if any issues arise in the future?

Undergoing the Dissolution Process

With all of the steps to dissolve an LLC, it almost seems harder than forming one in the first place! After years in business, your LLC may have a lot of baggage. In the end, dissolving your company is something akin to a divorce — the longer you have been married, the more you have to sort out. In this section I take you through the dissolution steps so you can file your one or two-page dissolution form with the secretary of state, knowing that you're completely protected from anything coming up in the future and biting you in the ass(ets).

Everyone must go through the following three-step process when dissolving an LLC:

1. **Acknowledge the end is here.**

   This is simple — the LLC is legally forced to dissolve, or the members vote to discontinue the business. In the preceding section I go over the logistics of creating a plan and making sure all of the members are on the same page.

2. **Wind up the affairs.**

   This process can be simple or long and arduous, depending on the sheer amount of paperwork, creditors, clients, and business associates that you have acquired over the years. In this stage you liquidate and distribute your company's assets.

3. **Terminate the company.**

   After all your bases have been covered, this is the easy part — you just file paperwork. You make the required filings to withdraw from whatever states you have registered to transact business in; then you file *articles of dissolution* with your local secretary of state.

Now that you have an overview of the entire process, in the following sections I go over some of the more important steps in greater detail.

Settling your debts: Paying creditors

When your LLC is formally dissolved, your liability protection diminishes substantially. Therefore you need to be as meticulous as possible in dealing with any current and possibly future creditors and claims.

The laws that dictate how an LLC manages its creditors vary from state to state, so you have to research your state's laws on the issue before taking any action. I collected all of the state laws (current at the time of publication) regarding the notification of creditors and posted them here: `www.docrun.com/dummies/dissolution` (password is **onesmartdummy**). Generally, most states recognize the distinction between creditors and claims that the LLC knows about *(known claims)* and those that it doesn't *(unknown claims)*.

Dealing with known claims

Any money that your LLC currently owes and any judgments that have been filed against your LLC generally fall into this category of *known claims*. All known claims must be dealt with properly before the company can be dissolved. You may even be required to include an affidavit to this effect in your articles of dissolution you file with the secretary of state.

Your state laws provide a specific process for you to deal with known claims. This procedure varies widely from state to state, but is probably a variation of this: You must notify the creditor in writing that your company will be dissolving and request that he submit his claim within a certain time frame. Generally, the deadline for a creditor to submit claims can be no less than 120 days.

Include the following information in the notification letter:

- A statement that you intend to dissolve, including an approximate dissolution date, if you have one.
- What information you want the creditor to give when they send in the claim (invoice numbers, dates, and so on).
- The deadline by which claims should be submitted (check state statutes for the minimum time frame you can allow).
- A paragraph stating that any claims received after the deadline won't be honored.
- The person and mailing address to which the creditor must send the claim (typically your registered agent's address).

Send all notification letters via certified mail. You need to have receipts proving you sent each letter.

The good news is that if a creditor fails to submit his claim(s) prior to the cut-off date, his claim no longer has merit and will not be honored, even by the courts. This means that when it comes time to distribute the proceeds from liquidating the assets, the money that would have gone to that creditor can instead go to other obligations, or even be distributed to the members!

If you are dissolving and don't want to give your hard-earned cash away to creditors, you may be tempted to transfer the assets into a safe place before dissolving, thereby preventing the claimants access to it. Unfortunately, as simple as this remedy sounds, it's also very illegal. It's called *fraudulent conveyance* of assets and is a very serious offence that the courts will undoubtedly not take lightly.

Accepting or rejecting claims

After you receive a claim, you have the option of either accepting it or rejecting it. If you choose to accept it, keep in mind that everything is negotiable. You can often settle a claim for less than the total amount. Just make sure that after you settle a claim with a creditor, you pay it.

If you choose to reject a claim — usually because you don't think it is valid — you have to use your discretion to consider whether the creditor will seek recourse. If you think the creditor may be a problem, talk to your attorney to prepare for any actions the creditor may take after the company has been dissolved. When you reject a claim, you should write a letter to the creditor stating that you are rejecting it. If possible, and if your attorney thinks it's a good idea, give a brief explanation as to why you are refusing the claim. This way the rejection will hold extra weight if it is ever brought for questioning in a court of law.

Dealing with unknown claims

While your LLC was in business, it likely left some sort of mark on the world. Even if the operating business has been dissolved, your products are still out in the world and/or your services have still made an impact, therefore there is still going to be residual liability. Any claims that could arise in the future from things like negligence or product liability fall under the category of unknown claims.

Because you can't notify these claimants in writing — after all, you don't know who's going to come out of the woodwork later on — the state provides a remedy: Publish a notice of dissolution in a local newspaper. With the advent of the Internet, it's a rather arcane remedy . . . but hey, it works in your favor! After all, who reads those notices, anyway?

Again, you have to check your state's laws for the details, but the publication should be published in the county where your business is located and should contain a description of the LLC and its business and specify that claims against the LLC must be filed within a certain period of time or the claim will be no longer enforceable. The publication should also clearly state the method that claims are to be filed.

If the claim is filed within the set time period, or prior to the statute of limitations, whichever is sooner, the creditors have the right to go after the members personally for the judgment to the extent of the amount of money that was distributed to the member upon the liquidation and termination of the company. Because of these sorts of unknown claims, I encourage you to rethink formally dissolving your company and instead, allow the statute of limitations to run out. (See "Keeping your LLC on life support," earlier in the chapter.)

If you are registered in multiple states, publish the notice of dissolution in every state that your LLC conducts business in. This can be time consuming, so I recommend that you get your multistate registered agent to help you.

The LLC can provide for unknown claims by obtaining insurance and/or setting aside some of its assets instead of distributing that portion of the proceeds to the members. This may be a good idea if your company has substantial liabilities and you just want to sleep better at night.

Giving each his due: Paying members

After the proceeds of the sale of your LLCs assets have gone to settle its debts (as discussed in the preceding section), you can now focus on distributing whatever is left (if anything) to the members. The Internal Revenue Code of the IRS directs a specific order in which the members are to be paid; however, this order can be overwritten in the operating agreement.

Generally, the first to be paid are the members who are owed distributions. For instance, if the LLC recognized a profit but for some reason didn't distribute that money to a member (the cash was needed for something else), then that member is first paid what he is owed. Also, if a member has made a loan to the company, then that member is paid back first.

After the members have been paid what they are owed, the remaining money is used to refund the members for their initial contributions. This may seem strange, but the money that you invested is returned to you before receiving any share of the actual profit. If there isn't enough money to return the member's initial contributions, then whatever profit is distributed is split into relevant proportions. However, this isn't set in stone and how members are reimbursed upon dissolution can be structured whichever way you like in your LLC's operating agreement. This usually requires the consent of at least a majority of the members, however. Check your state laws for clarification on this.

Did your investment in the company only consist of services? Well, services have a value too! Meet with the rest of the members in the company and decide what the value of your services was worth. You can look at current pay scales in your industry as a guideline. For instance, if you worked for free for the company for one year, and your peers were paid $50,000 for that same year, then you can reasonably ask for $50,000 as a return of your initial capital (services) contribution.

After the initial contributions have been returned to the members, any remaining cash is usually distributed to the members according to their percentage of ownership. If a member owns 30 percent of the company, then she gets 30 percent of the remaining cash. If you and the other members of your LLC want to vary this arrangement, you have to amend your operating agreement or create a formal resolution showing that all members are onboard. You also need to check that your plans are in line with your state's laws.

Wrapping up the government affairs

After the creditors have been paid and the members have been reimbursed — and perhaps even given some extra dough — you need to deal with taxes. In most cases, you have federal, state, and local tax forms to file.

To file your final federal return, you just file a normal return (or information statement, depending on how your LLC is taxed) and check the box at the top that indicates that this is a final return. If your state requires you to file a special LLC tax return, then you also need to file a final version of this return as well.

The numerous tax returns and addendums that you're required to file vary widely depending on the type of taxation your LLC has elected, so make sure to clear everything with your accountant before formally dissolving your entity with the state. I discuss tax returns in more detail in Chapter 14.

Only after you are in *good standing* — all filings are up to date and all taxes have been paid — in each state where your LLC transacts business can you start the withdrawal and dissolution process. Your registered agent should be able to provide you with your status in each state and tell you whatever steps you may need to take to get back into the state's good graces. Sadly, if you have failed to file your annual returns in many states, this can be a costly endeavor.

Making it official: Filing the dissolution

After your affairs have been completely wrapped up, you officially dissolve your LLC by filing articles of dissolution with your secretary of state (also referred to as a *cancellation*). When these articles have been formally filed, your company's record doesn't disappear altogether; instead, its public status is shown as *dissolved* or *terminated.*

If your LLC is registered to transact business in multiple states, you need to *withdraw* (often referred to as a "withdrawal" or "cancellation," depending on the state) from all other states before you can *dissolve* your company in your home state. The withdrawal process is similar to the dissolution process and usually requires a nominal fee. Just keep in mind that you don't file articles of dissolution to withdraw from a state. States have separate forms for this purpose. After you have withdrawn from all states you are foreign-filed in, only then can you formally dissolve your LLC in your home state.

If you have a multistate registered agent, you may benefit by letting him handle the entire withdrawal and dissolution process for you. Coordinating with many state agencies at one time can be a big hassle, especially because they all have different time frames for processing the paperwork. Leaving this job to the pros who already have relationships established with states' offices is definitely worth the extra fee.

Generally, articles of dissolution consist of

- The name of the company
- A list of the members of the company
- The reason the company is dissolving
- The date that you wish the dissolution to become effective
- Any information regarding unpaid taxes
- The members' signatures and the date the form was signed

You may also need to include a statement, signed by the managers (or members, if member-managed), that states that the LLC has handled all of its liabilities, distributions have been made to the members, no lawsuits are pending, and that payment arrangements have been made for all judgments (if any).

Some states have it backward and require you to file your dissolution papers before paying your creditors and winding up your affairs. You need to check your state's laws to see whether or not this is the case. To help you out, I collected all the state laws (current at the time of publication) on the issue. You can view them at `www.docrun.com/dummies/dissolution` (password is **onesmartdummy**).

Dealing with the tax consequences

The tax consequences can be good and bad for the members when dissolving an LLC. Your accountant can go over the pros and cons with you when you run your dissolution plan by her before dissolving. Remember that if your LLC isn't profitable, the losses can also be passed on to the members (assuming you elected partnership taxation), which can offset other income and save you and the other members a nice chunk of change come tax time!

If your LLC is canceling debt that the members were personally responsible for (for example, paying off bank loans), then the IRS treats these transactions as income to the members, which can cause some unexpected tax burdens. This is often referred to as *phantom income,* which I discuss in further detail in Chapter 14. You can also read more about this rule under Section 108 of the Internal Revenue Code, which I include at `www.docrun.com/dummies/irs_section_108` (password is **onesmartdummy**).

You have many other tax considerations if your LLC has employees. You must make sure that you're caught up on your federal and state payroll taxes and unemployment insurance. Again, your accountant is the best person to help you.

Following the dissolution checklist

Now that you have a good idea of what the dissolution process entails, you can feel confident that when you finally do commence the "beginning of the end," you'll have all your bases covered. If you have decided to *not* leave your company on life support, or you've reached the end of any common statutes of limitations (for example, the amount of time someone has to sue you for an incident), then you are ready to dissolve your company!

To help you along and make sure that no stone is left unturned, follow this checklist:

- ❑ Hold a meeting of the members and vote to terminate the LLC. Make sure this decision is reflected in the operating agreement or in a resolution signed by all members.
- ❑ Liquidate (sell off) all LLC assets for cash.
- ❑ Make any final federal tax deposits that are due
- ❑ File final quarterly or annual employment tax forms (IRS **Form 940**).
- ❑ Issue final wage and withholding info to employees (IRS **Form W-2**).
- ❑ Report W-2 information to the IRS (IRS **Form W-3**).
- ❑ If necessary, file the final IRS **Form 8027**, Employer's Annual Information Return of Tip Income and Allocated Tips.
- ❑ File federal tax returns.
- ❑ Issue payment information to subcontractors (IRS **Form 1099-MISC**).
- ❑ Report information from 1099s issued (IRS **Form 1096**).
- ❑ Report business asset sales (IRS **Form 8594**).

- ❑ Report sale or exchange of property used in the LLC (IRS **Form 4797**).
- ❑ File final employee pension/benefit plan (IRS **Form 5500**).
- ❑ If necessary, report the exchange of like-kind property (1031 exchange).
- ❑ Cancel all state and local business permits.
- ❑ Cancel all fictitious firm name filings.
- ❑ Transfer all intellectual property (domain names, patents, state and federal trademarks, and so on). You and your partners can decide who gets to be the lucky beneficiary of these things.
- ❑ File the last state tax return.
- ❑ Pay all current and past due franchise and corporate tax fees.
- ❑ If necessary, obtain a certificate of good standing with your state tax bureau.
- ❑ Send notification of dissolution to vendors/creditors.
- ❑ Publish a notice of dissolution in the local newspaper in each jurisdiction where you have transacted business.
- ❑ Pay or reject all creditor claims.
- ❑ Pay all debts that are owed to members, including distributions that were never made.
- ❑ Distribute any remaining profit to the members according to their ownership percentage.
- ❑ Pay any back fees that are owed to the secretary of state in each jurisdiction where you transact business.
- ❑ Withdraw from all states in which you are foreign-filed.
- ❑ File articles of dissolution with the secretary of state.
- ❑ If necessary, notify your customers of the dissolution.

Part V

LLCs on Steroids: Advanced Strategies

A Few Simple Strategies for Asset Protection

- Use a nominee to make it harder for others to find your assets.
- Use multiple LLCs to segregate your assets from one another so that if one asset — such as a piece of property — is engaged in a lawsuit, the others are safe from seizure.
- Form two companies in different states to separate your business's assets from the actual operations of the company.
- Transfer all your personal assets into a family LLC that keeps financial instruments, such as stocks, bonds, cash, and mutual funds, safe.

Visit `www.dummies.com/extras/limitedliabilitycompanies` for an article on how to use an LLC for estate planning.

In this part . . .

- Addressing the basics of liability protection for your business and personal assets.
- Using advanced strategies for asset protection.
- Discovering how LLCs and real estate were made for each other.
- Learn some pretty nifty strategies on how to protect your investment properties by using multiple entities.

Chapter 17

Using LLCs to Cover Your Assets

In This Chapter

- Recognizing who can come after your assets
- Understanding how LLCs protect your assets
- Looking at some easy asset protection strategies

This chapter very well may be the most important one you read. After all, why would you want to work so hard to build your future only to have someone else take away all the assets you've accumulated? If you think the fact that you observe good business practices means this chapter doesn't apply to you, think again. Lawsuits are getting out of hand in this society, and no one is exempt. Simply owning something of value puts you at a much higher risk than even the shadiest businessman. After all, the term *frivolous lawsuits* exists for a reason; lawsuits don't need to be soundly based or even well intentioned.

A lot of people are looking to get something for nothing. Unfortunately, that means that hardworking folks like you, who have built up a sizeable nest egg, are a target. Aside from buying expensive insurance policies that, when it comes down to it, may or may not have your back, the only thing that you can really do to protect yourself is to plan ahead and structure your assets so they're safe. Doing so now is important because when you're in a lawsuit, it's too late. From here on out, you must take steps to protect your assets every time you save money, start a new venture, register intellectual property, make any big purchases, get married, plan your estate, and so on.

Because LLCs have *dual liability protection* (where the company is also protected from the owner's personal lawsuits), they've been revolutionary for asset protection, especially personal asset protection. LLCs are such a big piece of the puzzle that, when an attorney sees you're protecting your assets in an LLC, she'll often advise her client not to sue you in the first place. No insurance company can match that sort of protection!

In this chapter, I show you how you can protect your assets for the rest of your life by forming an LLC and how you can safely own high-risk assets (assets that are very likely to be sued) while protecting everything else you've worked for.

Knowing the Dangers: What Can Happen without LLC Protection

More than 50,000 lawsuits are filed in the United States every day, and the numbers keep growing. Litigation has become a way of life for Americans; the collective mindset is shifting to that of "get somethin' for nothin'," and small businesses — the lifeblood of the American dream — can pay a heavy price. Although a large corporation may be able to cover the costs of an everyday lawsuit relatively easily, these legal fees may be debilitating to a small business.

You may think you're exempt, but chances are that if you haven't been sued yet, it won't be long. Although businesses tend to get sued most often, you're also likely to be sued personally. Actually, the law of averages say that within your lifetime, you'll be sued twice. And that's at today's numbers; can you imagine tomorrow's? As hard as paying the $75,000 legal bill on a frivolous lawsuit can be for a small business, it can be even harder for an individual. Even if you win, you may have nothing left! This fact is why using LLCs to protect assets and deter lawsuits is just as important for individuals as it is for businesses.

Often, attorneys tie in asset protection with estate planning. Although protecting your estate is imperative — making sure that it actually makes it to your kids and not into the hands of some Joe Schmo who tripped over a sprinkler on your front lawn — estate planning doesn't really have much bearing on protecting your assets from litigators. In other words, just because you have an estate plan does *not* mean that your assets are protected while you're alive. Find out more about using an LLC for estate planning at `www.dummies.com/extras/limitedliabilitycompanies`.

Lawyers and creditors come calling

The saddest thing about lawsuits is that even if you win, you lose. A lot of these lawyers who take on frivolous cases work on a *contingency basis,* meaning they don't charge the client unless they win the case. So ultimately you may be the victor, but you're the only one paying legal fees. Legal fees for defending a frivolous case can easily amount to hundreds of thousands of dollars, which can be debilitating for a small business. The only way to protect against having to pay outrageous sums of money for seemingly petty arguments is to stay out of court in the first place. I'm not saying that you should settle a lawsuit brought against you. I'm saying that you should make your assets either unapparent or unattractive to the wolves that are scoping them out. LLCs can do just that.

The people and businesses who loan you money — your creditors — also have their eyes on your hard-earned assets. Had a bad month and didn't keep up with your debt? Your creditors will no doubt be looking at how they can capitalize on their loss — and rightfully so. They lent you the money, and they need to get it back. If you let an angry creditor have his way with your assets, you'll be in a huge hole. To prevent this situation, make sure that you have an LLC in place that protects your assets. When you're in control of your assets, attractive creditor settlements are pretty easy to come by.

The rise of the frivolous lawsuit

According to the *Wall Street Journal,* frivolous lawsuits cost the average family approximately $3,520 per year. Don't be a statistic. Using LLCs to protect your investments and your assets is normally enough of a deterrent to keep you out of the courtroom in the first place!

Back in the old days, business was done on a word and a handshake. If a person didn't live up to his agreement, he would face the shame and disappointment of the people around him. That disgrace was enough to keep people in their place. Money was only associated with hard work, not simple accidents. If you slipped in the supermarket, you'd just be embarrassed. That's all. You wouldn't be thinking about all the free cash you could get from the local family business.

Nowadays, things have changed. Lawyers patrol hospitals, and commercials run on TV for class-action lawsuits. If you've ever been in a car accident, however minor, you've most likely received a flood of letters from personal-injury attorneys looking to make a buck.

If you back out of a parking spot too fast and get into a fender bender, an attorney will likely be looking to sue you. If you don't have deep enough pockets, or he can't get to your assets, he'll sue the insurance company, the car maker, your Aunt Margaret who purchased the car and loaned it to you to drive — basically, anyone and everyone who has money. Often, it doesn't matter whether you injured someone; all that matters is whether someone with deep pockets can be targeted. Lawyers play on jurors' emotions by making them sympathize with the plaintiff, who would rather make a quick buck in a lawsuit than earn it by working, and chastising you for being one of the lucky few who has struck it rich. The game is called Robin Hood, and it's one you needn't play.

The IRS stakes a claim

If you aren't at enough risk from lawsuits and creditors (see the preceding section), remember that you still have to worry about the IRS. When given the right authority, the IRS can impact your financial life more than any individual creditor can. It gets free reign, including seizing your belongings and bank accounts.

Now, although the IRS is part of the government — especially where individuals are concerned — it's subject to a few rules, all of which you can use to your advantage. When the IRS deals with an LLC, it must follow the same laws and restrictions as most creditors, except with a little bit more knowledge and disclosure. For instance, if the IRS goes after you personally, it can't seize your interests in the LLC and liquidate your company. It can only lay claim to your *economic interest* and must wait for you to pay out. This aspect is unique to the limited liability company and is due to the charging order protection benefit of LLCs I mention throughout this chapter. (Hit the later section "Taking charge of charging order protection" for a specific definition.)

Hiding your assets from the IRS can be difficult because you're most likely reporting them and/or depreciating them on your tax returns. You don't want to hide from the IRS (that's tax evasion), and you shouldn't have to. Your asset protection plan should be so solid that the IRS doesn't have the ability or, better yet, the justification to go after your assets to settle an IRS debt.

Liens are lurking

Some lawyers are really good, and the worst thing that can happen is to get sued by one of them without having any sort of asset protection plan in place. Imagine you get taken to court over a contract dispute, and the attorney talks the judge into placing a *prejudgment lien* on your assets; now you can't move, touch, or transfer your assets or even conduct business with them until the lawsuit has been decided.

Say the amount of the lien covers the entire amount due on a ten-year contract, and it's a pretty hefty amount. Your assets don't quite cover it, so your bank account is attached to the lien, and you aren't even able to write checks. If this happens, you may have a hard time buying necessities, such as gas and food, but the worst thing of all is that you most likely won't be able to pay your attorney to defend the case. Eek! You're trapped! If this happens, you may find yourself in a position to settle immediately and for unfavorable terms.

What about when this happens to your business? What if you're unable to move money, write checks, pay bills, pay your rent, pay on your business loans, or make payroll for two months or longer? Where would your business be then? Unless you have significant personal savings, this could be debilitating.

Even if you get through the lawsuit without a prejudgment lien, you aren't necessarily in the clear. If you win the lawsuit, you're okay, but what if you lose? Say someone gets a judgment on you for more than you can afford to pay at the moment. Unless you can immediately write a check for a big chunk of change, the judgment creditor can request to have a *judgment lien* placed on your assets, which leaves your bank account completely frozen. Your home, rental property, savings account, mutual funds, CDs, kid's college fund, *everything* is frozen and can be liquidated to pay the lien. Have equity in your house that you want to use to pay for the lawsuit? You can't refinance or sell your house to take advantage of the equity; you can't even collect income from your investment properties or invoice your clients in your business! Instead, your home will be put on the auction block, right before your eyes. Liens are the worst thing that can happen to you in business. Unless you have an LLC, that is. Read on to find out what strategies to use to protect you and your business.

You don't have to lose a lawsuit to have a judge impose a lien. Anyone can request a lien on your assets, including creditors or the IRS.

Getting the Best Asset Protection with LLCs

Some asset protection plans just try to hide your assets from prying creditors and potential plaintiffs. Although that should be the first line of defense, it isn't nearly enough. You see, if you do get dragged into court, you'll probably be subpoenaed for the information or asked about it while on the stand. In either case, you shouldn't lie. If you do, you'll have a lot more to lose than your assets; you can lose your freedom.

If predators see that you have hordes of cash and real estate sitting in an LLC, they very well may not go after the assets in the first place. Why? Because LLCs are very tough nuts to crack, and the predators know this. They also know that if you're smart enough, you can trap them in a situation where they're paying out money for *you!* And because most credit agencies work on commission and attorneys work on a contingency basis (as I describe in the earlier section "Lawyers and creditors come calling"), they don't want to waste their time on you if they know they aren't going to get paid.

Setting up a Fort Knox for your personal assets

As the old adage goes, "You aren't in business until you've been sued." Nowadays, as litigious as society is, you don't even need to be one of the bad guys to be dragged into court. By simply transacting business with the general public, you open yourself up for myriad potential lawsuits, and no matter how arbitrary the complaint is, the destruction it leaves in its wake can be crippling.

The states know that many fewer businesses would be started if entrepreneurs were forced to put their livelihoods at stake every time they began new ventures. Therefore, certain entity types are afforded *limited liability,* which protects the owners and managers of the business from being held personally responsible for the debts, obligations, and misdeeds of the business. Out of all the entities, LLCs offer the most comprehensive form of this protection (hence the name *limited liability company*).

An LLC protects you from the liabilities that you inevitably come across during the normal, everyday course of business. Should your business get sued or go bankrupt, your *personal assets* (home, car, investments, and so on) and other businesses (if they're in different LLCs) can't be taken away. Only the assets included in the LLC that got sued are at risk.

The one exception to the normal protection of LLCs is professional limited liability companies (PLLCs), because personal responsibility is essential to being a licensed professional. I discuss this unique entity type at length in Chapter 2.

If you want to use an LLC to protect your personal assets, you must do so in advance, not after you've already been sued. Too many victims of frivolous lawsuits have shown up at my office wondering what they can do to get out of them — asking how they can save their homes and bank accounts that are about to be taken away. Unfortunately, at that point, it's always too late. If only they had spent some time planning, such as reading this book or working with an advisor, they could've saved everything.

By establishing your new business or placing your existing business in an LLC, you sign your company up for the most cost-effective, ironclad insurance policy around. A business insurance policy may still have a role in keeping the business itself from having to pay for its own misdeeds. However, insurance policies are only effective in lawsuits arising from product or service liability and usually don't pay out to unsatisfied creditors if the company can't meet its debt obligations. Also, whereas insurance companies can be wishy-washy about paying out, the LLC is pretty fail-safe.

Here's the clincher: LLCs are so foolproof that most attorneys often avoid the time and cost of suing them in the first place and instead opt to negotiate a settlement. Now, that's protection!

An LLC's veil of liability protection isn't infallible. If you don't take certain measures to establish and maintain that your LLC isn't simply an extension of you (your *alter ego*), a court can disregard the LLC and allow the plaintiff or creditor access to your personal assets. This situation is called *piercing the veil* of liability protection. In Chapter 20, I show you ten important steps you can take to protect your veil of limited liability.

Although an LLC shields you from being held personally responsible for minor negligent acts, it does nothing for egregious criminal acts or willful misconduct. Also, the LLC does offer some protection against certain government creditors, such as the IRS, with one main exception: As a member or manager of an LLC, you can be held personally responsible for the failure to pay payroll taxes. Therefore, if you're withholding taxes from your employees' checks and for some reason fail to submit that money to the tax man, you're putting your personal assets at risk.

Taking charge of charging order protection

Many moons ago, when a creditor obtained a judgment against a partner of a partnership, the creditor could simply take the partner's interest in the business (and, proportionally, all related assets) and liquidate them to get paid, often leaving a ravaged business in his wake. Clearly, this scenario wasn't fair to the other, innocent, partner(s) in the partnership just going about their business when suddenly everything they worked for was destroyed!

To remedy these unfair acts, the courts amended the laws so that partners in an LLC, unlike owners of corporations, have another layer of liability protection called *charging order protection.* A member can have two different rights in an LLC: *economic rights* (the right to receive profit allocations and distributions from the company) and *other rights* (which include the right to vote on important matters or be involved in the management of the day-to-day business). Charging order protection grants only economic rights to the assignee, unless the operating agreement specifies otherwise. In other words, the creditor has no other choice but to shut his trap and sit back and receive whatever distributions you decide to grant him. You can stop profit distributions altogether, and the creditor has no say in the matter. Read on to find out how this arrangement works.

Seeing how corporations leave you vulnerable

To understand how a lack of charging order protection can leave you vulnerable, consider the example of Josh, who started a business, J.R. Marine, Inc., when he was only 23. To get started, he borrowed some money from his grandfather by selling him a 5 percent share in the business. He was smart and good with numbers, and the business grew steadily over the years. Ten years in, J.R. Marine had taken over the market. It was good timing too, because Josh had just met the love of his life and was eager to start a family.

One day, he was in the parking lot of the local supermarket and accidentally backed into a woman's car. The woman was friendly; they traded insurance information, and he helped her on her way. Two months later, Josh was served with a lawsuit. The woman claimed that she was severely injured in the accident and was unable to work and support her four kids (she was a single mom). She was suing Josh for wages and emotional trauma.

Josh found a decent litigation attorney and was forced to slap down $20,000 as a retainer to defend the case. Four months later, the case went to trial. They were counting on a settlement, but the woman wouldn't budge. Josh had to pay out another $40,000 for attorney fees. At trial, Josh couldn't believe how the woman's attorney made him seem like the big, wealthy, bad guy who thinks he can "drive all over" a struggling cocktail waitress/single mother, who can't afford to feed her kids and now will never get ahead in life. The woman, wearing a neck brace, cried on the stand. Her attorney asked the jury to "do the right thing." Of course, their idea of the "right thing" was to award the woman more than $2 million of Josh's money.

At first Josh thought he was okay; after all, he didn't have too much money in his bank account. However, what he did have was his stock of J.R. Marine, Inc., a corporation, which is considered a personal asset. Before long, the business was seized. They liquidated the inventory, the building, everything, just to pay off his judgment. Josh's livelihood and all his assets were destroyed.

If J.R. Marine, Inc., had been J.R. Marine LLC, Josh may not have been sued in the first place. As I note throughout this chapter, attorneys know that LLCs are notoriously hard to get to, and the smart ones will avoid them at any cost. When the waitress's personal-injury lawyer did an asset search to determine whether Josh had any seizable assets, he would've seen that Josh's business (or his share of the business) was held in an LLC.

Setting up the booby trap

Imagine it: a naïve creditor, instead of receiving her check in the mail, gets a notice that she has to pay thousands of dollars in taxes. But that's exactly what can happen if an attorney tries to seize assets in an LLC.

Take Josh's example from the preceding section. If Josh had set up an LLC and the plaintiff's attorney had never been bitten by an LLC before, the attorney may have tried to seize the LLC interests anyway. In that case, he would've hit a brick wall called a charging order. After the attorney obtained the charging order, his client would've received only the distributions that the LLC's manager (in this case, Josh's grandfather) decided to give to her. Josh — being the smart guy that he is — would've decided that instead of distributing the profits, he would just keep them in the company. (If the other members complain about having to pay taxes and not receiving any income for a while, they can just borrow money from the LLC and sort it out at a later date.)

This situation is the worst place for Josh's judgment creditor to be in because although profit distributions are being withheld from her, she's still required to pay taxes on whatever share of the profits are allocated to her. This share is called *phantom income*, which I dive into in Chapter 14, and it usually isn't a good thing. In this case, however it works in Josh's favor, allowing him to easily run a trap, forcing the whiny actress (ahem, waitress) to end up with nothing except the pleasure of paying down his tax bill! It's funny how this arrangement can make even the most bull-headed creditors call up, ready to negotiate an extremely favorable settlement! Josh's business would be safe.

You, too, can lay such a trap for someone trying to frivolously worm her way into your LLC. To ensure the creditor (also known as the unwelcome member) knows what's going on, here's what you do:

1. **Send a letter to the creditor making her aware of the tax debt that she owes and is obligated to pay.**
2. **Send a letter to the IRS folks letting them know how much the creditor owes.**

   Include in the letter a point stating that you want to keep your LLC current on its tax debt, and you suggest that, should the IRS not receive payment, an audit on the creditor may be required.
3. **Make sure to send a copy of the IRS letter to the creditor.**

I guarantee you that before long, the creditor will approach you with a settlement amount that is definitely in your favor.

Dual liability protection doesn't always fly for single-member LLCs

For many years, professionals and consultants argued about whether single-member LLCs were allowed the same dual liability protection as regular, multiple-member LLCs. Finally, in 2003, a case came up in the Colorado Bankruptcy Court, and the court decided that this dual protection (also called *charging order protection*) doesn't apply to single-member LLCs because there are no innocent partners to protect (the reason the charging order exists in the first place).

After this ruling, more states got on the bandwagon and restricted dual liability protection to LLCs with more than one member. Other states, however, decided to go against the grain and instead drafted charging order protection into their state laws — for *all* LLCs, even single-member ones.

Remembering that even charging order protection comes with rules

Charging order protection is pretty straightforward and comprehensive. The laws do vary substantially from state to state, so be sure to review your state's laws on the issue before forming an LLC for asset protection purposes. If you don't like what you see, you can always form your LLC in a state with more favorable laws and then register to transact business in your home state. I have collected a list of state laws addressing charging order protection at `www.docrun.com/dummies/charging_order_protection` (password is **onesmartdummy**).

However, you do have to play by a few rules, which I explain in the following sections. For charging order protection to be effective, you must have certain provisions in your LLC's operating agreement that provide for it. Don't leave it up to your state's laws to be in your favor when it comes to this. I show you how to draw up an ironclad operating agreement all through Part III of this book. Though making sure you guard your LLC's charging order protection may seem overwhelming or troublesome, it's worth it. By taking a few days to educate yourself and/or by hiring a qualified attorney to draft your LLC's operating agreement, you can establish an LLC that will provide an indomitable safe harbor for your business for years to come. No other entity offers dual-layer liability protection, protecting both your personal assets from the business liabilities and protecting your business from your personal liabilities. No wonder the LLC is by far the most popular entity formed today!

You must be a true partnership

If you're a single-member LLC (that is, an LLC with only one owner), you face a drawback: Substantiating case law from a Colorado bankruptcy case some years back established that single-member LLCs aren't afforded charging order protection. The logic is that because there isn't another partner in the partnership who needs protection, charging orders shouldn't be applicable for single-member LLCs. In certain states, this precedent should make you wary of forming an LLC for any sort of business or asset protection purposes with only one member. In community property states, adding your spouse as a second member doesn't count, so I recommend issuing a small percentage of your LLC to a close friend or relative as a safeguard (preferably someone who isn't the greedy or difficult type).

Membership can't be freely transferrable

Charging order protection relies heavily on restricting membership from easy access to the other rights — the management and control in the business. Each state has a default statute that dictates how membership interests are to be transferred and which rights are afforded to the new member (which is, on average, pretty restrictive). However, all states also give you some leeway, allowing you to lay out your own set of rules in your LLC's operating agreement. Just be careful that you aren't using this extra rope to hang yourself by allowing the free transference of membership shares and, in the process, inadvertently destroying your own charging order protection. When drafting your operating agreement, keep an eye out for this potential problem. In Chapter 9, I give you some suggestions for special rules and provisions you can add to the operating agreement to doubly uphold charging order protection for your LLC.

Your LLC must be manager-managed

Using charging order protection is a really powerful strategy for LLCs; however, a common mistake is for member-managed LLCs to rely on this strategy. The manager determines the profit and loss allocations, so if the LLC is manager-managed, then a creditor stepping in as a member may be able to actually determine these allocations on his own (depending on the operating agreement and the judge's decision). To avoid this risk entirely, don't make your LLC member-managed. Even if all the current members are managing, you should still designate your LLC as manager-managed; then name all the current members as individual managers.

The lawsuit prevention trap is based on charging order protection and therefore only works if your LLC has elected some form of pass-through taxation. So, though corporate taxation may appeal to you for other reasons (see Chapters 8 and 14), you may want to think twice before electing corporate taxation for your LLC because it doesn't allow taxes to be passed through.

What happens if your charging order protection fails you?

Lawsuits are still open to interpretation; thus, a judge can decide your case however she wants, depending on how she sees the evidence. Although uncommon, if a judge finds good cause, she can circumvent the charging order protections that LLCs offer and instead allow a creditor to foreclose on a member's interest. In this case, you and your partners can do a couple of things to minimize the damage:

- **You can draft a provision in the operating agreement that requires a debtor member to sell his membership shares back to the LLC or to the other members.** You have to give a formula that determines the value of those shares, or the buy-back can be done for the exact amount of the member's original investment in the LLC. This way, you and your partners are assured that you won't have to deal with any unscrupulous, transplanted members who don't have your company's best interests in mind. Ideally, this provision should be in place when your agreement is first written, but as long as the lawsuit isn't pending or on the immediate horizon, you and your partners can always amend your operating agreement, adding this provision in.
- **If a member is already in the process of having his membership shares seized, creating a huge problem for the other members, the remaining members can vote to dissolve the LLC and purchase all the assets upon liquidation.** They can also choose to form a new LLC without the indebted member and transfer the assets to the new entity. Any monies that would be given to the indebted member instead go to the creditor who holds those membership shares.

Like regular liability protection (which protects the owners from the debts of the business), charging order protection depends on your maintaining a proper separation of your LLC from yourself and keeping your records in an orderly manner. Chapter 13 is devoted to record keeping.

Exploring Strategies for Increased Security

Protecting your assets is so simple that I challenge you to come up with one good reason why you shouldn't do it — not later in the year, not in a couple of months, but *now.* Asset protection strategies work only if you do them before you ever get into trouble. After you're sued by a creditor (or if the IRS is after you), you can't transfer your assets into an LLC to protect them. Otherwise, you can be found guilty of *fraudulent conveyance of assets,* which means you set up your asset protection plan to defraud your creditors and prevent a specific claim. In this case, not only will you hand over your assets to the creditor on a silver platter, but you also may face some pretty steep fines and maybe even some jail time.

So you need to set up your asset protection plan when you don't have any lawsuits pending or creditors looming. After all, you never know what tomorrow may bring. Set up your defenses early and make sure that as you accumulate more and more in life, no one can take it away.

In the following sections, I go over a few simple strategies that you can use:

- Using a nominee to make it harder for others to find your assets
- Using multiple LLCs to segregate your assets from one another so that if one asset, such as a piece of property, is engaged in a lawsuit, the others are safe from seizure
- Forming two companies in different states to separate your business's assets from the actual operations of the company
- Transferring all your personal assets into a family LLC that keeps financial instruments, such as stocks, bonds, cash, and mutual funds, safe

Electing a nominee to protect yourself with privacy

Privacy is the first line of defense when it comes to asset protection. If people don't think you have anything, then they won't bother suing you in the first place. The saying goes, "Own nothing, control everything," but that doesn't mean that just because people will try to take your things, you shouldn't own and enjoy the finer things in life. You work hard, and you deserve to enjoy the fruits of your labor. And even if the world can see that you have money, you can keep people from knowing where it is. That's where privacy comes in handy.

Some states, such as Nevada, protect the privacy of the LLC's members. This protection means that the members don't need to be publicly listed in the articles of organization or the annual reports your company files with the secretary of state; only the managers have to be listed. If the members don't need to be listed in your state, then you can just hire a nominee to serve as your LLC's manager. A *nominee* is a person who can truthfully state on the stand that she's unrelated and unknown to you. Doing that ensures that your name, as owner of the LLC, remains private and off public record.

You can hire a nominee from a nominee company, usually for less than $500 per year. Keep in mind, though, that this move works only if your LLC is manager-managed.

If you're in a state that doesn't allow privacy protection for members, consider forming your LLC in another state, such as Nevada, that does allow it.

After you have a nominee manager in place, unless you broadcast to the world that you own the LLC, people won't even think to look into the issue further. Your name won't be on public record, and unless they ask you directly, creditors will have no way of knowing that you're even associated with the LLC.

If your LLC is currently member-managed, you need to amend your articles of organization to make it manager-managed. Otherwise, you have to list your members (namely, you) on your annual report — which is public record.

Privacy won't fully protect you. It's not a strategy in and of itself, per se, but more like an add-on. If you solely use a manager-nominee and think that you're completely protected, you'll get the shock of your life when you get dragged into court. The lawyers will ask you about your assets, and at that point, you have two choices: Give up the goods or perjure yourself. Considering that perjury is a pretty serious criminal offense, I would take door No. 1 — and that leads to you revealing the location of your assets so they can be taken.

Setting up multiple LLCs: The more, the merrier!

With an LLC, your business is protected from you, and you're protected from your business. But what protects your business from itself? When your business is sued, the creditors may not be able to go after your personal assets, but they can still go after the business's assets! You can fix that.

Any business or property that operates directly with the public is at risk of being sued. If you have all your business assets in your operating company and you get sued, all your business assets can be seized. The same goes for personal assets. If you own ten properties and put them all in the same LLC, and then someone slips and falls on your first property and sues you, everything in that LLC is up for grabs — all ten properties.

The best and easiest way to protect what's yours is by insulating each of your major assets in its own LLC. Doing so can be somewhat costly, but on large assets, it's a small price to pay. For instance, New York taxi cab companies often place each taxi in a separate LLC. That way, if one driver gets into an accident and the cab company gets sued, only that one cab can be seized and liquidated to pay off the claim. That LLC can then be dissolved, and the taxi company is still standing. You don't have to worry about million-dollar judgments now!

Make sure you aren't already facing a lawsuit when setting up a structure like this one. If you've been sued and start transferring entities to different LLCs to protect them from the creditor, you're engaging in fraudulent conveyance. Not only will it not hold up in court, but it's also illegal.

Following the dual-entity strategy

An easy way to protect your business's assets is to simply not keep them in the LLC that operates with the public. You can do so by creating a separate LLC that holds your primary LLC's assets, making this approach a *dual-entity* strategy. This protection strategy is my favorite by far; in addition to keeping your assets safe, you also save on some of your state and local taxes. You can set up your LLC this way no matter the tax or management structure.

An example of how dual entities work

Say you decide to start a local pizza delivery company. You live in the high-tax state of California. In this case, you form your LLC in the state of California (not much you can do about this; if you're located there, you have to register and pay taxes there, no matter what), but you then place all your assets, such as your pizza ovens, cash registers, and so on, into a Nevada LLC that has elected corporate taxation (see Chapter 8 to find out how to make tax elections). For extra protection, you make this Nevada LLC a completely private entity by hiring a nominee (see the "Electing a nominee to protect yourself with privacy" section earlier in the chapter).

Your Nevada LLC that owns the assets then leases them to your California LLC (your *operating company* — the one that deals with the customers, vendors, and so on). This way, your company's assets are 100 percent protected. Why? Because they're in a completely separate entity. Your California LLC controls the assets, but doesn't own them, which is the most powerful position to be in. If your California company gets into a legal predicament — for example if a customer gets injured — the inquiring attorney will see that it's completely devoid of assets. Even if he finds out that you own the Nevada LLC, he can't do anything.

If you choose to use this strategy, make sure the lease between the California LLC and the Nevada LLC is legitimate. You need to write up a contract and pay a reasonable leasing fee to the Nevada LLC every month or every quarter. This step may seem like a pain in the butt, but believe me, it ensures that your strategy is legitimate if you ever go to court.

The tax advantages

One of the main reasons you should form your LLC in Nevada is because Nevada has absolutely zero taxes. Zero business taxes, zero franchise taxes, zero personal income taxes — zilch. And you have to elect corporate taxation on that Nevada LLC because if you try this plan with an LLC with pass-through taxation, your assets are still protected, but the profits flow through to you personally, and you have to pay taxes on them in whatever state you live in.

So, here's how the tax reduction goes. If you have $100,000 in profit at the end of the year that you want to keep in the company, you can have the profit go to your Nevada LLC as a lease payment for the use of the assets instead of having it flow through to you and your partners and paying state and federal taxes on it. This $100,000 payment is a legitimate tax deduction, so it eliminates the profit in your LLC. After the money is in your Nevada LLC, it's only taxed at the federal corporate tax rate (which is usually just above 15 percent), as opposed to the personal income tax rate (which can be 35 percent or more!). This strategy is great if you want to save money for assets or other business-related items.

Nevada isn't the only state with a favorable tax climate. In Chapter 5, I list other pro-business states and show you how to select the one that works best for you.

Protecting your family with the family LLC

Although a family LLC sounds official, it's really just an LLC like any other; you don't have to do anything different when you file your articles of organization. It just serves a different purpose. The family LLC protects the assets you and your family will need in the future. If you're like the majority of folks, you have a savings or money-market account that is coupled with your checking account. Maybe you have some mutual funds. Regardless, everything is in your name. That's not good. Remember: *Own nothing, control everything*. Instead, your assets should grow under the protection of an LLC.

The usual arrangement for a family LLC is that you and your spouse both own 50 percent of the membership. After the LLC is set up, all savings accounts, insurance policies, brokerage accounts, mutual funds, CDs, bonds, and so on are transferred into the LLC in a nontaxable event.

Don't place your home in your family LLC. Your home can be the source of many lawsuits. For example, if a neighborhood kid sneaks onto your property and accidentally drowns in the pool (God forbid!), all the assets in the LLC can be taken. Instead, form a separate LLC for your home or get a homestead exemption (which I discuss in Chapter 18).

Now, if you or your spouse is sued, the assets are safe in the entity, and the creditor can only obtain a charging order. In this case, you use the booby-trap method I outline in the "Setting up the booby trap" section earlier in the chapter to resolve the situation.

Also, if your LLC acquires any debts or obligations, you (and your spouse) aren't liable for them. For instance, say you're extended a margin on your brokerage account and you make a few bad trades; unless you personally guaranteed the loan, you aren't responsible for it — although all your other assets in the LLC may be at risk of being liquidated to repay the debt.

The more that your family LLC is legally separated from you, the safer it is. You can use nominees and find a way to make your personal assets seem like a normal course of business. Create a paper trail that separates you from the assets in the LLC. For instance, if your vehicles are in the LLC, make sure to lease them to your family. This strategy is also a good way to have a legitimate purpose for transferring savings into the LLC on a regular basis. Make sure to document everything; have legitimate contracts and keep your records in order as if it were a real business. The less obvious it is that the LLC only serves to protect your assets, the more certain you can be that the LLC will be rock solid in the courtroom.

What's the deal with trusts?

A couple of years ago, trusts were the hot thing for asset protection, especially *spendthrift trusts* where your assets couldn't be touched by creditors. You just named yourself as the beneficiary and you were good to go! Unfortunately, thanks to a *New York Times* article that blasted these trusts for allowing the wealthy to avoid creditors and to Missouri senator Jim Talent, spendthrift trusts aren't what they used to be.

Here's the deal: Senator Talent slipped an act into a bankruptcy bill, right before it was about to pass, that allows creditors to get to any assets that were put into trusts within the ten years previous to the claim. Therefore, you can still create a spendthrift trust, but it doesn't do much good if anything happens within the next ten years. Not a good idea!

Unless you're looking to add a trust to your arsenal for estate-planning purposes, I'd just stick with an LLC.

Chapter 18

Protecting Real Estate with LLCs

In This Chapter

- Using an LLC to protect your real estate holdings
- Transferring the title and dealing with mortgage companies

Real estate offers the easiest path to success . . . and the easiest path to lawsuits. If someone is living in a rental property you own and is injured, he'll most likely sue, especially because he doesn't even have to do an asset search to know that you have at least one valuable asset — the property he's living in.

Even if you just own vacant land, you're still open to multitudes of liabilities. No matter how clear the signs are, trespassers will always end up on your property, and if an accident happens, you'll most likely be held responsible. Not to mention all the environmental liabilities that can occur with vacant land. Although real estate gives you good cause to be wary, all these potential liabilities aren't the end of the world. With some good advice (starting with this chapter!) and an LLC or two, you'll be fine!

Comparing LLCs to Other Possible Real Estate Entities

LLCs are the best entities for holding real estate, no doubt about it. They offer the most liability protection of any entity type out there (Chapter 2 goes into detail about the other entities), and when you're looking to protect valuable assets, this peace of mind is priceless.

Different people need different strategies. I'm writing in generalities, so keep in mind that you may be one of the few cases where a corporation or S corporation is your best bet. For instance, if you're flipping properties so often that it's considered an operating business, a corporation (more specifically, an S corporation) may not be such a bad thing. I go into more detail on that later in the chapter.

Before you create your plan for protecting your real estate investments, make sure to speak with a qualified professional. You need to get everything right in the beginning because if you've made a mistake, you probably won't find out until it's too late to fix it.

In the following sections, I go over a couple of the alternatives to using LLCs for holding your real estate (or land trusts) and explain why I don't think they're good options. Before you proceed, though, here's a quick reminder of some of the perks inherent in operating under an LLC:

- **LLCs are the most flexible entities around.** You decide how the property is managed; you make your own rules. You can put whatever you want in your operating agreement, including what rights, powers, and limitations the company's manager is subject to.
- **LLCs don't require the same intensive formalities that corporations require.** For LLCs, minutes, resolutions, and so on are optional (though highly recommended). For instance, if you don't do your annual meeting minutes, you won't have to worry about such dire consequences as your entity being disregarded in court and your personal assets seized.
- **Everyone involved in the LLC — all members, managers, and employees — is protected from liability for the actions of the company itself.** This situation is a stark contrast to the limited partnership, in which only the limited partners (not the general partners) are protected.
- **LLCs offer a second level of liability protection (called *charging order protection*) that protects the business from the creditors of the owners.** For instance, if your partner gets sued personally, you don't have to worry that the person suing will be able to seize your partner's interests and liquidate the company in order to get paid.

Holding real estate in corporations: The worst choice

When it comes to real estate, corporations are by far an inferior choice. Don't get me wrong; I don't dislike corporations at all. Actually, I recommend them to a lot of clients who are starting up small businesses. But when it comes to real estate, corporations are the worst! Corporations are to real estate like kryptonite is to Superman: They're poisonous. Don't do it.

Regardless of what I say, I always encounter a skeptic who needs more information, so here are some concrete, important things to keep in mind:

- **Less liability protection:** Corporations don't offer the same level of liability protection that LLCs do. They offer only one layer rather than two. Your personal assets are protected in the event that the corporation gets sued, but if you get sued personally, your corporation is toast — in other words, it's liquidated to pay off your judgment. Considering that real estate is normally pretty expensive and not something that you want to lose, this point may sway you to use an LLC instead.
- **Double taxation:** Double taxation — the term alone should make you want to run far, far away — is the main reason why you should never use a corporation to hold your real estate assets, especially if they're rental properties. All income that the property receives is first taxed at the corporate tax level and then taxed at the dividends tax rate after you take the cash out of the company.
- **Prevented from selling:** If you think double taxation of profits isn't bad enough, try to get the property *out* of the corporation after you sell it! Unlike LLCs, you can't move assets in and out of a corporation without triggering a taxable event. And don't think you can avoid this obstacle by simply selling the corporation along with the real estate it contains — any knowledgeable buyer will run far away from that deal! After all, who wants to be locked into the same high-tax situation you're currently facing?

Say you purchase an investment property in an LLC at $500,000. After holding it for four years, it appreciates to $1 million. At that point, you want to sell it; you know that the market can turn on a dime. You sell, which means that you realize a $500,000 profit that passes directly to you, to be reported on your personal tax return. This profit is taxed at a long-term capital gains rate, which currently stands at only 20 percent — a pretty good deal!

Now here's an example of how double taxation can hurt you: Say that instead of the preceding scenario, you choose to hold that same investment property in a corporation. First, the profit from the sale of the property is taxed at the corporate rate, which means your corporation pays about $170,000 in taxes (15 percent on the first $50,000 and then 34 to 37 percent on the remaining). Then, after you take the remaining $330,000 personally, you need to pay personal tax on the dividend income. That means you're paying an additional $66,000 in federal taxes (assuming the maximum dividend tax rate of 20 percent) for a grand total of $236,030 in taxes. Yikes — and you haven't even figured in state taxes yet!

At this point, clients often bring up the value of the *S corporation* (a corporation that has elected S corporation tax status with the IRS). After all, S corporations have similar pass-through taxation as the LLC and therefore aren't subject to double taxation, so what's the difference? Although the differences appear slight on the surface, you'll actually still dish out more cash for taxes with an S corporation than an LLC. Say you want to transfer the appreciated property out of the S corporation without selling it (maybe to convert it to a personal residence for the added tax benefits, for instance); you'll be taxed. LLCs, on the other hand, allow you to transfer property in and out of the entity without being taxed. LLCs also offer dual liability protection, so if you or your partner is sued personally, your investment property inside your LLC can't be seized.

If you decide that S corporation taxation is your best option, you can always form your real estate company as an LLC and elect S corporation taxation. That way, you can switch back to partnership taxation if necessary. I go over electing your LLC's taxation in Chapter 8.

If your business is operating as a corporation and wants to purchase some property for its operations, you should put the property into a separate LLC. Not only will holding the property in an LLC insulate it from any lawsuits filed against the business, but it can also save you from the whole double-taxation debacle. The corporation can be a member of that LLC and contribute the money for the purchase (which is a tax-free event). The corporation can then lease the office space, which is a deductible cost. As far as the LLC goes, the rental income it receives from the business is offset by the operating expenses of the property and its depreciation. You pay taxes only on what's left over.

Falling short with land trusts

If you're currently in real estate or have been heavily researching it, you've probably heard of *land trusts,* which are arrangements in which one person, the *trustee,* agrees to hold the title of the property for the benefit of another person, the *beneficiary.*

Although they seem like a newer thing and are gaining popularity, land trusts have been around for a while — a long while. They go back as far as the Roman Empire. They were heavily used during the Tudor period in England, when owning land came with many more burdens than just kooky tenants, such as serving in the military. Because land trusts offer such a thick veil of privacy, citizens of England hid their land ownership to get out of fighting the war of the week.

Today, land trusts are used to avoid a different type of war — legal battles. Land trusts not only allow you to keep your real estate out of your name but also let you avoid probate and have the property immediately pass on to your heirs upon death. Because of a trust's privacy protection, large corporations often use them to secretly buy up large plots of land in little chunks without anyone being the wiser.

However, land trusts don't offer more than superficial protection. Although they can serve at the front lines of your privacy, without the added assurances of an LLC, you and your assets are still vulnerable.

Understanding land trust protection

Like all trusts, land trusts have a trustee and a beneficiary. The *trustee* is the name on public record and can be a person, LLC, corporation, or other type of entity. The *beneficiary* is the land owner and indirectly owns and ultimately controls the trust; however, the beneficiary's name is kept private and can't be accessed by the roving eye of a litigation attorney looking to sue.

Sounds great, right? Well, the downside is that although land trusts sound really official, they're actually no more separate from you than a sole proprietorship. They aren't separate entities with separate identities. What does this mean for you? *Zero* liability protection. If one of your tenants burns himself while messing around with the water heater and decides to sue, the property in your land trust is fair game along with other assets. Also, if your neighbor sues you personally for running over her cat (accidentally, of course!), your land trust is considered personal property, and it and everything in it, including your real estate holdings, can be taken away. Your attorney may have you place your assets in a land trust for estate planning purposes, but considering the lawsuit statistics nowadays, your assets may not even make it past your retirement.

Clients often ask me how an attorney can take away the land trust if he doesn't know they own it. Well, that's easy. He gets you on the stand and asks you point-blank whether you own any real estate properties. You can't lie. After all, you're the land trust's beneficiary, also known as a beneficial *owner.* You have to tell the court that you own the real estate and also disclose any other assets you have, whether in land trusts or not. So as soon as you get dragged into court, the little protection that your land trust offered you disintegrates.

Assessing the pluses and minuses of land trusts

Land trusts do have their benefits. Privacy is a huge issue for some people nowadays. If you don't want to use a *nominee* (a person who allows you to maintain your privacy as the LLC's owner) for your LLC (see Chapter 17) but do want to protect your privacy, a land trust is perfect for you as long as it's paired with a good ol' LLC that can deliver on its shortcomings. Put an LLC and land trust together, and they make double trouble for anyone who wants to get at your hard-earned assets. The LLC has liability protection, and the land trust offers privacy and estate planning advantages.

The best way to maximize the benefits of both the land trust and the LLC is to make the LLC the beneficiary of the land trust. That way, if you need to take the stand, you can honestly say that you don't own the land trust; your LLC does. If the plaintiff wants to continue to sue you, great! Then you can just snag him in the awesome LLC booby trap that I outline in Chapter 17. But that will rarely come to pass. The attorney probably won't want to mess with you any further, and he'll most likely drop the case or offer a reasonable settlement.

Holding your real estate in a land trust with an LLC as the beneficiary has some other pluses and minuses. Because going over them all would take pages and pages to, I just give you a brief overview.

Here are some advantages:

- The property's sales price can be kept off public record. This act can help keep property taxes lower than they'd be at the property's fair-market value.
- You can sell or gift the property quickly and efficiently. You don't have to record a new deed; you just name a new beneficiary.
- You can easily continue the project in the event that a partner dies.

Here are the disadvantages:

- Some states don't allow you to do a tax-free, like-kind (IRS Section 1031) exchange with property in a land trust. You must transfer the land out of the trust for the like-kind exchange to be possible. This move may involve sizeable fees and taxes and also removes the veil of privacy during the transfer.
- Trustees are often unwilling to take certain necessary actions on your behalf, such as signing mortgage documents. The mortgage may need to be placed in your name, which eliminates all privacy protection.
- Land trusts are often created by attorneys who are very specialized in their field. Although that specialization means you'll be in great shape if the viability of your trust is ever questioned, the (often sky-high) attorney fees can also make forming one in the first place cost prohibitive.

Looking at LLC Property Logistics

Like many things, putting property into a newly formed LLC sounds easier than it actually is. Instead of just figuring it out as you go, you need some real-world advice to guide you. The reality is that mortgage companies are skittish about loaning money to newly formed LLCs. Wouldn't you be? The LLC has no financial history, no assets, no credit score to go by . . . the bank would probably be better off lending money to a 4-year-old. Transferring the title on property you already own can also quickly become a sticky situation. You need to prepare for these situations, among others, when setting up your asset protection plan.

Protecting your home

I know that with all the benefits of LLCs that I lay out in this book, you're going to be tempted to put your personal residence into an LLC. After all, you know that LLCs can protect your assets from creditors and lawsuits — and what more important asset do you have than the home you've built your life in? Well, as tempting as it may be, don't do it.

Owning a home comes with a lot of amazing tax benefits that you lose if you transfer it out of your name. (To better understand all the benefits of home ownership, I recommend you read *Home Buying Kit For Dummies* by Eric Tyson and Ray Brown [Wiley].) For instance, when you sell the property, you won't get the tax-free benefit that you currently have. You also won't be able to take advantage of the Universal Exclusion that allows you and your spouse to exclude up to $500,000 in gain.

Most states have laws that automatically protect your home in the event of a lawsuit or lien, so you don't need the protection of an LLC. This shield is called a homestead exemption and only applies to your personal residence; investment properties don't count. Check your state laws to see whether this exemption is automatic or whether you have to file a claim to acquire it. With the exception of a possible small filing fee, homestead exemptions are free.

Depending on your state, your homestead exemption may cover all or part of the equity you have in your home. Some states, such as Florida, Texas, and Oklahoma, cover 100 percent of your home, but other states only cover it up to a certain dollar amount.

Deciding which state to form in

Unfortunately, in the case of rental properties, you don't gain too many tax benefits by forming the LLC that holds the property in a tax haven, such as Nevada or Wyoming (unless, of course, the property is actually located in Nevada or Wyoming — in that case, good thinking!). Renting a property to someone may be considered "doing business," and therefore you're required to register in that state and also pay *franchise fees* (a common term for state business taxes or fees). For your convenience, I've collected all state laws that address what exactly constitutes doing business. You can find them at `www.docrun.com/dummies/transacting_business` (password is **onesmartdummy**).

Also, for the most part, the lawsuits against your property will be handled in the state where the property is and where the incident occurred. So even if your LLC is domiciled in another state with better laws, you may not be able to take advantage of them.

You may be able to avoid registering to transact business in a particular state if all you're doing is holding vacant land. Holding onto land isn't considered conducting business as long as you haven't started the development process and aren't receiving any rent payments. In this case, you can probably form your LLC in Nevada or Wyoming and not have to worry about foreign filing or paying taxes in the state where the property is actually located. However, if you decide to develop the land in the future, you'll likely have to register in that state at that time.

If your rental property is going to make a lot of profit and your state imposes some pretty hefty taxes, I suggest using the dual-company strategy that I outline in Chapter 17 to reduce the amount of state taxes you pay. In this case, you follow a few steps:

1. **Form an LLC in the state where your property is located and then transfer the property to that LLC.**
2. **Form a Nevada or Wyoming corporation and set it up as a management company that you pay to manage the property.**
3. **Pay a reasonable percentage of the LLC's profits to the management company.**

   These profits are now safe and secure in a tax-free entity and away from the potential creditors and lawsuits of the property.

Getting lenders to loan to an LLC

If you just formed your LLC yesterday, you may have a hard time getting your banker to loan it money. After all, when banks loan money, they have certain criteria that they use to evaluate credit-worthiness. For instance, with businesses, they look at cash flow and assets. With individuals, they look at income and credit scores. Your LLC has none of these. From the bank's perspective, your LLC has no credit history, no track record, and no assets. Therefore, you'll most likely be required to personally guarantee the loan.

You also have to try to persuade the bank to allow the LLC to hold the property's title, the legal document that shows the ownership of the property. Banks obviously don't like this. They want the person guaranteeing the loan to hold the title. However, the bank usually relents in certain instances.

I guarantee you that the worst way to get the bank to let the LLC hold the title is to tell your banker you want to transfer the property into the LLC for "asset protection purposes." Banks hate that phrase. After all, they're some of the biggest creditors around. However, bankers do understand (and respect!) estate planning issues. Let your banker know that you want to transfer the property into the newly formed LLC for estate planning purposes. If your banker isn't savvy enough to understand what you're doing, shop around. I'm sure you can find a bank that's willing to accommodate you.

After you get a banker on board, you get the loan personally. Then, when the title is in your name, you can transfer it into the LLC's name. The whole process shouldn't take more than a few days to complete. You're still personally guaranteeing the loan; however, the title is in the name of your LLC and protected from creditors.

If you're currently financed and want to transfer the title into your LLC, check with your mortgage company first. Transferring the title may trigger a due-on-sale clause in your contract, which means that you'll have to pay your mortgage back in full. That will force you to refinance. Mortgage companies often enforce this clause when you've locked in a really low fixed rate and they want you to refinance at a higher rate.

If your mortgage company won't allow you to transfer your property into an LLC, you may want to see whether it will allow you to transfer the property into a living trust for estate planning purposes. Most mortgage companies have policies that accommodate this sort of thing. If so, have an attorney form a *living trust* (a trust that a grantor creates while he is still alive), and then make your LLC the trust's beneficiary. With this arrangement, you still get the protection that an LLC offers and you don't trigger a due-on-sale clause when you transfer your property.

Transferring the title

After you've formed the LLC and you're in the clear to transfer the title of the property to the LLC, you're ready to prepare a *deed,* a document that transfers the ownership of a property. You can choose from a lot of different types of deeds. Some make the original owner responsible for all current defects or liabilities of the property, whereas others waive the previous owner from all responsibility (the property is just transferred as-is). If you're transferring the property from your own name to an LLC that you control, I recommend you use the latter, which is called a *quit-claim deed*. After all, it's a much easier deed to draft. You can find out more about quit-claim deeds at `www.docrun.com/dummies/quit_claim_deed` (password is **onesmartdummy**).

The deed needs to be in the LLC's name and be signed by you and anyone else who will be authorizing the transfer of the property, and it will most likely have to be notarized. Then you're ready to file! The deed must be filed in the county that the property is located in. As to exactly where you file it, the exact office differs from county to county, so you need to do a little bit of research to get the office's name and address. Start with the county recorder's office or the county clerk's office and go from there. Keep the following advice in mind when considering a title transfer:

- **Your property should be held in the name of your LLC.** For instance, your county recorder should show that your parcel number is titled to your LLC. If this info isn't recorded properly, your assets may be in jeopardy.
- **Make sure to check with your title insurance company before transferring the title.** Some insurance companies cancel coverage if the title has been transferred to a new entity.
- **Although contributions to an LLC are tax-free, some states impose a separate transfer tax.** It often depends on why the property is being transferred, and in some circumstances, the tax burden can be pretty hefty. To find out the details in your case, I recommend you do a quick phone consultation with a real estate attorney or tax advisor who specializes in the county that the property is located in.

Part VI
The Part of Tens

the part of tens

Enjoy an additional Part of Tens list online at www.dummies.com/extras/limitedliabilitycompanies.

In this part . . .

- Why you should form an LLC
- Keep your LLC intact and impenetrable from outside forces

Chapter 19

Ten Good Reasons to Form an LLC

In This Chapter

- Protecting your real estate, intellectual property, and personal assets with an LLC
- Raising capital with your LLC
- Running your business in an LLC

By now, you've probably figured out that I think the LLC is the best entity structure around. And for good reason! LLCs are flexible — you can use them for practically any purpose — and they offer more benefits than any other entity type. They have a favorable pass-through tax status, and with the dual liability protection that LLCs offer, corporations and limited partnerships can't compare.

What I love most about LLCs is that they are completely customizable. You can draft pretty much whatever rules you want in your operating agreement, even overriding many state laws with a simple paragraph. You can also choose whichever tax structure you want; LLCs can elect to be taxed like corporations or even S corporations.

LLCs are a departure from all previous ways of doing business. They are the future, and that's a good thing! Too many people simply form an LLC without realizing its power. They adopt a fill-in-the-blank operating agreement (yuck!), if they bother to make one at all, and they rarely look critically at their tax situations to see where money can be saved. So much can be done with LLCs, and yet most people don't know or don't bother because they stick to their comfort zone, either dealing with older entity types that they're more familiar with or mentally limiting the LLC to the same restrictions as, say, a corporation. This chapter reminds you of the awesome capabilities of LLCs so that you never forget to make the most of a good situation.

To Customize Your Small Business

LLCs are great for small businesses because they're adaptable to all situations. No matter whether you have 100 silent investors or are a two-person small-business operation, the LLC is so flexible that you can pretty much write the operating agreement to suit your needs; you can make your own rules and tailor your entity to suit the intricacies of your business. With a corporation, you're limited to stiff corporate formalities and the weighty, unbending infrastructure of shareholders, directors, and officers.

If you're operating as a sole proprietorship (which is how most small businesses are structured) or general partnership, I have no doubt that reading this book will convince you to form an LLC today, because a sole proprietorship or general partnership is the most dangerous form of doing business. It offers zero protection from creditors and lawsuits and therefore leaves your personal assets on the table for pretty much anyone to grab. Not to mention that neither of these entities can raise capital (and you won't go very far when it comes to impressing people).

By combining a lot of the advantages of corporations and S corporations with their own special attributes, LLCs have become exceptionally attractive to small-business owners. They take the liability protection that corporations offer and build on it, adding an extra layer of protection by way of the charging order (see Chapter 17). They also offer a pass-through tax structure similar to S corporation tax status, but with *zero restrictions.* Any person or entity can be an owner, and your LLC can have an unlimited number of members.

To Protect Real Estate Assets

The LLC is a perfect entity for real estate holdings — you just can't beat it! One advantage is that an LLC has dual liability protection that shields your investments from the frivolous lawsuits filed against people like you every day. So if you rear-end someone in a parking lot and he sues you personally, he can't seize and liquidate your investment properties to settle the claim if they're held in an LLC. If that's not reason enough to convince you to form an LLC, turn to Chapter 18, where I show you all the powerful ways a limited liability company can protect real estate holdings.

Another huge benefit of the LLC over other entity types is its taxation. With an LLC, you can easily transfer your property in and out, because taxes aren't imposed on contributions or withdrawals of assets as long as no money changes hands. Individual members can also gain a tax benefit from recourse loans that they've guaranteed for the company. Considering that there's a good chance you'll have a mortgage on your property, that provision is a very good thing! Of course, before taking any big steps, speak with your CPA about any hidden tax issues that could crop up. After all, with more than 2,500 pages of federal tax code, you never know what you could be walking into.

LLCs are so great at holding real estate that I advise my clients to form one LLC per property that they own. This way, each property is isolated from the others, so if one property is sued, the others are safe from being seized. With the ease of operation and the limited record-keeping requirements, having multiple LLCs isn't as difficult as you may think.

To Shield Intellectual Property

I am a firm believer in keeping your intellectual property as far away from your operating business as possible. After all, what's more valuable than your brand, which you have worked so hard to build? Or the patents around which you centered your business? You need to protect those things with your life. Or with an LLC. Your choice.

Unless you have a bunch of important patents, placing all your intellectual property in separate LLCs is overkill. You don't want your intellectual property to operate with the public; that's your operating company's job. So how do you link your intellectual property in your LLC to your operating company? Have the LLC that holds your intellectual property *lease* the patents, trademarks, or copyrights to the operating company for its use. You need to sign paperwork and transfer money to make the arrangement official. After all, if it doesn't look legit, then there's no point in doing it in the first place.

Because of the charging order protections (see Chapter 17), it doesn't really matter too much who owns the LLC with the intellectual property. But investors generally like to have the intellectual property of the business owned by the business; therefore, the best setup is for the operating company to own the LLC. To be on the safe side, a common holding company can be the owner of both the operating company *and* the LLC with the intellectual property. The investors invest in the holding company, and voilà! They're happy, and the property is safe from lawsuits and angry creditors.

Only LLCs should be used for holding intellectual property, not corporations. If that corporation is owned by the operating business and the business is sued, then the corporation that owns the intellectual property is considered an asset of the business and subject to liquidation. Corporations don't have the same charging order protections that LLCs have. Therefore, if the intellectual property is in a corporation and the owner (in this case, the business) gets sued, then the intellectual property is toast. If the intellectual property was instead held in *an LLC* owned by the operating company, then this wouldn't be a concern.

To Raise Seed Capital for Your Business

The LLC is quickly becoming the entity of choice for raising *seed* or *angel capital* — early-stage investments under $500,000 or so. Whereas venture capital firms — I'm talking about the big, big guys here — generally prefer to invest in corporations because they're most familiar with them, smaller investors *love* limited liability companies. The partnership pass-through taxation allows investors to deduct their contributions, and if your little start-up doesn't turn a profit, they can use the losses to offset other income. That is a *huge* benefit to investors. If the business fails, they may not get their investment back, but they'll still get a nice deduction.

S corporations also offer pass-through taxation; however, the result and implications aren't even close to being the same. Investors can deduct their contributions only if the business fails, not immediately, and S corporations restrict who can and can't be an investor. Why limit yourself? LLCs can have as many investors as you choose — even hundreds of thousands! — and anyone can invest. One investor can be a small business in Wichita, and another can be a newly formed hedge fund based out of London.

According to the laws of most states, the entire membership interests in an LLC cannot be transferred freely; only the economic interests can. This is the foundation for the second layer of liability protection — charging order protection — that LLCs offer. Although this restriction is a good thing, it can be a bit intimidating to old-school investors who are comfortable with the ownership structure of the corporation.

If you're dealing with a wary investor, you can simply remind her that an LLC is incredibly flexible. Assuming that the laws of your state allow it (most do!), you can structure your membership shares to be freely transferable as they are in a corporation. Granted, if you're ever sued personally and are relying on the charging order protection, you may face some problems in court. In the worst-case scenario, your LLC is treated as a corporation. In the best-case scenario, you get the best of both worlds: freely transferrable ownership interests, favorable pass-through partnership taxation, and dual liability protection.

With an LLC, you can have different *classes* of membership. For example, you can give members with Class A membership full voting rights and members with Class B membership absolutely no voting rights. Or you can allow one class of membership shares to be transferable, whereas the other class of membership shares can't be transferred without the approval of all the members.

To Plan Your Estate

Don't overlook the value of the LLC when you plan your estate. Although it's a simple entity in comparison to some of the über-complex trusts that your attorney may recommend, the LLC provides powerful asset protection. LLCs protect you not only from creditors, but also from probate lawyers and court costs. They allow you to avoid probate altogether, which means that your estate isn't subject to the nickel-and-diming (I wish they were just nickels and dimes!) that probate attorneys siphon from estates as the court divvies up assets.

With an LLC, you can structure the management however you like, which is useful if you're minimizing your estate (to reduce or eliminate estate taxes) while you're alive by gifting a little bit of your assets to your heirs each year. An LLC is especially convenient for gifting property; you can just gift some membership interests. It beats having to retitle the property each year! You can be the LLC's sole manager as the membership interests are transferred so that you control the property, but your heirs get to own it. Set it up so that when you die, your heirs become managers, or name someone else as a temporary manager until your heirs reach a certain age.

Additionally, you can structure your LLC in such a way that the membership interests have less value than the underlying assets you are gifting. This means that you can squeeze more into the $13,000 the IRS lets you gift each year tax-free. You do so by putting all your assets into an LLC, then devaluing the membership of that LLC (usually by taking away voting and management rights) before slowly gifting it away to your children. If estate planning is your goal and you want more information, go to `www.dummies.com/extras/limitedliabilitycompanies` to find out more on the topic.

LLCs are commonly used with different types of trusts. Trusts are great and definitely have their place in most estate plans, but don't make the mistake of looking at your estate only from a tax-saving perspective. Trusts don't offer anything in the way of liability protection, and if you don't use an LLC to cover your assets, you may not have anything left to leave your heirs. Those assets may go to the dogs (er, I mean creditors)!

To Do a Short-Term Project

LLCs were made for short-term projects. When these entities were first introduced, they were never supposed to live forever like corporations do. That's why, when you create your articles of incorporation, you state a specific dissolution date or *term,* the number of years that the LLC is to be in existence. Although most states allow you to extend the LLC beyond this term with a simple vote of the members, this scheduled termination of the company is convenient for short-term projects such as real estate development and film financing.

Because of their pass-through taxation for investors, LLCs are especially great for flash-in-the-pan projects for which you have to raise money. Investors can come together, pool their money, do the project, make the profit, and then dissolve the company. Upon dissolution, all the assets are liquidated, the creditors are paid off, and the remaining profit is split among the members according to their ownership percentages. All profits flow through to the investors' personal tax returns, so they don't have to worry about double taxation. (Chapter 16 covers the dissolution process in more detail.)

In the meantime, you and the other members can allocate the company's profits and losses however you like. This makes investors happy, because you can get more creative with the structure of the investment. For example, a common agreement for LLCs raising financing for a film is that, upon earning revenue, each investor gets her money back plus 10 percent. Afterward, all members share profits according to their membership share in the company. The limited liability company is the only entity that offers this sort of flexibility.

When you're doing a short-term project, all members must be on the same page from the get-go. When bringing on members, make sure that you give plenty of information about the project, specify that the LLC will be liquidated and dissolved, and tell them when you expect the dissolution to take place. Remember that you need a vote of the members to dissolve on a date other than the dissolution date specified in the articles of organization. If all members aren't in agreement, you'll have trouble moving forward with your plans.

To Segregate Assets

Segregating assets is vital in business. By segregating your business assets into individual LLCs, you put them out of the reach of your company's creditors or people who may want to sue you.

A lot of people incorrectly think that if they're operating as a corporation or an LLC, then their assets are safe, but that's not necessarily true. If you're like most entrepreneurs, your business is your biggest asset. If you lose the ability to operate, you're doomed. Your business may be protected from your personal creditors, and you may be protected from your business's creditors; however, what protects your business from its own creditors? If your LLC gets sued, everything inside it can be seized and liquidated. Even worse, the courts can put a lien on your company and then do an *asset freeze,* which means that you have zero access to your operating capital — you can't write checks or receive funds from clients. How stable will your business be after three months or more of an asset freeze?

The best way to fully protect your assets (and your access to them) is to keep no assets in the operating company. Instead, the company uses leased assets. Now, I don't mean that you have to start looking for furniture- and equipment-leasing companies. In this case, *you* own the leasing companies (or your business does). Each asset is put into a different LLC, and each LLC then leases these assets back to the operating company. When the operating company is sued, it has no assets with which to settle the claim. So, in the worst-case scenario, you dissolve the operating company and form a new one. You again set up the lease agreements with the various LLCs, and you're back in business!

The leasing aspect of this strategy is essential. Not only does it create an official transaction record, which is of vital importance if the strategy is ever questioned in court, but it also serves to pull extra profit out of your operating LLC; don't forget that cash is also an asset that may be seized in the event of a lawsuit! In Chapter 17, I go into all the many ways that an LLC can be used to protect your assets.

To Minimize Your Tax Burden

When you first go into business, chances are your company won't be profitable right away. Building up a business takes time, and in the first year or two, you probably will incur thousands of dollars in losses. A lot of entrepreneurs, eager to soften the financial blow of the startup phase, decide to form an LLC. With an LLC and its default partnership taxation, the losses of the business flow through to the members so that they can use them as deductions for other income.

Say, for example, that your business incurs $40,000 in losses in the first year of operation. If you and your partner each own 50 percent of the company, then you each get a $20,000 business deduction on your personal tax returns.

That could save each of you as much as $6,000 in federal income taxes alone! When starting up your company, every dollar counts; and an extra 6,000 of them can really help get things off the ground.

To Change the Profit Distributions

An LLC's profits can be paid out disproportionately to the actual ownership percentages, so you and your partners can set up the company so that you receive all the profits and losses — even if you own only 10 percent of the company. Why would you want to do that? Well, a common reason for changing the distributions is to provide an extra incentive for investors. For example, if one investor contributes all the capital, he gets 50 percent of the company. However, the profit distributions can be varied so that he receives 100 percent of the profits until his investment has been paid back (plus 10 percent in some cases). Then the profit distributions return to normal, and the profit is split equitably among the members.

The only contingency that the IRS places on altering the allocations is that it must deliver *substantial economic effect.* This is just a fancy way of saying that you need to have a decent reason for changing up the allocations. In the above example, you have proven substantial economic effect; that is, you aren't varying the allocations for no other reason than to egregiously avoid taxes. Another good example of substantial economic effect is giving a higher portion of the allocations (and thus, distributions) to a particular investor because he invested during a riskier time in the life of the business.

You can get yourself into some serious tax trouble if you act without taking the whole picture into account. So if you want to vary your profit distributions, work with an accountant who knows all the applicable IRS rules. Tax law is complicated, so it's better to pay someone who spends all day learning and understanding it than to try to grasp it all yourself.

When varying your allocations, document such arrangements in your operating agreement or by resolution of the members. After all, you can't refuse to send a minority partner a check one year simply because you and the majority of the members suddenly decide to take all the profit. Well, okay, you *can* do that, but only if that sort of power is afforded to you in the company's operating agreement, which has to be signed off on by all members. For more on the very important topic of creating membership rules in your operating agreement, flip to Chapter 10.

To Protect Your Personal Assets

Although I don't recommend putting your home into an LLC (you may lose some of the great tax breaks that you get as an individual), I do recommend putting all your other personal assets into one. When you spend your entire life saving for retirement, your children's education, or even that second home you've long dreamed about, nothing is more crippling than losing it all in a lawsuit.

Rockefeller once advised people to own nothing and control everything. You don't have to be a billionaire to walk in his footsteps. If you're like most people, you currently hold all your personal assets in your own name: your savings account, your cars, and your mutual funds, stocks, and bonds. This means that the reverse of Rockefeller's advice is true — you own everything yet control nothing, and it can all be taken away from you.

If you really want to follow in the footsteps of financial giants, start by forming an LLC. Better yet, form a series of LLCs. Then contribute all your personal assets to those LLCs and make sure that they're isolated from one another. That way, if a debt arises pertaining to one of your assets — for example, you get a margin call that you can't quite pay for — then all your other assets are safe. LLCs are cheap; I form them for clients every day for less than $200. You don't have to be a millionaire to take advantage of strategies of the rich. After all, whatever your net worth is at the moment, you worked hard for it and deserve to keep it safe.

Chapter 20

Ten Ways to Keep Your Liability Protection Intact

In This Chapter

- Keeping all the paperwork in order
- Watching where the money goes (and comes from)

Now, really, what is the point of a limited liability company without the *limited liability* part? Without limited liability, it's no better than an expensive sole proprietorship — no special protections, no special tax treatment, no ability to issue shares of ownership. If you don't take the simple steps necessary to keep your limited liability intact, you may as well save yourself the filing fee for creating your LLC and be prepared to kiss your hard-earned personal assets goodbye if you're sued.

Before you even think about taking extra steps to protect your limited liability, I ask you to do one thing: Be on your best behavior. No, I don't mean keep your elbows off the dinner table and say "please" and "thank you." I mean don't lie, cheat, or steal in the name of your LLC. Wrongful misconduct on the part of a member is the easiest way for your LLC's veil of limited liability to be pierced. Don't think that your company will protect you from purposeful fraud that you initiate.

File the LLC Properly

The first step to obtaining liability protection is filing the LLC. I know this point may sound elementary, and I don't want to insult your intelligence, but plenty of extremely intelligent and accomplished individuals have failed at this first step and ended up being taken to the cleaners. Often, entrepreneurs get too busy and distracted; after all they're running a business! They start their LLC paperwork and then leave it to sit on their desk, collecting dust, until they find the time to get around to filing it.

If this description makes you think I've been spying on you (I haven't), you should hire a formation company to file the documents for you. You don't even have to sign anything (except maybe the check to pay the company!). In most states, your formation company can list itself as the *organizer* — a temporary position that only lasts until the company is filed — and handle the entire process for you. The fee is normally small, and it can get this incredibly important task off your plate.

Situations often come up when you want to file quickly and don't have any time for preparation. Keep in mind that when you rush to file, you run the risk of getting your articles of organization rejected because you didn't do the requisite research and preparation. Also, you need to take time to attach to your articles certain provisions, such as the limited liability provision and the charging order provision, that are never included on the state's generic articles of organization.

Find a Partner

Because LLCs were initially created as partnerships, some states don't even allow you to form an LLC with only one member (called a *single-member LLC*). Even if your state does allow the formation of a single-member LLC, don't blur the line between what is *allowed* and what is *advised.* You may be able to form and operate a single-member LLC without a problem; however, when a business lawsuit comes up, depending on the state, the court may treat you differently than it would a standard, multimember LLC. Namely, it may not give you the benefit of charging order protection.

Charging order protection is a form of liability protection unique to LLCs that keeps your business safe in the event you get sued personally. If you're like most entrepreneurs, your business *is* your biggest personal asset, so this shield may be more important to you than the standard form of liability protection!

Charging order protection has a caveat: It exists to protect partners in the business from each other, not just to protect you. After all, if you get sued and your portion of the business is seized, it isn't fair for your business partner to suddenly be in business with some stranger, is it? Charging order protection was created to remedy this injustice, and as you can see, it only applies to true partnerships. And the one thing you need to be a partnership is a partner!

If you want a surefire way to completely protect your LLC, you should have more than ten members. Historically, any organization that has more than ten members has never had its veil of liability pierced or its charging order protection tossed aside by the courts. If you have more than ten members, you should be in the clear, no matter what.

If you're totally intent on having a single-member LLC and you're in a state where single-member LLCs aren't offered the same level of liability protection (see Chapter 17), then you must do what you can to look like a legitimate LLC by following all the tips in this chapter — especially the ones about having meeting minutes and a good, solid operating agreement. Don't have a partner but still want to assure the benefit of charging order protection? I recommend that you do one of two things:

- **Find a friend or family member whom you can trust, and issue her a small membership percentage.** Make sure you have a contract or your operating agreement states that she can't sell or transfer the shares without your approval. Because she isn't contributing anything to the business, you can also state in your operating agreement that she gets a very small percentage of the distributions.
- **Form a corporation that you can control — preferably in a tax-free state — and make the corporation your second partner in the business.** Remember, LLCs can have anyone as a member, and members don't even need to live in the same country.

Create an Operating Agreement

If you've read any part of this book, you may have a pretty good idea of how absolutely necessary I feel an operating agreement is. Your operating agreement is the backbone of your company. It creates the infrastructure and acts as an operations manual that you and your partners will fall back on time and time again to sort out the gray areas and disputes that occur during the normal course of business.

Until your operating agreement has been created, your LLC isn't complete. Creating a comprehensive, foolproof operating agreement for your LLC should be at the top of your to-do list. LLCs are very flexible entities, and in your operating agreement you can tailor your LLC to whatever your needs are. Whether you're raising capital, building a business, or flipping a real estate property, you'll want different people in your organization to have different authority, and you can create a system for keeping everyone on the same page.

State law gives LLCs an incredible amount of leeway for how they want to be structured and operated, but without an operating agreement in place that includes all specifications, your LLC must abide by the state's default laws. These laws are often strict, unfavorable, and offer very little liability protection. That's why you *must* create an operating agreement for your LLC before engaging in any sort of business. You can create a customized agreement in less than a day, so don't put it off because you think it will be difficult! In Chapter 9, I get you started on creating this über-important document.

Capitalize the Company

The phrase *capitalizing the company* means investing money into your business. A business without even a little bit of money isn't really a business at all. Although I don't like to trot out the old adage that it takes money to make money, usually you need to invest *some* capital to get your business going. I'm not the only one who thinks this; the courts agree.

The easiest way for a court to determine whether your company is a separate operating business or an *alter ego* (a company put into place to protect its owners) is to see whether you've invested in the business. After all, most small businesses aren't profitable when they're starting out, so the courts can't base their decision on profitability. They must go on capitalization.

What if you're starting small and didn't invest any money into your LLC? In this case, if you can show substantial cash flow and prove that your business is operational and deals regularly with the public, then you have a good chance of being in the clear. Make sure that you have a reason for your shares being issued to you, though — whether for services rendered, assets given, or money invested. You must put this information in your meeting minutes.

File Your Annual Reports

You must file your annual reports on time each year. If you fail to file your reports, you'll go out of good standing with the secretary of state. If you remain out of good standing for a certain amount of time (usually a year), then your LLC will automatically be revoked, and you'll have no limited liability protection at all. Not good!

The filings are often one page and require minimal information, such as the names and addresses of the LLC's members and/or managers, the name and address of the LLC's registered agent, and the corporate office address (Chapter 13 has more details about annual reports). You either file your annual report with the same state office that you filed your articles of organization with — in most states, it's the secretary of state — or you file it with the state tax board. Your registered agent should be able to provide you with the exact information regarding what's required to maintain your LLC in a particular state. (Flip to Chapter 5 for details on registered agents.)

Hold Member Meetings Regularly

Although annual meetings are only required for corporations and not LLCs, you must hold them anyway. If a creditor of your LLC wants to attach your personal assets to a lawsuit, he will attempt to prove one of two things:

- Your LLC is an alter ego.
- Your LLC appears to be a sole proprietorship or general partnership and should be treated as one.

The best defense against these attacks is to choose to go through the same formalities that corporations are required to go through. I know what you're thinking: You're a busy entrepreneur! How on earth can you find the time to draft meeting minutes and issue financial reports? Rest assured, though, that it won't take as much time as you think. Not only does all this documentation help designate the LLC as a separate entity (and disprove it's an alter ego), but it also helps prevent your LLC from being classified as a sole proprietorship or general partnership, both of which have no meeting minutes at all.

You must have annual meetings, but you also must hold a meeting whenever a major action affecting the company is to take place. When you have meetings, you must keep a record of the minutes and resolutions that take place. Meeting *minutes* are a record that shows that important business decisions, the *resolutions,* were made after a successful vote of the members. These records prove that an action of the company isn't something some rogue member decided himself (in which case he'd likely be personally liable), but rather by the company as a whole, with all in agreement as to the course of action.

The IRS also will look to your meeting minutes to show that certain loans and financial transactions were approved. In other words, if you issue yourself a loan from the company, the IRS folks may not allow it if they don't see it properly documented in the company's minutes or some other form of agreement.

Minutes are also good to have when requesting a ruling from the IRS, such as a 1031 exchange (for real estate investors), or defending a position to the IRS or Department of Revenue during an audit of the company or an LLC member. The minutes must also authorize any major salaries and pension contributions, contractual relationships, and elections of managers.

In addition to all these things, minutes also can be used to explain any mistakes or company oversights that may have occurred. You can state what actions the company has taken to remedy the situation. Minutes are also good for justifying why the company took a certain questionable action, such as changing the income distributions to be disproportionate to the ownership percentages. (For more information about meetings, minutes, and resolutions, see Chapter 13.)

Obtain Your Licenses and Permits

Before opening your doors and taking orders from customers, you need to make sure that you're squared away in the eyes of the law. Many state governments require businesses to have licenses and permits in an effort to control various industries and obtain tax revenue. Most companies only need to file a state and city (or county) business license. However, if you're in a heavily regulated industry, such as gambling, alcohol, or land development, you need to inquire as to which licenses and permits you must obtain. (Chapter 13 covers licenses and permits in more detail.)

When you aren't in good standing with the state and its departments, you won't be held in high favor with the judge when he is determining whether to disqualify your LLC. If you find the ordeal of determining which business licenses you must file a bit overwhelming, contact your registered agent; she can either file the business licenses for you or point you in the right direction.

While you're applying for your state licenses and permits, don't forget the ever important federal *employer identification number* (also called an EIN or a tax ID number). Think of it as a Social Security number for your LLC. Until you obtain an EIN, you can't do much business. Applying for a number online at the IRS's website (`www.irs.gov`) is incredibly easy, as I explain in Chapter 8.

Avoid Commingling Funds and Assets

Commingling, treating your business's funds and assets as your own, is the biggest way, by far, to kill your LLC's liability protection. Here are a few examples of commingling:

- **You use the funds from your business for obvious personal expenses without documentation.** For example, unless you're a model or a newscaster, getting your teeth bleached is *not* a business expense. Good try!
- **Your personal bank account and your business bank account are the same.**
- **You endorse checks to yourself that are made payable to your business.**
- **You often move money between your business and personal accounts without keeping proper records.**

If you're treating your company account as your personal piggy bank, stop. Not only do you run the risk of being heavily penalized by the IRS, but you also risk losing your personal assets and your livelihood should you ever get dragged into court. If the courts decide you're treating your money and the company's money as one and the same, they can easily disregard your entity as not being separate from you — hence the term *alter ego.*

The best way to stay on the safe side and avoid mixing your personal and business funds is by taking the following advice:

- **Make sure your LLC has its own bank account.**
- **Don't use the business money to pay for personal items.** If you absolutely must, then carefully document it on the company's books.
- **Don't pay yourself indiscriminately.** The money you receive from the company should be in the form of a loan, salary, or distributions.

Sign Your Documents Correctly

In the course of business, you'll have to sign stuff. Lots of stuff. When you're doing business under your company name, you must sign as a representative of the company. What this rule means is that under your signature, you must include your title and the company name, or you must write "on behalf of" and your company name. Also, always use "LLC" or "Limited Liability Company" after your company name.

Your signature should look something like this:

Your signature

Your name

Your title (Manager or Member)

Your LLC Name, LLC

The *Wurzburg Bros. Inc versus James Coleman* case shows how important signing documents correctly is. In this case, James Coleman was the president of Coleman American Moving Services, Inc. When the company was behind on its payments to Wurzburg Bros., Inc. (one of its vendors), Mr. Coleman decided to send over a promissory note to ease the tensions. When he signed the promissory note, he failed to put his title and the company name under his signature. Wurzburg Bros. successfully sued James Coleman, the person, and succeeded in taking his personal assets to cover the judgment.

Give Up Some Control

To avoid having the courts determine that your company is an alter ego, you need to limit your control somewhat. If you have 100 percent control over all the company's decisions and finances, and your company does something wrong, the courts could easily hold you personally liable. This scenario is one of the most common ways to lose your liability. It happens most often in civil cases; however, the IRS has been known to force members to pay for their company's debts on this basis.

If you're a very small company, you often don't have too many people making decisions on a day-to-day basis because you're likely controlled by a small handful of people. In this case, just make sure that you don't have any nonfunctioning managers — that is, anyone who can be viewed as your puppet — and that you observe all formalities.

Glossary

allocation (noun): The amount of company income and deductible expenses that are assigned to each member and reported to them on their Schedule K-1.

alter ego (noun): When the courts determine that an entity is fully controlled by an individual and its only function is to provide a legal shield for a person. Although it's hard to prove an entity is an alter ego, the liability protection that the entity provides could be disregarded.

amendment (noun): An approved and ratified change to the articles of organization or the operating agreement.

articles of organization (noun): The document created and ratified by the LLC's organizers. The articles define the name of the LLC, the initial managers and/or members, the organizers, the state of formation, the LLC's purpose, the duration of the company, and other important information.

beneficiary (noun): The future recipient of all or part of an estate, trust, or insurance policy.

blue sky laws (noun): Securities laws that protect the public from fraudulent companies that don't offer investments of substance.

board of directors (noun): Elected by the entity's shareholders or members, the directors set company policy and choose the corporation's officers.

buy-sell agreement (noun): An agreement that outlines the terms of the purchase of a shareholder's interest in an entity.

bylaws (noun): The document created and ratified by the shareholders and/or board of directors of a corporation that outlines basic corporate policy.

C corporation (noun): An entity, unlike a partnership, which is completely separate from its owners. Corporations have their own level of taxation, which varies greatly from personal income tax.

capital (noun): The total amount of assets that an individual or entity owns, which includes liquid cash, real estate, equipment, stocks and bonds, and so on.

capital assets (noun): All assets, including real estate, equipment, and cash, that are owned by an entity.

capital gains (noun): In real property, the sale price minus the purchase price, plus improvements.

case law (noun): Interpretations of the law by the courts that can be used as precedents in future cases.

cell (noun): A unit in a series LLC that acts like a separate LLC but is still under the same common umbrella.

charging order (noun): A type of court order that restricts the claim of certain assets, such as property or securities, to their fiscal income only. Under charging order protections, assets can't be liquidated or sold.

common law (noun): The laws brought over from England that are still generally accepted.

company kit (noun): A binder that contains the items essential for the running and maintaining of a limited liability company. Items can include sample minutes and operating agreement, membership certificates, a company seal, and membership transfer ledger.

consolidation (noun): The act of two companies coming together to form a new entity that they both operate under.

corporation (noun): A separate entity that has been accepted by the government and does business or other activities, can offer ownership shares to raise capital (except in the case of a nonprofit), and can sue and be sued in a court of law.

deed: 1. (noun) In the case of real property, the document that transfers the ownership from one party to another. 2. (verb) The act of transferring ownership of real property by use of a deed.

dissolution (noun): The winding up of affairs and termination of an entity either voluntarily by the entity's owners or by a government action.

distribution (noun): An actual distribution of the profit in the form of cash, usually proportionate to the number of shares in the corporation.

doing business (verb): Normally a term that connotes whether an entity is carrying out normal and regular business activities within a jurisdiction. If an entity is "doing business" in a foreign state, it may be subject to state taxes and required to register with the Secretary of State in that jurisdiction.

domicile (noun): The state in which an entity is registered and headquartered — its home state.

double taxation (noun): When a corporation pays taxes on the profits, then distributes those profits to shareholders in the form of dividends, which are taxed again on a personal level.

Employer identification number (EIN) (noun): Used to differentiate entities, such as corporations or LLCs, from others; the company equivalent of a Social Security number.

entity (noun): A general legal term for any company, corporation, LLC, partnership, institution, government agency, educational body, or any other form of organization that has a completely separate identity from that of the individuals behind it.

face value (noun): The number of shares of stock, as shown on the certificate, multiplied by the stock's par value, also shown on the certificate.

foreign corporation or LLC (noun): An entity that is formed in a different state or nation than the one it is doing business in. Foreign entities must register with all states that they are conducting regular business in.

franchise tax or fees (noun): A common state-level tax imposed on businesses.

fraudulent conveyance (noun): The act of transferring assets to another party for the sole purpose of making them inaccessible to a creditor or the party of a lawsuit or divorce. If the assets are transferred before the knowledge of any such lawsuit exists, then the assets are not being fraudulently conveyed.

general partner (noun): One of the managers of a limited partnership. The business's liability is shared by all general partners in a limited partnership.

general partnership (noun): A business partnership that has two or more partners wherein each partner is equally liable for any of the business's debts.

holding company (noun): A company whose sole purpose is to own the stock or membership shares of other entities to simultaneously oversee the management and policies of all entities.

impute (verb): The act of holding one person responsible for the acts of another. If someone in business has knowledge of another's actions, such as an employee, then they are imputed to that person and held responsible for their acts.

incorporate (verb): To obtain the Secretary of State's approval of the articles of incorporation. When you incorporate, your company is now officially a corporation. When forming an LLC, this act is loosely termed *organizing.*

joint liability (noun): When two or more parties (or entities) are held equally responsible for a debt or judgment.

joint venture (noun): When two or more people (or entities) create an entity for a limited time and for a specific project, such as raising funds or a shorter-term real estate transaction. After the business has been completed and the affairs have been wound up, the joint venture is terminated, and the entity is dissolved.

judgment creditor (noun): When a person or organization sues you and wins (the court decides that you owe that party money), that party becomes a judgment creditor until you pay them what you owe.

judgment debt (noun): When a lawsuit is lost, the judgment debt is the money owed to the winning party by the losing party.

liability (noun): A legal term for responsibility and one of the most common words used in corporate and partnership law. When you have liability for yourself, your business, or even your partners, you are held personally responsible for the acts of those parties, meaning you can be subject to a lawsuit or criminal charges.

lien (noun): A legal claim against an asset that is used to secure a loan or debt.

limited liability protection (noun): The protection of an owner, manager, or employee of a business against being responsible for the debts and/or obligations of the business.

limited partner (noun): One of the two kinds of partners in a limited partnership; a limited partner has no say in the day-to-day management of the company and isn't personally responsible for the liabilities and debts of the company.

limited partnership (noun): A type of partnership that consists of one or more limited partners, who are silent in the day-to-day management and aren't personally liable for the LLC's debts, and one or more general partners, who manage the business but *are* personally responsible for the company's debts.

living trust (noun): A trust created by the trustor during that person's lifetime, where the trustor is distributed profits from his assets in the trust until his death, when the trust continues on and instead gives those distributions to the new beneficiaries — typically the trustor's children. (***Note:*** This is not to be confused with a *living will,* which comes into effect only during a person's lifetime if he becomes incapacitated in any way.)

member (noun): An individual or entity that has an ownership interest in the LLC with or without voting rights.

membership certificate (noun): An official document, issued by the LLC to a member that states the LLC's name and state of formation. When issued, it is signed by the managers and/or members and lists the number of shares and the member's name.

membership interest (noun): A member's percentage of ownership in the company.

membership or shareholder register (noun): The record of members (in an LLC) or shareholders (in a corporation) that lists current and past issuances and transfers.

merger (noun): The instance in which two businesses decide to become one and transfer all assets into one of the entities (the surviving entity) and then dissolve the other.

minutes (noun): The official record of the events that took place at a company meeting.

nominee (noun): 1. The successor to one person's rights and obligations on a contract; 2. The person or entity that acts on another's behalf, either to protect the privacy of that individual or entity or to handle the affairs during an absence.

nonprofit corporation (noun): Also called a *not-for-profit corporation,* an organization incorporated and ratified by the state that operates for purposes of charity or public benefit. A nonprofit corporation has no shareholders and can apply for federal and state tax-exempt status.

off-shore corporation or LLC (noun): Any corporation or LLC that is created and domiciled in any country other than the United States.

operating agreement (noun): A contract among the members of the LLC that governs the company's operation, management, membership, and distribution of the company's profits.

organize (verb): See ***incorporate.***

pass-through tax status (noun): A type of taxation, inherent in LLCs, that passes the income or loss generated by the business to the partners to be reflected on their personal income tax returns.

phantom income (noun): Income that is allocated to a partner that he must pay tax on but doesn't actually receive in the form of cash.

piercing the veil (noun): When a judge allows the plaintiff to hold the members of the LLC, otherwise immune, personally responsible for the damages caused by the LLC under their control.

provision (noun): A clause or stipulation in a document or agreement.

quorum (noun): During a corporation or LLC's annual or special meetings, the number of people required to be present so voting can take place. Unless otherwise stated in the bylaws or operating agreement, a quorum is usually just a majority.

registered agent (noun): A person or company designated in the articles of organization as authorized to receive service of process and other important documents from the state on behalf of the company. In most states, an LLC is required to have a registered agent.

regulatory law (noun): Rules and regulations created by government agencies that are based on statutes.

resolution (noun): An agreement of policy, rules, and guidelines that have been voted on by the corporation's board of directors or the LLC's managers and/or members.

S corporation (noun): A designation made by a corporation that elects a pass-through tax status, thereby eliminating the double taxation that corporations are normally subject to.

series LLC (noun): A unique type of LLC, available in only certain states, under which you can create numerous cells that act as separate entities and can own separate assets.

service of process (noun): When sued, the initial delivery of a legal summons, or the delivery of other legal documents such as a subpoena, complaint, and so on.

several liability (noun): When multiple people are responsible for a debt; however, if they fail to pay and the burden falls on only one person, that person is severally liable (as in "joint and several").

silent partner (noun): An investor who puts in money but doesn't deal with the business's day-to-day operations nor makes any operational decisions. In a limited partnership, this person is called a *limited partner.*

single-member LLC (noun): An LLC that is wholly owned by one person or institution — typically also the manager.

sole proprietorship (noun): An unincorporated business owned and managed by a single person (or husband and wife).

statutory law (noun): Laws and statutes that have been enacted by the legislative branches of state or federal governments.

stock certificate (noun): An official document, issued by the corporation, that states the name of the corporation, the state of incorporation, the type of stock the certificate represents, as well as the number of shares of stock in the corporation and the par value of that stock. When issued, it's normally signed by the president and secretary and lists the number of shares and the shareholder's name.

trademark: 1. (noun) A name, tag line, slogan, or symbol that identifies a product officially registered and legally restricted by use of the registrant only. 2. (verb) To register a name, tag line, slogan, or symbol as a trademark.

trust (noun): A legal arrangement in which an individual or enterprise (the trustor) gives economic control of assets to an individual or institution (the trustee) for the benefit of the beneficiaries.

trustor (noun): An individual who creates a trust; also called a *grantor.*

winding up the affairs (verb): Prior to dissolving, the process of liquidating the entity's assets, paying the final bills, distributing remaining assets to the members/shareholders, and then filing a formal dissolution with the Secretary of State.

Index

• A •

• E •

• F •

• G •

• H •

• I •

• K •

• L •

• M •

N

• P •

• Q •

• R •

• S •

• T •

• Z •

About the Author

Jennifer Reuting is one of the foremost experts on corporate structuring and limited liability companies. She has been entrusted by thousands of companies over the years to address their individual corporate needs. In 2001, she founded InCorp®, a registered agent and compliance firm. Now one of the "Big Four" national registered agent companies, InCorp services more than 200,000 clients nationwide. InCorp specializes in servicing medium to large businesses, accountancy firms and law firms.

To service the needs of individuals, upstarts, and small businesses, Jennifer founded MyLLC.com, a company that focuses on offering affordable business formation solutions. Jennifer lends her corporate structuring talents to the clients at MyLLC.com, providing affordable yet comprehensive solutions for their business needs.

Jennifer's newest venture, DocRun.com, was born out of the need to provide the readers of this book with an easy, affordable way to create attorney-level operating agreements and other business-related contracts.

Jennifer speaks regularly on television and radio shows across the U.S., addressing common business issues such as the formation and management of limited liability companies and corporations. You can also read her articles at MyLLC.com and DocRun.com.

Dedication

Another one for you, Dad.

Author's Acknowledgments

I'd like to thank Amanda Graham for your awesome attitude and working your magic! To Vanja Habekovic, Esq. for being the best tax wiz I know, and taking the time to make this book solid.

My sincere thanks to my agent, Andy Barzvi, at Empire Literary, whose time and effort has made this opportunity possible. Whoever said agents aren't likeable has obviously never met Andy.

A million thanks to Doug Ansell. You rock, my friend. Simple as that.

And to Chris Baldwin . . . for keeping me smiling.

Publisher's Acknowledgments

Acquisitions Editor: Stacy Kennedy

Project Editor: Amanda Graham

Copy Editors: Pam Mourouzis and Megan Knoll

Technical Editor: Vanja Habekovic

Project Coordinator: Patrick Redmond

Cover Image: ©iStock.com/Talaj

Math & Science

Algebra I For Dummies, 2nd Edition
978-0-470-55964-2

Anatomy and Physiology For Dummies, 2nd Edition
978-0-470-92326-9

Astronomy For Dummies, 3rd Edition
978-1-118-37697-3

Biology For Dummies, 2nd Edition
978-0-470-59875-7

Chemistry For Dummies, 2nd Edition
978-1-118-00730-3

1001 Algebra II Practice Problems For Dummies
978-1-118-44662-1

Microsoft Office

Excel 2013 For Dummies
978-1-118-51012-4

Office 2013 All-in-One For Dummies
978-1-118-51636-2

PowerPoint 2013 For Dummies
978-1-118-50253-2

Word 2013 For Dummies
978-1-118-49123-2

Music

Blues Harmonica For Dummies
978-1-118-25269-7

Guitar For Dummies, 3rd Edition
978-1-118-11554-1

iPod & iTunes For Dummies, 10th Edition
978-1-118-50864-0

Programming

Beginning Programming with C For Dummies
978-1-118-73763-7

Excel VBA Programming For Dummies, 3rd Edition
978-1-118-49037-2

Java For Dummies, 6th Edition
978-1-118-40780-6

Religion & Inspiration

The Bible For Dummies
978-0-7645-5296-0

Buddhism For Dummies, 2nd Edition
978-1-118-02379-2

Catholicism For Dummies, 2nd Edition
978-1-118-07778-8

Self-Help & Relationships

Beating Sugar Addiction For Dummies
978-1-118-54645-1

Meditation For Dummies, 3rd Edition
978-1-118-29144-3

Seniors

Laptops For Seniors For Dummies, 3rd Edition
978-1-118-71105-7

Computers For Seniors For Dummies, 3rd Edition
978-1-118-11553-4

iPad For Seniors For Dummies, 6th Edition
978-1-118-72826-0

Social Security For Dummies
978-1-118-20573-0

Smartphones & Tablets

Android Phones For Dummies, 2nd Edition
978-1-118-72030-1

Nexus Tablets For Dummies
978-1-118-77243-0

Samsung Galaxy S 4 For Dummies
978-1-118-64222-1

Samsung Galaxy Tabs For Dummies
978-1-118-77294-2

Test Prep

ACT For Dummies, 5th Edition
978-1-118-01259-8

ASVAB For Dummies, 3rd Edition
978-0-470-63760-9

GRE For Dummies, 7th Edition
978-0-470-88921-3

Officer Candidate Tests For Dummies
978-0-470-59876-4

Physician's Assistant Exam For Dummies
978-1-118-11556-5

Series 7 Exam For Dummies
978-0-470-09932-2

Windows 8

Windows 8.1 All-in-One For Dummies
978-1-118-82087-2

Windows 8.1 For Dummies
978-1-118-82121-3

Windows 8.1 For Dummies, Book + DVD Bundle
978-1-118-82107-7

Available in print and e-book formats.

Available wherever books are sold. **For more information or to order direct visit www.dummies.com**